THE PRAYER MANUAL

COMPILED FROM ANCIENT, MEDIEVAL,
AND MODERN SOURCES

BY

FREDERICK B. MACNUTT

LONDON
A. R. MOWBRAY & CO LTD

© A. R. Mowbray & Co Ltd 1961

Printed in Great Britain by
Alden & Mowbray Ltd at the
Alden Press, Oxford

SBN 264·65288·6

First published in 1951
Second edition, 1952
Third edition, 1954
Fourth edition, 1968

FOREWORD

I AM compelled to write this foreword without having had any chance of studying this *Prayer Manual*. Perhaps it is as well, as study of it might distract me from the two relevant things which I wish to say.

In the first place, to all who knew him the fact that Canon Macnutt compiled this book of prayers is commendation enough in itself. It was in the First World War that he first began to collect prayers for public and private use which proved singularly helpful to himself and others. From then onwards he drew all his studies and his sensitive spiritual insight this way. The perfection of his collection became his absorbing interest after his retirement from his canonry in Canterbury Cathedral: I wish his collection could have been printed in full. I am sure that the fruits of his long and sanctified labours as here presented will inspire as they will reflect the true spirit of approach to God in prayer, and will teach how 'to make prayers, and supplications, and to give thanks, for all men.'

And, secondly, there is great spiritual value in having resort in our prayers to those which have been composed by saintly men in the past. We must, indeed, never cease to put the emotions and petitions of our hearts before God in our own words also. Nothing can ever replace the outpouring of our offering of prayer in such simple ways and words as come most easily to us. It is a grave loss to think that God must always be approached in elevated language or in carefully phrased and thought out periods. We must pray for ourselves, and generally we do so best in words that are simple, sincere, and short. And yet there is a very necessary place for such prayers as this manual contains. In public prayer, the language should be thoughtful, dignified, and uplifting.

And by the use in private of the chosen prayers of good men, we are helped to fulfil our duty of intercession for all sorts and conditions of men; we find utterance when we are tongue-tied; and we catch from their spirit and from their phrases spiritual insights which become part of our own spiritual possession and so enrich us unto God.

Into this manual the author has put a life's experience of 'growing up into Christ.' I am sure many will find, in its careful use, a portion of his spirit coming to aid them in their spiritual growth and expression.

GEOFFREY CANTUAR:

LAMBETH PALACE
October, 1951

PREFACE TO 1968 EDITION

SINCE it was first published in 1951, the *Prayer Manual* compiled by Canon Macnutt has continued to enjoy a high reputation, having proved itself worthy of its place in the worship of the Church.

In publishing a further edition of the manual, it was felt that it would be helpful to revise the presentation of the prayers. But the many who are familiar with their content and order can be assured that these differ in no way from those of the original compilation.

A. R. MOWBRAY & CO LTD

EDITORIAL PREFACE

IT was in 1915 that my husband, while serving as a Chaplain to the Forces, made his first collection of prayers in a small note-book. This inspired him to draw upon the literature of prayer for private devotions and for public use. Year by year his store was enlarged. He always had it in mind to publish a comprehensive volume of prayers for use in church 'especially after the Third Collect,' as well as for guidance in meditation and stimulation to private prayer.

With this end in view, on his retirement in 1945 he spent much of his time in research, translation, and correspondence. A month before his life on earth was over he had collected some 1,400 prayers and completed his work, with thanksgiving to God. He realized that it might be necessary to reduce the number when the time came for publication. After careful thought a selection of the prayers, together with some rearrangement of their form, has now been made. I am deeply grateful to Canon R. W. D. Lee, Vicar of Horsham, for the unsparing help he has given me in the work of rearrangement, indexing, and correction of proofs. He has willingly shouldered the heavier burden in this task.

The Prayer Manual is in succession to my husband's *War Primer*, which he hastily put together in 1939, a few weeks after hostilities began, at the suggestion of Archbishop Lang. The wide welcome given to *The War Primer* encourages me to hope that his own great wish will be fulfilled in offering *The Prayer Manual* to the service of the Church.

And so to the dedication he gave to this book I now add my own to his memory whose passing into the nearer presence of Christ seems to me, in the words of Dr. J. W. Suter, 'to shorten the distance all prayer must cover.'

E. M. MACNUTT

HORSHAM
August, 1951

DILECTISSIMAE MEAE
E. M. M.

Into thy hands, O Lord, we commit these prayers of thy servants, which we offer before thee in time of crisis when thy judgements are seen in the earth. Incline thine ear to our thanksgivings, accept our confessions, and grant our petitions according to thy gracious will, who hast taught us to pray, and ever livest to intercede for us in heaven, world without end.

CONTENTS

Prayer is speaking to God; so the first necessity is that you should be directing your minds towards God. That is the best part and the most important part of prayer anyhow, and without it all the rest is useless. . . . Our Lord says that when you come into the presence of God you should forget all about yourself and your needs, even your sins; you should be so filled with the thought of God that what you want above all things is that God's Name may be hallowed—reverenced—throughout the world. You are to ask for that first, because you ought to want it most. And next, that He may be effectively King of the world He has made. so that all men obey His law; and then that His whole purpose of love shall be carried out unspoiled by the selfishness of men.

WILLIAM TEMPLE
From 'Christian Faith and Life'

It is highly necessary, to provide against the inconstancy of our hearts, by having at hand such forms of prayer as may best suit us when our hearts are in their best state, and also be most likely to raise and stir them up, when they are sunk into dullness. For as words have a power of affecting our hearts on all occasions, as the same thing differently expressed has different effects upon our minds; so it is reasonable that we should make this advantage of language, and provide ourselves with such forms of expressions, as are most likely to move and enliven our souls, and fill them with sentiments suitable to them.

WILLIAM LAW
From 'A Serious Call'

INTRODUCTION

OUR day-to-day experiences of life bring with them
from time to time matter for depression or a
wandering mind. Not infrequently we find that praying
is impossibly hard and unfruitful. The right atmosphere
for prayer is not always easy to create in one's own room
alone. There is an absence of that 'togetherness' which
is so helpful 'in the great congregation.' Indeed,
although a man may pretend for practical purposes that
he is the centre of his own world, he is certainly not the
centre of the real one. In building up a self-centred
existence he is only constructing a world of fictions.

It is here that the prayers of the Divine Society
throughout the ages can help us to realize our true part
and function in the real world, and to feel that our feet
are indeed set in a large room. The common prayers of
the Divine Society may seem at first too general and too
remote for our private use. During church services our
minds may not have time to appreciate their content as
we listen to their recital. Yet when used in our private
prayer-time, which gives time to reflect, we can ponder
them clause by clause and phrase by phrase. Thus in
'slow motion'—and that is the only way to pray—the
words will speak and we shall hear through them what
the Lord will say concerning us.

The first section of this manual has been arranged
with this view in the hope and prayer that it will assist
day by day those who would lift up their hearts to God
as members of Christ—to speak and to listen.

The remainder of the book is intended to help clergy
and others, whether in the Daily Offices or otherwise,
to find appropriate words of approach, petition, or praise,
by which they can express aloud the thoughts of all on
the infinite variety of facets of our common life.

It may well be that many prayers appearing in the latter section will be right for use in private daily prayer too; and conversely that the prayers allotted to private use will be suitable for united and public prayer. For example, preachers may find some appropriate for utterance at the end of the sermon to lead from exhortation up to aspiration.

In the Notes and Index following the Prayers, the sources and authorship of nearly all have been stated. In a few cases their origin has not been traced. The Notes should be read in conjunction with the attributions beneath the prayers. The word 'adapted' has been used in a number of cases, where in translation or paraphrase an attempt has been made to improve the prayer for purpose of use. In other instances new translations have been made by the compiler where the current form seems hardly to provide in English a worthy equivalent of a noble original, or where the old translation employed archaic language which upon our lips to-day would be unnatural and out of date.

I should like to add that the Notes which appear in this volume are a very abbreviated form of the Notes left in manuscript by Canon Macnutt.

R. W. D. Lee

THE VICARAGE
HORSHAM
August, 1951

INDEX OF PRAYERS

PART ONE
MORNING AND EVENING PRAYERS FOR A MONTH

PART TWO
PRAYERS FOR PUBLIC OR PRIVATE USE

PART ONE

MORNING AND EVENING PRAYERS
FOR A MONTH

THE BREASTPLATE OF ST. PATRICK   1

I arise to-day with the power of God to guide me, the might of God to uphold me, the wisdom of God to teach me, the eye of God to watch over me, the ear of God to hear me, the word of God to give me speech, the hand of God to protect me, the way of God to prevent me, the shield of God to shelter me, the host of God to defend me; against the snares of devils, against the temptations of vices, against the lusts of nature, against every man who meditates injury to me, whether far or near, with few or with many.   *St. Patrick*

DEDICATION   2

My Lord, I offer myself as a sacrifice of thanksgiving. Thou hast died for me, and I in turn make myself over to thee. I am not my own: Thou hast bought me; I will by my own act and deed complete the purchase. My wish is to be separated from everything of this world; to cleanse myself simply from sin; to put away from me even what is innocent, if used for its own sake and not for thine. I put away reputation and honour, and influence and power, for my praise and strength shall be in thee. Enable me to carry out what I profess.   *Cardinal Newman*

BROTHERLY LOVE   3

O merciful Father, whose will it is that we should love one another: give grace to us thy children, that we may look each to the good of others in word and deed; and hallow all our friendships by the blessing of thy Spirit, for his sake who loved us and gave himself for us, Jesus Christ our Lord.

STRENGTH AND PEACE   4

O God, our loving Father, we pray thee to keep us ever close to thyself, that we may find in thy love our strength and our peace.   *William Temple*

THE BREASTPLATE OF ST. PATRICK 5

Christ with me, Christ before me, Christ behind me,
Christ within me; Christ beneath me, Christ above me;
Christ at my right, Christ at my left; Christ in my lying
down, Christ in my sitting, Christ in my rising up; Christ
in the heart of every man who thinks of me, Christ in the
mouth of every man who speaks to me, Christ in every eye
that sees me, Christ in every ear that hears me.   May thy
salvation, O Lord, be ever with us.   *St. Patrick*

HUMILITY 6

O God, who resistest the proud, and givest grace unto the
humble: grant us the virtue of true humility, of which
thine only-begotten Son himself gave us the perfect
example; that we may never offend thee by our pride, and
be rejected for our self-assertion; through Jesus Christ
our Lord.   *Leonine Sacramentary*

AT ALL TIMES 7

Grant us, Lord, to know in weakness the strength of thy
Incarnation: in pain the triumph of thy Passion: in poverty
the riches of thy Godhead: in reproach the satisfaction of
thy sympathy: in loneliness the comfort of thy continual
presence: in difficulty the efficacy of thy intercession: in
perplexity the guidance of thy wisdom; and by thy glorious
death and resurrection bring us at last to the joy of seeing
thee face to face.   *Unknown*

8

Unto him that loveth us, and loosed us from our sins by
his Blood; and he made us to be a kingdom, to be priests
unto his God and Father; to him be the glory and the
dominion for ever and ever.   *Revelation 1. 5-6*

9

The everlasting Father bless us with his blessing everlasting.

B

ADORATION AND THANKSGIVING   10

O good Lord Jesus Christ, I pray thee to open my mouth, that therewith I may praise thee, and give unto thee thanks for all thy goodness towards me: and I beseech thee to keep it from all vain speech, from all leasings, and from all manner offences that thereby might come.

The Primer, 1557

FAITH, HOPE, AND LOVE   11

Christ, our Saviour, come thou to dwell within us, that we may go forth with the light of thy hope in our eyes, and thy faith and love in our hearts.   *Gregorian Sacramentary*

INWARD PEACE   12

Set free, O Lord, the souls of thy servants from restlessness and anxiety: give us the peace and power which flow from thee; and keep us in perplexity and distress, in griefs and grievances, from fear or faithlessness; that so, upheld by thy power and stayed upon the rock of thy faithfulness, through storm and stress we may abide in thee.

BOLDNESS   13

Grant us, O Lord, such boldness for thee, that we may set our face as a flint and not be ashamed: but contending valiantly for the truth out of weakness we may be made strong and conquer in the fight; through Jesus Christ our Lord.   *Wells Office Book*

COURAGE, WISDOM, POWER   14

O God, grant that looking upon the face of the Lord, as into a glass, we may be changed into his likeness, from glory to glory. Take out of us all pride and vanity, boasting and forwardness; and give us the true courage which shows itself by gentleness; the true wisdom which shows itself by simplicity; and the true power which shows itself by modesty.   *Charles Kingsley*

THANKSGIVING 15

All praise, all glory be to thee, my Lord and my God, for hearing my prayers in the time of my trouble. Praise the Lord, O my soul: while I live will I praise the Lord; as long as I have my being, I will sing praises unto my God. I called upon the Lord in my trouble, and the Lord heard me at large; therefore will I praise him. Thou art my God, and I will thank thee; thou art the Lord, and I will praise thee. Praised be the Lord, who hath not cast out my prayer, nor turned his mercy from me. O give thanks unto the Lord, for he is gracious, and his mercy endureth for ever. I will not only praise thee in secret, O Lord, but I will tell abroad what thou has done for my soul. Accept, O my God, this my sacrifice of praise and thanksgiving; and since the longer I live, the more I experience thy most adorable boundless goodness, the more devoutly may I daily praise thee, the more fervently may I daily love thee, through Jesus Christ, thy beloved. *Thomas Ken*

INWARD PEACE 16

O Lord Jesus Christ, who didst say that in thee we may have peace, and hast bidden us to be of good cheer, since thou hast overcome the world: give us ears to hear and faith to receive thy word; that in all the tensions and confusion of this present time, with mind serene and steadfast purpose, we may continue to abide in thee, who livest and wast dead and art alive for evermore.

Frederick B. Macnutt

WORSHIP 17

Unto him that is able to guard you from stumbling, and to set you before the presence of his glory without blemish in exceeding joy, to the only God our Saviour, through Jesus Christ our Lord, be glory, majesty, dominion, and power, before all time, and now, and for evermore.

St. Jude 24-25

MORNING   18

Into thy hands, O heavenly Father, I commit myself, body
and soul.   Let thy holy angel be with me, that the evil one
may have no power over me.   Help and bless thy Church;
hold thy protecting hand over this land and people: have
pity upon those who are in distress and need.   O God, let
the light of thy truth shine upon us, and bring us at last to
thy heavenly Kingdom; through Jesus Christ our Lord.
                                              Luther

DEDICATION   19

O God, who hast revealed thyself to be our King and
Saviour: grant us grace to yield ourselves to thine obedience; that we may be built upon the sure foundation of
thy Christ, and grow up before thee into a living temple,
where righteousness, mercy, and love abound and flourish,
and thy people offer unto thee a holy worship; through
Jesus Christ our Lord.   *Frederick B. Macnutt*

STRENGTH AND INSPIRATION   20

Inspire and strengthen us, O Lord God, by thy Holy
Spirit, to seek thy will and uphold thine honour in all
things; in the purity and joy of our homes, in the trust and
fellowship of our common life, in daily service of the
good; after the pattern and in the power of thy Son our
Lord Jesus Christ.   *E. Milner-White*

LOVE OF GOD   21

My God, my love: thou art all mine, and I am all thine.
Enlarge me in love; that with the inner mouth of my heart
I may taste how sweet it is to love.   Let me love thee more
than myself, and myself only for thee, and in thee all that
love thee truly: as the law of love commandeth shining
forth from thee.   *Thomas à Kempis*

INVOCATION 22

O God the Holy Ghost, who hast called us to thy service, as thou hast begun thy work, so also continue and finish it in us. Save us from our besetting sins, from pride, and bitterness, and faintness of heart, from sloth and self-deceit, and the curse of an unsubdued will; and grant us to know and to follow, to do and to suffer thy will; who with the Father and the Son livest and reignest, one God, for ever and ever. *R. W. Church*

FAITH 23

O holy Jesus, meek Lamb of God; bread that came down from heaven; light and life of all holy souls; help me to a true and living faith in thee. O do thou open thyself within me with all thy holy nature, spirit, tempers, and inclinations, that I may be born again of thee, in thee a new creature, quickened and revived, led and governed by thy Holy Spirit. *William Law*

BROTHERLY LOVE 24

O God of love, who through thy Son hast given us a new commandment that we should love one another, even as thou didst love us, the unworthy and the wandering, and gavest him up for our redemption: we pray thee, Lord, to give us thy servants, in all time of our life on earth, a mind forgetful of past ill-will, and a single heart to love our brethren; for the sake of thy Son, Jesus Christ our Lord. *From the Coptic*

ASPIRATION 25

I beseech thee, good Jesus, that as thou hast graciously granted to me here on earth sweetly to partake of the words of thy wisdom and knowledge, so thou wilt also vouchsafe that I may some time come to thee, the fountain of all wisdom, and always appear before thy face; who livest and reignest, world without end. *The Venerable Bede*

INVOCATION 26

Most great and glorious Lord God, accept my imperfect repentance, and send thy Spirit of adoption into my heart, that I may again be owned by thee, call thee Father, and share in the blessings of thy children. *John Wesley*

DEDICATION 27

O Lord Jesus Christ, who hast created and redeemed me, and hast brought me unto that which now I am, thou knowest what thou wouldst do with me; do with me according to thy will; for thy tender mercy's sake.
King Henry VI

ADORATION 28

O God, who requirest that we should seek thee and makest us to find thee, and openest to us when we knock: O God, from whom to be averted is to fall, and to whom to be turned is to rise; in whom to abide is to be established: O God, whom to know is to live, whom to serve is to reign; I praise thee, I bless thee, I adore thee, my God.
St. Augustine

WORK AND REFRESHMENT 29

O God, the strength of them that labour and the rest of the weary: grant that when we are strained and harassed by our work we may be renewed and recreated by thy Spirit, to serve thee gladly in health and vigour of body and mind; through Jesus Christ our Lord.

INWARD PEACE 30

O God, the consolation of them that be sorrowful, and the salvation of all who put their trust in thee: grant unto us in this dying life the peace for which we humbly pray, that we may hereafter attain unto thy presence and enter into thine unending joy; through our Lord Jesus Christ.

FREEDOM FROM SELF 31

O God, set our hearts at liberty from the service of ourselves, and let it be our meat and drink to do thy will.

HELP AND CORRECTION 32

Merciful God, to thee we commend ourselves and all those who need thy help and correction. Where there is hatred, give love; where there is injury, pardon; where there is doubt, faith; where there is despair, hope; where there is sadness, joy; where there is darkness, light. Grant that we may not seek so much to be consoled, as to console; to be understood, as to understand; to be loved, as to love; for in giving we receive, in pardoning we are pardoned, and dying we are born into eternal life. *St. Francis*

THE STUDY OF RELIGION 33

Almighty God, our heavenly Father, without whose help labour is useless, without whose light search is vain: invigorate my studies, and direct my inquiries, that I may by due diligence and right discernment, establish myself and others in thy holy faith. Take not, O Lord, thy Holy Spirit from me; let not evil thoughts have dominion in my mind. Let me not linger in ignorance, but enlighten and support me; for the sake of Jesus Christ our Lord.

Dr. Johnson

THANKSGIVING 34

Thine, O Lord, is the greatness, and the power, and the glory, and the victory, and the majesty: for all that is in the heaven and in the earth is thine; thine is the kingdom, O Lord, and thou art exalted as head above all. Both riches and honour come of thee, and thou rulest over all; and in thine hand is power and might; and in thine hand it is to make great, and to give strength unto all. Now therefore, our God, we thank thee, and praise thy glorious name. *1 Chronicles* 29. 11-13

INVOCATION   **35**

O Holy Spirit the comforter, who art everywhere present
and fillest all things, treasury of blessings and giver of life:
descend and remain upon me, most blessed one, and cleanse
me from all that is impure within.   *S. Baring-Gould*

FAITH, HOPE, AND LOVE   **36**

My God, I believe in thee: increase my faith.   I hope in
thee: strengthen my hope.   I love thee, and desire to love
thee more and more, and above all things, and all others
for thee: quicken my love and make me wholly thine.
                                              Unknown

GROWTH IN KNOWLEDGE   **37**

O Lord, whom to know is to live, I beseech thee to
increase in me the knowledge of thy truth.   In the truth
which I know, establish me; whatsoever things I ought to
know, teach me; in truths wherein I waver, confirm me;
in those things wherein I am deceived, correct me; in
things hard to understand, guide me; and from untruths,
false and noisome, deliver me.   Send out thy light and thy
truth, and let them lead me, till I know as I am known.

ENLIGHTENMENT   **38**

O God, who clothest thyself with light as with a garment,
and makest the outgoings of the morning and evening to
praise thee: mercifully grant that, as by thy created light
we perceive the wonders of thy universe, so by the un-
created light of thy Spirit we may discern the adorable
majesty of thy being; and that, our hearts and minds being
illumined by his presence, we may walk in thy paths
without stumbling, until at last all shadows flee away, and
in thy perfect light we see light; who with the Son and the
Holy Spirit art God for everlasting.   *W. R. Matthews*

OPENING PRAYER   39

O Almighty God, from whom every good prayer cometh,
and who pourest out on all who desire it the spirit of grace
and supplication: deliver us, when we draw nigh to thee,
from coldness of heart and wanderings of mind, that with
steadfast thoughts and kindled affections we may worship
thee in spirit and in truth; through Jesus Christ our Lord.
William Bright

EVENING   40

Into thy hands, O Lord and Father, we commend our
souls and our bodies, our parents and homes, friends and
servants, neighbours and kindred, our benefactors and
brethren departed, all thy people faithfully believing, and
all who need thy pity and protection. Enlighten us with
thy holy grace, and suffer us never to be separated from
thee, who art one God in Trinity, God everlasting.
St. Edmund Rich

ADORATION   41

O thou, in whom all things live, who commandest us to
seek thee and art ready to be found: to know thee is life,
to serve thee is freedom, to praise thee is our souls' joy. We
bless thee and adore thee, we worship thee and glorify thee,
we give thanks to thee for thy great glory. Maker and
preserver of all things visible and invisible, keep, we
beseech thee, the work of thine own hands, now and at all
times; through Jesus Christ our Lord.   *St. Augustine*

GUIDANCE IN STUDY   42

We beseech thee, O God, the God of truth, that what we
know not of things we ought to know thou wilt teach us;
that what we know of truth thou wilt keep us therein; that
what we are mistaken in, as men must be, thou wilt
correct; that at whatsoever truths we stumble thou wilt yet
establish us; and from all things that are false, and from all
knowledge that would be hurtful, do thou evermore
deliver us.   *After St. Fulgentius*

AT DAYBREAK   43

Lord Jesus Christ, very Sun of the world, ever arising and
never going down; who by thine appearing givest health
and gladness, creating, preserving, and nourishing all
things in heaven and in earth; I pray thee graciously to
enlighten my spirit, that the night of sin and the mists of
error may be driven away by thine inward shining; so that
I may go all my life long without stumbling, and walk as in
the daytime, pure and undefiled by the works of darkness;
who with the Father and the Holy Spirit livest and
reignest for ever.   *Erasmus*

GUIDANCE   44

O God, by whom the meek are guided in judgement, and
light riseth up in darkness for the godly: grant us, in all our
doubts and uncertainties, the grace to ask what thou
wouldest have us to do; that the Spirit of wisdom may save
us from all false choices, and that in thy light we may see
light and in thy straight path may not stumble; through
Jesus Christ our Lord.   *William Bright*

BROTHERLY LOVE   45

Enable us, O Lord, to love thee with all our heart and soul
and mind and strength, and our neighbours as ourselves;
that so the grace of thy love may dwell in us for ever.
Grant that all envy, jealousy, and mistrust may die in us,
and that suspicion and harsh judgements may be put
away from us, while we live in continual fellowship with
thee; through Jesus Christ our Lord.   *W. A. Knight*

DEDICATION   46

Lord, grant us grace, to make thy goodness our trust:
shutting our hearts against pride, our mouths against evil
words, our ears against foul knowledge, and using thy
gifts to the promotion of thy glory and of man's salvation;
for his blessed sake, in whom we have all and are full and
abound, Jesus Christ.   *Christina Rossetti*

BIBLE-READING   47

Grant, O Lord, that we may be diligent to read thy word,
wherein is wisdom, wherein is the royal law, wherein are
the lively oracles of God; and that reading it, we may daily
increase in the knowledge of thyself, and love and serve
thee with more perfect heart.   *Unknown*

INVOCATION   48

God the Father bless me, Christ guard me, the Holy Spirit
enlighten me, all the days of my life! The Lord be the
defender and guardian of my soul and my body, now and
ever, and world without end! Amen. The right hand of
the Lord preserve me always to old age! The grace of
Christ perpetually defend me from the enemy! Direct,
Lord, my heart into the way of peace. Lord God, haste
thee to deliver me, make haste to help me, O Lord.
                                    The Book of Cerne

INWARD PEACE   49

O God of peace, who hast taught us that in returning and
in rest we shall be saved, and in quietness and in confidence
shall be our strength: by the might of thy Spirit lift us, we
pray thee, to thy presence, where we may be still and
know that thou art God; through Jesus Christ our Lord.
                                            J. W. Suter

EVENING THANKSGIVING   50
φῶς ἱλαρὸν ἁγίας δόξης

O Jesu Christ, thou joyous light of the holy glory of the
Father, deathless, celestial, hallowed, blest: as we come to
the setting of the sun and behold the light of evening, we
hymn thee, Father, Son, and Holy Spirit of God. Worthy
art thou at all times to be hymned with hallowed voices,
Son of God, who givest life; therefore praise from the
whole world is thine.   *Greek Vesper Hymn*

DEDICATION   51

Send out thy light and thy truth, that I may live always
near to thee, my God. Let me feel thy love, that I may
be—as it were—already in heaven, that I may do all my
work as the angels do theirs; and let me be ready for every
work, be ready to go out or go in, to stay or depart, just as
thou shalt appoint. Lord, let me have no will of my own,
or consider my true happiness as depending in the smallest
degree on anything that can befall me outwardly, but as
consisting altogether in conformity to thy will.

Henry Martyn

INVOCATION   52

O God the Holy Ghost, most loving comforter of the faint-
hearted, I beseech thee to turn that which is evil in me into
good and that which is good into that which is better; turn
my mourning into joy, my wandering feet into the right
path, my ignorance into knowledge of thy truth, my luke-
warmness into zeal, my fear into love, all my material
good into a spiritual gift, all my earthly desires into
heavenly, all that is transient into that which lasts for ever,
everything human into that which is divine, everything
created and finite into that sovereign and immeasurable
good, which thou thyself art, O my God and my Saviour.

Thomas à Kempis

MORNING: COMMENDATION   53

Be, Lord, within me to strengthen me, without me to
preserve, over me to shelter, beneath me to support,
before me to direct, behind me to bring back, round about
me to fortify.   *Lancelot Andrewes*

                                                        54

Almighty and merciful God, Father, Son, and Holy
Spirit, vouchsafe to bless, aid, and bring us at last to the
life eternal.   *Sarum Breviary*

BIBLE-READING 55

O God, heavenly Father, from whom cometh every good and perfect gift, by whose inspiration all scripture is given, for doctrine, for reproof, for correction, and for instruction in righteousness: enable me to take thy word as a lamp unto my feet and a light unto my path; open my eyes that I may behold wondrous things out of thy law; and make me a doer as well as a hearer of thy word; through Jesus Christ our Lord.

TEMPORAL AND ETERNAL 56

Almighty and everlasting God, who hast set thine eternity in our hearts, and awakened within us desires which the world cannot satisfy: lift our eyes, we pray thee, above the narrow horizons of this present world, that we may behold the things eternal in the heavens, wherein is laid up for us an inheritance that fadeth not away; through Jesus Christ our Lord. *G. W. Briggs*

GUIDANCE 57

Lord God Almighty, open my heart and enlighten me by the grace of thy Holy Spirit, that I may seek what is well-pleasing to thy will; direct my thoughts and affections to think and to do such things as may make me worthy to attain to thine unending joys in heaven; and so order my doings after thy commandments that I may be ever diligent to fulfil them, and be found meet to be of thee everlastingly rewarded. *The Venerable Bede*

GLORIA 58

Almighty God, whose glory the heavens are telling, the earth thy power, and the sea thy might, and whose greatness all thy creatures that think and feel everywhere proclaim: to thee belong all glory, honour, might, greatness, and splendour, now and for ever, world without end. *Liturgy of St. James*

ON WAKING   59

Thou who sendest forth the light, createst the morning,
makest the sun to rise on the good and on the evil:
enlighten the blindness of our minds with the knowledge
of the truth: lift thou up the light of thy countenance upon
us: that in thy light we may see light, and, at the last, in the
light of grace the light of glory.   *Lancelot Andrewes*

DEDICATION   60

Blessed to thy name, O Lord God, who hast set before me
life and death, and hast bid me choose life. Behold, Lord,
I do with all my heart choose life; I choose thee, O my God,
for thou art my life. Save, Lord, and hear me, O King of
heaven, and accept my sacrifice, even the sacrifice of my
whole heart, which I now give thee. O my God, I offer
thee my senses and passions, and all my faculties; I offer
thee all my desires, all my designs, all my studies, all my
endeavours, all the remainder of my life; all that I have, or
am, I offer up all entirely to thy service.

Lord, sanctify me wholly, that my whole spirit, soul,
and body may become thy temple. O do thou dwell in
me, and be thou my God, and I will be thy servant.
    Thomas Ken

GLORIA   61

Glory be to thine all-blessed providence, O Lord, glory to
thy care for men, glory to thy condescension, O thou who
alone lovest mankind. Glory, O Christ, to thine uprising,
glory to thy dominion, glory to thine ordering of all things;
giver of life, O Christ our God, thou only lover of mankind, O Lord our resurrection and our life, glory be to thee.
    Eastern Orthodox

62

May God give us light to guide us, courage to support us,
and love to unite us, now and evermore.   *Unknown*

BIBLE-READING   63

O Lord Jesus Christ, who art the truth incarnate, and the
teacher of the faithful; let thy Spirit be present with us in
reading thy word, and conform our hearts to thy revelation: that learning of thee with honest hearts, we may be
rooted and built up in thee; who livest and reignest with
the Father and the Holy Spirit, one God, world without
end.   *Anon.*

FAITH   64

O Lord God, suffer us not to lean to our own wisdom, nor
to believe as blind flesh fancieth, nor to seek salvation
where superstition dreameth; but let our faith only be
grounded on thy word, and give us grace truly to believe in
thee, with all our heart to put our trust in thee, to look for
all good things of thee, to call upon thy blessed name in
adversity, and with joyful voices and more merry hearts to
praise and magnify it in prosperity.   *Thomas Becon*

EVENING   65

Watch thou, O Lord, with those who wake, or watch, or
weep to-night, and give thine angels charge over those who
sleep. Tend thy sick ones, O Lord Christ; rest thy weary
ones; bless thy dying ones; soothe thy suffering ones; pity
thine afflicted ones; shield thy joyous ones. And all, for
thy love's sake.   *St. Augustine*

TEMPORAL AND ETERNAL   66

Grant us, O Lord, not to mind earthly things, but to love
things heavenly, and while now we dwell among things
that are passing away, to cleave to those that shall abide for
ever; through Jesus Christ our Lord.

                                                          67

The Lord bless us, and preserve us from all evil, and bring
us to everlasting life; and may the souls of the faithful,
through the mercy of God, rest in peace.   *Sarum Primer*

SELF-MASTERY AND SERVICE   68

O Lord, help us to be masters of ourselves, that we may be
servants of others.   *Sir Alexander Paterson*

DAILY WORK   69

O Lord, our heavenly Father, by whose providence the
duties of men are variously ordered: grant to us all such a
spirit that we may labour heartily to do our work in our
several stations, as serving one master and looking for one
reward. Teach us to put to good account whatever talents
thou hast lent to us; help us to overcome all sloth and
indolence; and enable us to redeem our time by zeal and
patience; through thy Son, our Saviour. *Bishop Westcott*

AGAINST WORLDLINESS   70

O Lord, take from me a careful heart in all wordly things,
and grant that neither poverty oppress me and drive me to
despair or falsehood, neither wealth nor prosperity lift me
up to forget thee or myself; but that in prosperity I may be
thankful, and in adversity patient and humble. Make me
merry without lightness, sad without mistrust, sober
without dullness, fearing thee without desperation,
trusting in thee without presumption.   *Henry Bull*

GLORIA   71

Glory be to thee, O Lord, glory be to thee. Glory to thee
and glory to thine all-holy name, for all thy divine per-
fections therein: for thy goodness to us sinners and
unworthy, and mercy beyond all expression and imagination. Yea, O Lord, glory and praise and blessing and
thanksgiving, by the voices and concert of voices as well of
angels as of men, and of all thy saints in heaven, and of all
thy creation withal on earth, world without end.
                                        Lancelot Andrewes

BIBLE-READING   72

Grant to us, Lord, grace to hear thy Word with devout attention, with deep reverence, and with a true desire both to practise what it commands and to obtain what it promises. Imprint it upon our minds, and write it upon our hearts; and grant that, contemplating thy glory in this bright mirror of thy gospel, we may be changed into the same image through thy Spirit.   *Benedict Pictet*

HUMILITY   73

O Lord Jesus Christ, who didst humble thyself to become man, and to be born into the world for our salvation: teach us the grace of humility, root out of our hearts all pride and haughtiness, and so fashion us after thy holy likeness in this world, that in the world to come we may be made like unto thee; for thine own name's and mercies' sake.
    Bishop Walsham How

DEDICATION   74

O Lord, I give thee humble and hearty thanks for thy great goodness and mercy towards me. What thou hast further for me to do or to suffer, thou alone knowest. Give me patience and courage, and a firm resolution to do thee service, with grace to do it. And let me not live longer than to honour thee; through Jesus Christ.
    Archbishop Laud

THE WAY, THE TRUTH, THE LIFE   75

Lord Jesus Christ, the way by which we travel: shew me thyself, the truth that we must walk in: and be in me the life that lifts us up to God, our journey's ending.
    Frederick B. Macnutt

76

Blessing, and honour, and glory, and power, be unto him that sitteth upon the throne, and unto the lamb for ever and ever.   *Revelation* 5. 13

C

INVOCATION   77

Keep me, O my God, from the great offence; quench in
me all vain imaginations and sensual desires; sanctify and
supply my heart with the dew of thy Holy Spirit; refresh
it with the streams of thy grace, that it may bring forth
fruit in due season, and not cumber the ground nor be cut
off in thy anger.   *Henry Vaughan*

GUIDANCE   78

O Lord, who hast taught us that the way of man is not in
himself, and hast mercifully promised to keep the feet of
thy saints: direct our thoughts and inspire our actions, we
humbly pray thee, to the good of thy Church and the
fulfilment of thy eternal purpose; through Jesus Christ our
Lord.   *J. Armitage Robinson*

DEDICATION   79

Lord, I give and offer up unto thee myself and all that is
mine, actions and words, repose and silence; only do thou
preserve and guide me, and direct my hand and mind and
tongue to things that are honest and acceptable to thee,
and withdraw me from anything from which it were better
to abstain, by and for the sake of Jesus Christ our Lord.
                                     Archbishop Laud

FAITH   80

O Father, I will trust thee: for all the known and all the
unknown good that I have ever had has come from thee.
Sweet Saviour, I will trust thee: thy grace is all-sufficient
for my soul, as mighty as thy power and as matchless as
thy love.   Blest Spirit, I will trust thee: how can I ever
dare to trust myself, to think, or speak, or act apart from
thee ? O God, my God, my hope and stay, who knowest
and orderest all that is best, I know not what to will or do
aright; then make me ever love to choose and do thy will.
                                       Bishop Frere

BIBLE-READING 81

O Lord God, who hast left unto us thy holy Word to be a lantern unto our feet, and a light unto our steps: give unto us all thy Holy Spirit, that out of the same word we may learn what is thy eternal will, and frame our lives in all holy obedience to the same, to thy honour and glory and increase of our faith; through Jesus Christ our Lord.

Edward Dering

LOVE AND SERVICE 82

O God, the God of all goodness and all grace, who art worthy of a greater love than we can give or understand: fill our hearts with such love toward thee as may cast out all sloth and fear, that nothing may seem to us too hard to do or to suffer in obedience to thee; and grant that in loving thee we may become daily more like thee, and may finally obtain the crown of life which thou hast promised to them that love thee; through Jesus Christ our Lord.

Anon.

GLORIA 83

Glory be to God in the highest, and on earth peace, goodwill towards men: for unto us is born a Saviour, who is Christ the Lord. We praise thee, we bless thee, we glorify thee, we give thanks unto thee, for this greatest of thy mercies, O Lord God, heavenly King, God the Father Almighty. O Lord, the only-begotten Son Jesus Christ, O Lord God, Lamb of God, Son of the Father, who wast made man to take away the sins of the world, have mercy upon us by turning us from our iniquities. Thou who wast manifested to destroy the works of the devil, have mercy upon us by enabling us to renounce and forsake them. Thou who art the great advocate with the Father, receive our prayer, we humbly beseech thee.

Thomas Ken

ON WAKING   84

Most blessed Trinity, and one eternal God, as thou hast
this day awaked me from this bodily sleep, so awake my
soul from the sleep of sin; and as thou hast given me
strength after sleep, now again to watch, so after death
give me life; for what is death to me is but sleep with thee;
to whom be ascribed all glory, wisdom, majesty, dominion,
and praise, now and for ever.   *Henry Vaughan*

DEDICATION   85

O heavenly Father, subdue in me whatever is contrary to
thy holy will. Grant that I may ever study to know thy
will, that I may discover how to please thee. Give me a
true understanding and love of thy word, that it may be to
me bread which nourisheth to eternal life. Grant also that
I may never run into those temptations which in my
prayers I desire to avoid; and never permit my trials, O
Lord, to be above my strength; through Jesus Christ our
Lord.   *Bishop Thomas Wilson*

HOPE IN GOD   86

O God, who never forsakest those that hope in thee: grant
that we may ever keep that hope which thou hast given us
by thy Word as an anchor of our souls, to preserve us sure
and steadfast, unshaken and secure in all the storms of life;
through Jesus Christ our Lord.   *Unknown*

INVOCATION   87

We thank thee, O Lord, for the revelation of thy will
which thou hast given us in the blessings which thou
thyself hast pronounced upon those who love thee. Send
to us thy Holy Spirit to guide and teach us, that we may be
made worthy of thy heavenly kingdom, and live now as
fellow-citizens of the saints. O Lord, hear us: O Lord,
have mercy upon us: O Lord, make us like unto thee.
                                            Bishop Westcott

BIBLE-READING 88

O Lord God Almighty, who art the source of knowledge
and of truth; look down, we beseech thee, upon us thy
servants gathered here for the study of thy Word, and of
whatsoever helps to the understanding of it. Fill us with
the grace of thy Holy Spirit, who alone leadeth into all
truth; and grant us a right judgement in all things;
through Jesus Christ our Lord.

INWARD PEACE 89

O thou who art peace eternal, and givest peace to those
who are steadfast in heart: let thy peace be upon us thy
servants, that in the doing of thy will we may ourselves
find peace, and ever be ministers of peace to others;
through Jesus Christ our Lord.   *Frederick B. Macnutt*

GLORIA 90

Glory be to thee, O Lord, my creator. Glory be to thee,
O Jesus, my redeemer. Glory be to thee, the Holy Ghost,
my sanctifier, my guide, and comforter. All love, all glory,
be to the high undivided Trinity, whose works are
inseparable, and whose dominion endureth world without
end; to thee, to thee alone, and to thy Son, and Holy
Spirit, be glory for ever and ever. *Bishop Thomas Wilson*

DEDICATION 91

Take, Lord, all my liberty. Receive my memory, my
understanding, and my whole will. Whatever I have and
possess thou hast given to me; to thee I restore it wholly,
and to thy will I utterly surrender it for thy direction.
Give me the love of thee only, with thy grace, and I am
rich enough; nor ask I anything beside.

St. Ignatius of Loyola

INVOCATION   **92**

O God our Father, who hast sent thy Son to be our
Saviour: renew in us day by day the power of thy Holy
Spirit; that with knowledge and zeal, with courage and
love, with gratitude and hope, we may strive manfully in
thy service: may he keep our vision clear, our aspiration
high, our purpose firm, and our sympathy wide; that we
may live as faithful soldiers and servants of our Lord Jesus
Christ.   *William Temple*

DEDICATION   **93**

O Lord Jesu Christ, Son of the living God, grant me, a
weak and wretched sinner, to have ever before the eyes of
my heart thy life and character, and as far as in me lies to
imitate them. Make me to go forward in them and to
grow up into a perfect man and into an holy temple in the
Lord. Enlighten, I pray thee, my heart with the brightness of thy grace, and let it continually prevent and follow
me; that having thee as my guide in all my ways, I may do
such things as please thee and shun what is displeasing in
thy sight. Direct, I beseech thee, my thoughts, words,
and actions in thy law and in thy precepts, O Most High;
so that in all things I may do thy will, and may be
accounted worthy to be saved by thee both here and for
ever.   *Ludolphus of Saxony*

GLORIA   **94**

Glory to our ascended Lord, that he is with us always.
Glory to the word of God, going forth with his armies,
conquering and to conquer. Glory to him who has led
captivity captive, and given gifts for the perfecting of his
saints. Glory to him who has gone before to prepare a
place in his Father's home for us. Glory to the author and
finisher of our faith; that God in all things may be glorified
through Jesus Christ. To whom be all worship and praise,
dominion and glory; now and for ever and ever.   *Anon.*

CLOSING PRAYER   **95**

O Lord, hear my prayer, fulfil my desire to my good, and
to the praise of thy holy Name.   *Sarum Breviary*

DEDICATION **96**

O merciful Lord God, heavenly Father, whether we sleep or wake, live or die, we are always thine. Wherefore we beseech thee heartily that thou wilt vouchsafe to take care and charge of us, and not suffer us to perish in the works of darkness, but to kindle the light of thy countenance in our hearts; that thy godly knowledge may daily increase in us through a right and pure faith, and that we may always be found to walk and live after thy will and pleasure.

The Primer

97

O God, my protector, enlighten, I beseech thee, my inward eyes, that I consent not to sin; strengthen all my powers, that I may overcome mine enemies. Lord, subject all my senses and all my members to my spirit, in order to serve thee alone. Cleanse thou my heart, inflame my spirit, enlighten my understanding, collect my thoughts, unite all my powers, and bind them together with the chain of thy love and the fetters of thy fear, so that nevermore may I be estranged from thee, but that, ever subject and united to thee, I may cleave unto thee and faint not, but rather fear, and love, and thank, and praise, and bless thee now and for ever.

John Tauler

INWARD PEACE **98**

O Father of lights, with whom there is no variation nor shadow of turning, who abidest steadfast as the stars of heaven: give us grace to rest upon thy eternal changelessness, and in thy faithfulness find peace; through Jesus Christ our Lord.

G. W. Briggs

EVENING **99**

Preserve me, Lord, while I am waking, and defend me while I am sleeping, that my soul may continually watch for thee, and both body and soul may rest in thy peace for ever.

Bishop Cosin

DEDICATION   100

Grant, O Lord, that I may be so ravished in the wonder
and love of thee that I may forget myself and all things;
may feel neither prosperity nor adversity; may not fear to
suffer all the pain in the world rather than be parted and
pulled away from thee. O let me find thee more inwardly
and verily present with me than I am with myself; and
make me most circumspect how I do use myself in the
presence of thee, my holy Lord. Lord, I desire nothing
neither in myself nor in any creature, save only to know
and execute thy blessed will; saying alway in my heart,
Lord, what wouldst thou have me to do? Transform my
will into thine.   *Robert Leighton*

THE WAY, THE TRUTH, THE LIFE   101

Lord Jesu Christ, who hast said that thou art the way, the
truth, and the life: we pray thee suffer us not at any time to
stray from thee, who art the way; nor ever to distrust thy
promises, who art the truth; nor to rest in any other thing
than thee, who art the life; for thou hast taught us what to
believe, what to do, what to hope, and wherein to rest.
                                                Erasmus

THE LIKENESS OF LOVE   102

O blessed Jesus, who knowest the impurity of our affection,
the narrowness of our sympathy, and the coldness of our
love, take possession of our souls and fill our minds with
the image of thyself; break the stubbornness of our selfish
wills and mould us in the likeness of thine unchanging
love, O thou who only could, our Saviour, our Lord and
our God.   *William Temple*

                                                        103

To God, the Father of our Lord Jesus Christ; to the
eternal Son, that was incarnate and born of a Virgin; to the
Spirit of the Father and the Son; be all honour and glory,
worship, and thanksgiving, now and for ever.
                                            Jeremy Taylor

BIBLE-READING 104

O holy and eternal Jesus, who hast begotten us by thy Word, renewed us by thy Spirit, fed us by thy sacraments, and by the daily ministry of thy Word; still go on to build us up to life eternal. Let thy most Holy Spirit be present with me, and rest upon me in reading or hearing thy sacred Word, that I may do it humbly, reverently, without prejudice, with a mind ready and desirous to learn, and to obey, that I may be readily furnished and instructed to every good work, and may practise all thy holy laws and commandments, to the glory of thy Name.

Jeremy Taylor

LOVE OF GOD 105

Lord, give me what thou willest, only deny me not thyself; let me not possess thee less, love thee less, than, if faithful, I should have loved thee; be it that here I must be a wreck of myself; but bind me up, remake me, that I contain not for ever less of thee and of thy love.

Edward Bouverie Pusey

THE INWARD CHRIST 106

O God, who madest me for thyself, to show forth thy goodness in me: manifest, I humbly beseech thee, the life-giving power of thy holy nature within me; help me to such a true and living faith in thee, such strength of hunger and thirst after the birth, life, and spirit of thy holy Jesus in my soul, that all that is within me, may be turned from every inward thought or outward work that is not thee, thy holy Jesus, and heavenly working in my soul.

William Law

107

Unto him who is the blessed and only potentate, the King of kings, and Lord of lords; who only hath immortality, dwelling in the light which no man can approach unto, whom no man hath seen, nor can see: be honour and power everlasting. Amen. *1 Timothy* 6. 15-16

ON RISING   108

O God, who dividest day from night, give us hearts and
minds unshadowed by the gloom of evil; that we may
think continually upon things that are good and wholesome, and be always pleasing in thy sight; through Jesus
Christ our Lord.   *Gelasian Sacramentary*

INVOCATION   109

O Eternal God, the fountain of wisdom and the giver of
grace, who didst send thy Spirit to dwell with our fathers
and to guide them into the way of truth: grant to us in our
difficulties and dangers that we also may be guided by the
light and power of the same Spirit, to know thy mind and
to do thy will, for the glory of thy Name and the enlightenment of thy Church; through Jesus Christ our Lord.

                                    Arthur W. Robinson

SYMPATHY   110

Blessed Lord, who for our sakes wast content to bear
sorrow, and want, and death, grant unto us such a measure
of thy Spirit that we may follow thee in all self-denial and
tenderness of soul. Help us, by thy great love, to succour
the afflicted, to relieve the needy and destitute, to comfort
the feeble-minded, to share the burdens of the heavy laden,
and ever to see thee in all that are poor and desolate.

                                    Bishop Westcott

THANKSGIVING   111

O thou, who art the hope of all the ends of the earth, and
on whom the eyes of all do wait, who crownest the year
with thy goodness, and openest thine hand and fillest all
things living with plenteousness: every day we give thanks
unto thee, and praise thy Name for ever and ever; through
Jesus Christ our Lord.   *W. A. Knight*

EVENING 112

O Lord Jesus Christ, our watchman and keeper, take us to
thy care: grant that, our bodies sleeping, our minds may
watch in thee, and be made merry by some sight of that
celestial and heavenly life, wherein thou art the King and
Prince, together with the Father and the Holy Spirit,
where thy angels and holy souls be most happy citizens.
O purify our souls, keep clean our bodies, that in both we
may please thee, sleeping and waking, for ever.

Elizabethan

INVOCATION 113

O most Holy Spirit of God, from whom alone floweth the
fullness of wisdom and life: come in thine everlasting
power and glory, we beseech thee, upon thy Church and
into the hearts of men; to bring to the world a new birth of
holiness, new interpretations of truth, and new unity in
love; in the Name of Jesus Christ our Lord, who with the
Father and thee liveth and reigneth, one God, world
without end. *E. Milner-White*

ENLIGHTENMENT 114

O God, who by thine almighty Word dost enlighten every
man that cometh into the world: enlighten, we beseech
thee, the hearts of us thy servants by the glory of thy grace,
that we may ever think such things as are worthy and well-
pleasing to thy Majesty, and love thee with a perfect heart;
through Jesus Christ our Lord. *Alcuin*

115

To God the Father, who first loved us, and made us
accepted in the beloved: to God the Son, who loved us,
and washed us from our sins in his own blood: to God the
Holy Ghost, who sheds the love of God abroad in our
hearts: be all love and glory for time and for eternity.

Thomas Ken

MORNING   116

O heavenly Father, in whom we live and move and have
our being, we humbly pray thee so to guide and govern us
by thy Holy Spirit, that in all the cares and occupations of
our daily life we may never forget thee, and remember that
we are ever walking in thy sight; through Jesus Christ
our Lord.

THANKSGIVING   117

It is meet and right to worship the Father, the Son, and
the Holy Spirit, Trinity of one substance and undivided:
it is meet and right to hymn thee, to bless thee, to praise
thee, to give thanks to thee, to worship thee, ever being
and being the same, thee, and thine only-begotten Son,
and thy Holy Spirit.   For thou art God, ineffable,
inconceivable, invisible, incomprehensible, being ever and
being the same, thou and thine only-begotten Son, and
thy Holy Spirit.   Thou didst bring us into being out of
nothing, and when we had fallen thou didst raise us up
again, and didst leave nothing undone till thou hadst led
us up to heaven, and didst bestow upon us thy kingdom
that shall come.   For all these things we give thanks to
thee, and to thine only-begotten Son, and thy Holy
Spirit, for all things that we know and know not, for thy
benefits manifest and hidden, which thou hast freely
given to us.   *Liturgy of St. Chrysostom*

SERVICE   118

Teach us, good Lord, to serve thee as thou deservest; to
give and not to count the cost; to fight and not to heed the
wounds; to toil and not to seek for rest; to labour and not
to ask for any reward, save that of knowing that we do thy
will; through Jesus Christ our Lord.
                                    St. Ignatius of Loyola

GOD'S PROTECTION   119

The Lord enrich us with his grace, and further us with
his heavenly blessing; the Lord defend us in adversity and
keep us from all evil; the Lord receive us our prayers, and
graciously absolve us from our offences.
                                    Gregorian Sacramentary

BIBLE-READING   120

Take away, O Lord, the veil of my heart while I read the
Scriptures. Blessed art thou, O Lord: O teach me thy
statutes: give me a word, O Word of the Father: touch my
heart: enlighten the understandings of my heart: open my
lips and fill them with thy praise. Be thou, O Lord, in my
spirit and in my mouth: in my mouth that lawfully and
worthily I may show forth thine oracles by the hallowing
power of thy thrice Holy Spirit.   *Lancelot Andrewes*

THE GOAL OF SERVICE   121

Enlighten thy people, O Lord, and inflame their hearts
with thy love: that they may daily follow thy steps, as thou
commandest, and last behold thee face to face in heaven
where thou art; who with the Father and the Holy Spirit
livest and reignest, world without end.
                                    Frederick B. Macnutt

EVENING: THANKSGIVING   122

Most gracious, almighty God, thou preserver of men,
what shall I do unto thee? What shall I render unto my
Lord for all the mercies and loving-kindnesses showed
unto thy servant this day, and all the days of my life
hitherto? I will offer unto thee the sacrifice of thanksgiving, and call upon the Name of the Lord. I will ever
love thee, fear thee, praise thee, and trust in thee. My
song shall be of thee in the night-season, and in the daytime I will be speaking of thy wondrous works, thy most
merciful and liberal arm; I will make thee my delight in the
house of my pilgrimage, and I shall always with all my
strength, with all my heart, and with all my soul, ascribe
unto thee all glory, wisdom, majesty, dominion, and
honour, this day and for evermore.   *Henry Vaughan*

ASCRIPTION   123

Glory be to thee, O Lord, glory to thee, O Holy One,
glory to thee, O King!   *St. Chrysostom*

INVOCATION   124

O Holy Spirit, who abhorrest all uncleanness and rejoicest
and delightest to dwell in pure and innocent hearts: I
beseech thee by thy mercies that, as I owe to thy loving-
kindness this glorious treasure which I carry in an earthen
vessel, so I may keep it safe by thy goodness, and daily
pleasing thee more and more with undefiled soul and body,
may come to that life which knows no corruption, in
which thou livest and reignest with the Father and the
Son.   *Elizabethan*

INWARD PEACE   125

O thou lover of mankind, send down into our hearts that
peace which the world cannot give, and give us peace in
this world.   O King of Peace, keep us in love and charity;
be our God, for we have none other beside thee; grant
unto our souls the life of righteousness, that the death of
sin may not prevail against us, or against any of thy
people.   *W. F. Hook*

ENLIGHTENMENT   126

We beseech thee, Lord Jesus, to enlighten us thy people
and set our hearts aflame with the fire of thy love: that we
may ever acknowledge thee as our Saviour and inwardly
behold thee as our Lord; who with the Father and the
Holy Spirit livest and reignest, ever one God, world
without end.

BROTHERLY LOVE   127

Almighty and most merciful God, who hast given us a new
commandment that we should love one another, give us
also grace that we may fulfil it.   Make us gentle, courteous,
and forbearing.   Direct our lives so that we may look to the
good of others in word and deed.   And hallow all our
friendships by the blessing of thy Spirit; for his sake who
loved us and gave himself for us, Jesus Christ our Lord.
                                        Bishop Westcott

BEFORE STUDY   128

O God, who hast ordained that whatever is to be desired, should be sought by labour, and who, by thy blessing, bringest honest labour to good effect; look with mercy upon my studies and endeavours. Grant me, O Lord, to design only what is lawful and right; and afford me calmness of mind, and steadiness of purpose, that I may so do thy will in this short life, as to obtain happiness in the world to come; for the sake of Jesus Christ our Lord.

Dr. Johnson

HEROIC LOVE   129

O Jesus, Master and Lord, pour into our hearts thine own heroic love, that being filled with love we may know the love which passeth knowledge, and live in the unknown power of love to win men to trust in love, to the glory of God who is love.   *William Temple*

NIGHT   130

To my weariness, O Lord, vouchsafe thou rest, to my exhaustion renew thou strength. Lighten mine eyes that I sleep not in death. Deliver me from the terror by night, the pestilence that walketh in darkness. Supply me with healthy sleep, that I may pass through this night without fear. O keeper of Israel, who neither slumberest nor sleepest, guard me this night from all evil, guard my soul, O Lord. Shelter me with the wing of thy pity; awaken me at the fitting time, the time of prayer; and give me to seek thee early, for thy glory, and for thy service.

Lancelot Andrewes

PURITY   131

Eternal God, who hast taught us by thy holy Word that our bodies are temples of thy Spirit, keep us, we most humbly beseech thee, temperate and holy in thought, word, and deed, that at the last, with all the pure in heart, we may see thee, and be made like unto thee in thy heavenly kingdom.

Bishop Westcott

DEDICATION   132

O King of glory and Lord of valours, our warrior and our
peace; who hast said, 'Be of good cheer, I have overcome
the world,' be thou victorious in us thy servants, for
without thee we can do nothing. Give us both to will and
to perform. Grant thy compassion to go before us, thy
compassion to come behind us: before us in undertaking,
behind us in our ending. And what shall I more say,
unless that thy will be done, who dost will that all men
should be saved? Thy will is our salvation, our glory,
and our joy.   *Alcuin*

THANKSGIVING   133

Praised be God in his power and glory; the Father, creator
of all, from everlasting to everlasting; the Son, our saviour
and redeemer; the Holy Spirit, our helper and comforter.
We praise him, for that he judges the world in righteousness; we praise him, in that he waits upon us in his
eternity; we praise him, who will bring to an end all that is
temporal; we praise him, who will perfect the thing which
he has begun.   *From the German*

TOUCHING LIVES   134

All through this day, O Lord, may I touch as many lives as
thou wouldst have me touch for thee; and those whom I
touch do thou with thy Holy Spirit quicken, whether by
the word I speak, the letter I write, the prayer I breathe, or
the life I have.   *Unknown*

THE HOLY TRINITY   135

God the Father, who didst create us: God the Son, who hast
redeemed us: God the Holy Spirit, who dost sanctify us:
bless us and keep us, O Blessed Trinity, in body, soul, and
spirit, unto life everlasting.   *From the German*

FOR BIBLE-READING   136

Let not thy Word, O Lord, become a judgement upon us,
that we hear it and do it not, that we know it and love it
not, that we believe it and obey it not: O thou, who with
the Father and the Holy Spirit livest and reignest, world
without end.   *Thomas à Kempis*

GIFTS OF GRACE   137

O Lord, increase in me faith and devotion; replenish my
heart with all goodness, and by thy great mercy keep me
in the same. Give me godly zeal in prayer, true humility
in prosperity, perfect patience in adversity, and continual
joy in the Holy Ghost; even for Jesus Christ his sake, my
only Lord and saviour.   *Archbishop Laud*

INWARD PEACE   138

O Lord God, heavenly Father, who didst give up thine
only-begotten Son into grief and sorrow, that we might
have peace through him: grant us so surely to found our
faith upon him alone that we may have peace in our souls.
Quicken us with thy Word; grant already here on earth the
peace which is a foretaste of the rest that remaineth for thy
people. And while the cares and tumults of this life beset
us round about, guide us in all our undertakings by thy
Holy Spirit, that we may abide in thy peace; through
Jesus Christ our Lord.   *Swedish Liturgy*

THANKSGIVING   139

We thank thee, O Lord, for all who have chosen poverty or
solitude for thy sake, for men of prayer, for saints in
common life who have borne suffering for noble ends, and
for those who have endured pain with patience and purity
of life, in the strength of him who for the joy that was set
before him endured the cross, even Jesus Christ our Lord.
    Unknown

D

THANKSGIVING   140

We give thee thanks, holy Lord, Father Almighty, eternal
God, who hast been pleased to bring us through the night
to the hours of morning: we pray thee graciously to grant
that we may pass this day without sin, so that at eventide
we may again give thanks to thee; through Jesus Christ
our Lord.   *Gelasian Sacramentary*

THE FINDING OF LOVE   141

O Lord Jesus Christ, thou Word of God, creator and
redeemer, possess our mind and conscience, our heart and
imagination, by thine indwelling Spirit; that we and all
men, being purged of pride, may find and rest in that love
which is thy very self.   *William Temple*

SERVICE   142

O Lord Jesus Christ, who when on earth wast ever
occupied about thy Father's business; grant that we may
not grow weary in well-doing. Give us grace to do all in
thy Name; be thou the beginning and the end of all; the
pattern whom we follow, the redeemer in whom we trust,
the master whom we serve, the friend to whom we look for
sympathy. May we never shrink from our duty through
any fear of man; make us faithful unto death: and bring us
at last into the eternal presence, where with the Father and
the Holy Ghost thou livest and reignest for ever.
                                    Edward Bouverie Pusey

COMMENDATION   143
In Manus Tuas

Into thy hands I commend my spirit, soul, body: thou
hast created, redeemed, regenerated them, O Lord of truth:
and with me all mine and all things mine: thou hast
bestowed them upon me, O Lord, in thy goodness.
Preserve us from all evil, preserve our souls, I beseech
thee, O Lord: keep us from falling and present us faultless
before the presence of thy glory in that day. Let the words
of my mouth and the meditation of my heart be alway
acceptable in thy sight, O Lord, my rock and my redeemer.
                                        Lancelot Andrewes

DAY AND NIGHT   **144**

O Christ, who art the keeper of all, let thy right hand guard and overshadow me by day and by night; when I sit in the house, and when I walk abroad; when I lie down, and when I rise again, lest at any time I fall; to the glory of thy Name.   *St. Nerses*

LOVE OF GOD   **145**

My God, I love thee thyself above all else, and thee I desire as my last end. Always and in all things, with my whole heart and strength, and with unceasing labour, I seek thee. If thou give not thyself to me, thou givest nothing: if I find not thee, I find nothing. Grant to me, therefore, most loving God, that I may ever love thee for thyself above all things and seek thee in all things in this life present, so that at last I may find thee and keep thee for ever in the world to come.   *Thomas Bradwardine*

TEMPORAL AND ETERNAL   **146**

O Lord Jesus Christ, exalt me with thee so to know the mystery of life that I may use the earthly as the appointed expression and type of the heavenly; and by using to thy glory the natural body, I may be fit to be exalted to the use of the spiritual body.   *Charles Kingsley*

BENEDICTUS   **147**

Blessed be he who in his love stooped to redeem mankind! Blessed be the King who made himself poor to enrich the needy! Blessed be he who came to fulfil the types and emblems of the prophets! Blessed be he who made creation rejoice with the wealth and treasure of his Father! Blessed be he whose glory the dumb sang with hosannas! Blessed be he to whom little children sang new glory in hymns of praise! Blessed be the new King who came that new-born babes might glorify him! Blessed be he unto whom children brought faltering songs to praise him among his disciples!   *Ephraem of Edessa*

MORNING 148

O almighty God, who sittest upon the throne, make all things within us new this day. Renew our faith, and hope, and love; renew our wills, that we may serve thee gladly and watchfully with all our powers; renew our delight in thy truth and in thy worship; renew our joy in thee, our longing that all may know thee, our desires and labours to serve others. And so take care of us thy people, who embrace the cross of thy Son and desire to walk in the light and power of thy Spirit, now and evermore.

Unknown

DEDICATION 149

Use me, my saviour, for whatever purpose and in whatever way thou mayest require. Here is my poor heart, an empty vessel: fill it with thy grace. Here is my sinful and troubled soul: quicken it and refresh it with thy love. Take my heart for thine abode; my mouth to spread abroad the glory of thy Name; my love and all my powers for the advancement of thy believing people; and never suffer the steadfastness and confidence of my faith to abate.

Dwight L. Moody

ADORATION AND THANKSGIVING 150

Thou, O God, art praised in Sion and unto thee shall the vows be performed. Thou art worthy, O Lord our God the holy one, to receive glory and honour and power. Thou that hearest the prayer unto thee shall all flesh come: this withal shall come. But my misdeeds prevail against me: O be thou merciful unto my sins: that I may come to give thanks unto thee with all thy works and with thy holy ones. O Lord, thou shalt open my lips and my mouth shall show thy praise.

Lancelot Andrewes

GUIDANCE 151

Teach me, O my Lord Jesus, instruct me, that I may learn from thee what I ought to teach concerning thee.

Archbishop Laud

BIBLE-READING   152

Grant me of thy grace, O Christ, I beseech thee, that thy
good Spirit may lead me in the right way, and remove far
from me him who cometh to destroy; that casting away all
malice of evil, I may search into the commandments of
my God, and with the eyes of my mind awakened go
forward faithfully to read and to weigh the marvels of thy
holy law.   *The Venerable Bede*

TEMPORAL AND ETERNAL   153

O Lord our God, who dost guide those who seek thee
through the vain shows of earth into the knowledge of thy
heavenly reality: let thy goodness uphold us and thy right
hand lead us, that we may obediently reject the illusions of
things temporal and walk without faltering in the light of
things eternal; through Jesus Christ our Lord.
                                        Frederick B. Macnutt

DEDICATION   154

Lord, who hast called me with a holy calling; O Word of
God, living and active, be thou quick to discern the thoughts
and intents of my heart, that I may not glory save in the
cross, that I may not tire in well-doing, and not wax weary
in soul.   Lord, I lack wisdom, make me wise, who ask in
faith and doubt neither thy power nor thy love; may my
inner man be renewed day by day, fashioned after the
image of God.   And this I pray that love may abound in
knowledge and all discernment, to learn to know thy will
and thee, my God, in all wisdom and spiritual understanding and orderly prudence.   *Archbishop Benson*

                                                 155

Blessing and honour and thanksgiving and praise, more
than we can utter, more than we can conceive, be unto
thee, O holy and glorious Trinity, Father, Son, and Holy
Ghost, by all angels, by all men, all creatures, for ever and
ever.   *Thomas Ken*

MORNING **156**

Into thy hands, O Lord, we commend ourselves this day.
Let thy presence be with us to its close. Strengthen us to
remember that in whatsoever good work we do we are
serving thee. Give us a diligent and watchful spirit, that
we may seek in all things to know thy will, and knowing it,
gladly to perform it; to the honour of thy Name.

Unknown

FAITH, HOPE, AND LOVE **157**

Lord, give me faith that tries and tests the things unseen,
and assures itself of thee who art the truth, that doubt
may not overwhelm nor darkness cover me; give me hope,
that I may follow the light of thy sure promises, and lose not
the way nor fall into byways; give me love, that I may give
thee myself as thou givest; for thou, O Lord God, art the
thing that I long for; and thou art blessedness beyond all
thought and heart's desiring. *Frederick B. Macnutt*

LIBERATION AND SERVICE **158**

O God, who knowest our hearts and seest our temptations,
our struggles, and our deep distress: have pity upon us, and
deliver us from the evil that wars against our souls. Thou
art all-powerful, and we are weak and sinful; but our hope
is in thee, O faithful and good God. Release us from
bondage to evil, and grant that henceforth we may serve
thee in the freedom of thy holy love. *Eugène Bersier*

BROTHERLY LOVE **159**

O God, who of thy great love to man didst reconcile earth
to heaven through thine only-begotten Son: grant that we
who by the darkness of our sins are turned aside from
brotherly love, may be filled with his Spirit shed abroad
within us, and embrace our friends in thee and our
enemies for thy sake; through Jesus Christ our Lord.

Mozarabic

DEDICATION   **160**

Lord Jesus, all-pure, purify us that we may behold thee.
All-holy, sanctify us that we may stand before thee.
All-gracious, mould us that we may please thee. Very love,
suffer us not to set at naught thy love; suffer not devil,
world, flesh, to destroy us; suffer not ourselves to destroy
ourselves; us with whom thou strivest, whom thou desirest,
whom thou lovest.   *Christina Rossetti*

FAITH   **161**

Almighty God, who in thy wisdom hast so ordered our
earthly life that we needs must walk by faith and not by
sight; grant us such faith in thee that, amidst all things
that pass our understanding, we may believe in thy
fatherly care, and ever be strengthened by the assurance
that underneath are the everlasting arms; through Jesus
Christ our Lord.   *Unknown*

THANKSGIVING: FOR THE CHURCH   **162**

O God, most glorious, most bountiful, accept, we humbly
beseech thee, our thanksgivings for thy Holy Catholic
Church: for the light of the faith which it has handed on to
us, and for the mercies by which thou hast redeemed us
from the power of sin; for the love which thou hast shed
abroad upon the earth, and for the holy lives in which thou
hast revealed thyself to mankind. Glory be to thee, O
blessed Trinity; and to thee be ascribed all honour, might,
majesty, and dominion, now and for evermore.   *Anon.*

WORSHIP   **163**

Worthy art thou, our Lord and our God, to receive the
glory and the honour and the power: for thou didst create
all things, and because of thy will they were, and were
created.   *Revelation* 4. 11

DEDICATION   164

Lord Jesu, I give thee my body, my soul, my substance,
my fame, my friends, my liberty, and my life; dispose of
me, and of all that is mine, as it seemeth best to thee, and
to the glory of thy blessed Name. Be thou a light unto
mine eyes, music to mine ears, sweetness to my taste, and
a full contentment to my heart. Be thou my sunshine in
the day, my food at the table, my repose in the night, my
clothing in nakedness, and my succour in all necessities.

Bishop Cosin

BEFORE UNDERTAKING DAILY DUTIES   165

O Lord, I have a busy world around me; eye, ear, and
thought will be needed for all my work to be done in that
busy world. Now ere I enter upon it I would commit eye,
ear, and thought to thee. Do thou bless them and keep
their work thine; such as, through thy natural laws my
heart beats and my blood flows without any thought of
mine for them, so my spiritual life may hold on its course
at those times when my mind cannot consciously turn to
thee to commit each particular thought to thy service.
Hear my prayer for my dear redeemer's sake.

Dr. Arnold of Rugby

LOVE AND FAITH   166

Lord, I believe in thee; help thou mine unbelief. I love
thee, yet not with a perfect heart as I would; I long for
thee, yet not with my full strength; I trust in thee, yet not
with my whole mind. Accept my faith, my love, my longing to know and serve thee, my trust in thy power to keep
me. What is cold do thou kindle, what is lacking do thou
make up. I wait thy blessing; through Jesus Christ our
Lord.   *Malcolm Spencer*

                                              167

Blessing, and glory, and wisdom, and thanksgiving, and
honour, and power, and might, be unto our God for ever
and ever.   *Revelation 8. 12*

BIBLE-READING 168

O God, our heavenly Father, who hast made known unto us through the Gospel the way of redemption for the forgiveness of our sins: grant unto us, we pray thee, that we may not contemn thy Word, but receive it from our hearts and put our sole trust in thy mercy and in the merits of thy dear Son, Jesus Christ. *Lutheran Liturgy*

HUMILITY 169

Lord Jesu Christ, whose whole life was nothing but humility and meekness, who only art our very righteousness; grant us to serve and honour thee, with humble and meek hearts, and in all our life and conversation to desire to be occupied in the works of righteousness; which livest and reignest. *The Primer*

GOD OUR PORTION 170

My God, I take thee for my portion: from mere prudence I turn from the world to thee; I give up the world for thee. I renounce that which promises for him who performs. To whom else should I go? I desire to find and feed on thee here; I desire to feed on thee, Jesu my Lord, who art risen, who hast gone up on high, who yet remainest with thy people on earth. I look up to thee; I look for the living bread which is in heaven, which comes down from heaven: give me ever of this bread. Destroy this life, which will soon perish, even though thou dost not destroy it; and fill me with that supernatural life which will never die. *Cardinal Newman*

GOD OUR GUARDIAN 171

May God Almighty direct our days in his peace, and grant us the gifts of his blessing; may he deliver us in all our troubles, and establish our minds in the tranquillity of his peace; may he so guide us through things temporal that we finally lose not the things eternal. *Gregorian Sacramentary*

DEDICATION   172

Lord, here I am, do with me as seems best in thine own
eyes; only give me, I humbly beseech thee, a penitent and
patient spirit to expect thee. Make my service acceptable
to thee while I live, and my soul ready for thee when I die.
Archbishop Laud

MORNING   173

O Lord, who hast brought us through the darkness of
night to the light of morning, and by thy Holy Spirit dost
lighten the darkness of ignorance and sin: we beseech thee
of thy loving-kindness to pour thy holy light into our souls,
that we may ever be devoted to thee, by whose wisdom we
were created, by whose mercy we were redeemed, and by
whose providence we are governed; to the honour and
glory of thy Name.   *The Book of Hours*

DEPENDENCE UPON GOD   174

Grant, O God, that amidst all the discouragements,
difficulties, dangers, distress, and darkness of this mortal
life, I may depend upon thy mercy, and on this build my
hopes, as on a sure foundation.   Let thine infinite mercy in
Christ Jesus deliver me from despair, both now, and at the
hour of death.   *Bishop Thomas Wilson*

THANKSGIVING: FOR ALL SAINTS   175

Here, O Lord, we do give unto thee most high praise and
hearty thanks for the wonderful grace and virtue declared
in all thy saints from the beginning of the world: and
particularly in the glorious and ever-blessed Virgin Mary,
Mother of thy Son, Jesus Christ our Lord and our God;
and in the holy patriarchs, apostles, martyrs, confessors;
whose examples, O Lord, and steadfastness in thy faith and
keeping thy holy commandments, grant us to follow.

Non-Jurors' Prayer Book

EVENING   176

Merciful God, who of thine abundant goodness towards us
hast made the day to travail in, and ordained the night
wherein to take our rest: grant us such rest of body that we
may continually have a waking soul, to watch for the time
when our Lord shall appear to deliver us from this mortal
life. Let no vain or wandering fancy trouble us; let our
ghostly enemies have no power over us, but let our minds
be set wholly upon thy presence, to love, and fear, and rest
in thee alone; that, being refreshed with a moderate and
sober sleep, we may rise up again with cheerful strength and
gladness to serve thee in all good works.   *Bishop Cosin*

THE VISION OF CHRIST   177

O Lord, the fulfilment of them that love thee, and the light
that shineth upon them unto perfect day, who giveth rest
and refreshment to them that fall asleep in thee: grant unto
us in all time of our service here on earth such a vision of
thyself as shall guide us through the world's confusions,
and support us in our conflicts and temptations. Then,
Lord, in thy mercy receive us into the company of thy
saints, and unveil thy glory, where thou reignest in thy
everlasting kingdom, world without end.
                                 Frederick B. Macnutt

DEPENDENCE UPON GOD   178

Be unto me, O Lord, alway thy mighty hand for defence:
thy mercy in Christ for salvation: thy all-true word for
instruction: the grace of thy life-bringing Spirit for comfort, until the end and in the end.   *Lancelot Andrewes*

THE COMFORT OF GOD   179

The blessing of the Lord rest and remain upon all his
people, in every land, of every tongue; the Lord meet in
mercy all that seek him; the Lord comfort all who suffer
and mourn; the Lord hasten his coming, and give us, his
people, peace by all means.   *Bishop Moule*

DEDICATION   180

God almighty, eternal, righteous, and merciful, give to us
poor sinners to do for thy sake all that we know of thy will,
and to will always what pleases thee; so that inwardly
purified, enlightened, and kindled by the fire of the Holy
Spirit, we may follow in the footprints of thy well-beloved
Son, our Lord Jesus Christ.   *St. Francis of Assisi*

HAPPINESS IN GOD   181

O God, who art all goodness, make me to love thee for
thyself and my neighbour for thee. Bless me in this life
with but peace of my conscience, command of my affections, the love of thyself and my dearest friends, and I shall
be happy enough to pity Caesar. These are, O Lord, the
humble desires of my most reasonable ambition, and all I
dare call happiness on earth; wherein I set no rule or limit
to thy hand or providence. Dispose of me according to
the wisdom of thy pleasure: thy will be done, though in my
own undoing.   *Sir Thomas Browne*

GLORIA   182

Glory be to the Father of mercies, the Father of men and
angels, the Father of our Lord Jesus Christ. Glory be to
the most holy and eternal Son of God, the blessed saviour
and redeemer of the world, the advocate of sinners, the
prince of peace, the head of the Church, and the mighty
deliverer of all them that call upon him. Glory be to the
holy and eternal Spirit of God, the Holy Ghost the
comforter, the sanctifying and life-giving Spirit. All glory
and thanks, all honour and power, all love and obedience,
be to the blessed and undivided Trinity, one God Eternal.
The heavens declare thy glory, the earth confesses thy
providence, the sea manifests thy power; and every spirit,
and every understanding creature celebrates thy greatness
for ever and ever. All glory and majesty, all praises and
dominion be unto thee, O God, Father, Son, and Holy
Ghost, for ever and ever.   *Jeremy Taylor*

BIBLE-READING 183

O Lord, who hast given us the Scriptures to be a lamp unto our feet and a light unto our paths, grant that thy Holy Spirit, who proceedeth from thee, may enlighten our minds and kindle our hearts, and that as thy Son has promised, he may lead us into all truth; through Jesus Christ our Lord.

INVOCATION 184

O heavenly Father, the author and fountain of all truth, send, we beseech thee, thy Holy Spirit into our hearts, and lighten our understandings with the beams of thy heavenly grace. We ask this, O merciful Father, for thy dear Son, our saviour, Jesus Christ's sake. *Bishop Ridley*

FAITH, HOPE, AND LOVE 185

O Lord, perfect for me that which is lacking of thy gifts: of faith, increase my littleness of faith: of hope, stablish trembling hope: of love, kindle its smoking flax: shed abroad thy love in my heart, withal to love thee, my friend in thee, mine enemy for thee. Let me fear one thing only, the fearing aught more than thee. *Lancelot Andrewes*

EVENING 186

O Lord, thou keeper of Israel, which in thy watch over thy servants dost neither slumber nor sleep; be my keeper, and preserve me this night. O keep my soul.
Archbishop Laud

187

To almighty God, whose glory the heavens are telling, the earth his might, and the sea his power, and whose majesty every feeling and thinking creature everywhere proclaims: to him belong glory, honour, might, greatness, and magnificence, now and for evermore. *Liturgy of St. James*

FAITH   188

O Sweet Jesu, increase our faith daily in us more and
more; that at the last, through thy goodness, we may be
made perfect and strong men in thy holy religion, and
show ourselves both before thee and before the world truly
faithful, by bringing forth plenty of good works, unto the
glory and honour of thy Name.   *Thomas Becon*

DEDICATION   189

Grant me, O Lord, to know that which is worth knowing,
to love that which is worth loving, to praise that which
pleaseth thee most, to esteem that highly which to thee is
precious, to abhor that which in thy sight is evil and
unclean. Suffer me not to judge according to the sight of
the eyes, nor to give sentence according to the hearing of
the ears of the ignorant; but with a true judgement to
discern between things temporal and things spiritual, and
above all else to fulfil the good pleasure of thy will; through
Jesus Christ our Lord.   *Thirteenth Century*

VISION   190

Come to us, O Lord! open the eyes of our souls, and show
us the things which belong to our peace and the path of
life; that we may see that, though all man's inventions and
plans come to an end, yet thy commandment is exceeding
broad—broad enough for rich and poor, for scholar,
tradesman, and labourer, for our prosperity in this life and
our salvation in the life to come.   *Charles Kingsley*

JOY IN GOD   191

O Christ our God, who art thyself the fulfilment of the law
and the prophets, and didst fulfil all the ordered purpose of
the Father, always fill our hearts with joy and gladness, now
and for ever, world without end.
                                    Liturgy of St. Chrysostum

DEDICATION   192

Truly, O Lord, because thou madest me, I owe unto thy
love my whole self; because thou didst redeem me, I owe
thee my whole self; because thou makest me such great
promises, I owe thee my whole self, nay more, I owe unto
thy love more than myself, insomuch as thou art greater
than I, for whom thou didst give thyself, to whom thou
dost promise thyself. Make me, I beseech thee, O Lord,
to taste by love that which I taste by knowledge; to perceive by affection what I perceive by understanding. I
owe more than my whole self to thee, but I have no more
than this, neither can I of myself render even all this to
thee. Draw me, O Lord, into thy love, even this whole
self of mine. All that I am is thine by creation: make it to
be all thine by love.   *St. Anselm*

UNION WITH CHRIST   193

Most loving Saviour, we would abide in thee: make our
hearts thy dwelling-place; fill our minds with the thought
and our imaginations with the picture of thy love; take
away whatever in us of selfishness or weakness hinders our
hearing or obeying thy call; teach us day by day to live
closer to thy side, which was pierced that we might live.
                                     William Temple

                                                194

Now the God of all grace and glory send the Spirit of his
Son plentifully into our hearts, that we may abound in the
fruits of godly living, to the praise of his grace, our present
comfort in this life, and the eternal salvation of our souls in
the day of our Lord Jesus Christ.   *Robert Sanderson*

THE HOLY TRINITY   195

God the Father, maker of men; God the Son, born
amongst men; God the Holy Spirit, sanctifying men;
bless, preserve, and keep us, all whom we love, and all for
whom we pray, now and for evermore.

ON RISING   196

Into thy almighty hands I do here resign my body and my
soul, with all the faculties thou hast bestowed upon both.
Guide thou them in the works of thy law; turn my eyes
from all transitory objects to the things which are eternal,
and from the cares and pride of this world (as thou hast
said) to the fowls of the air and the lilies of the field.
                                              Henry Vaughan

SEEKING GOD   197

Lord, thou art in me and shalt never be lost out of me, but
I am not near thee till I have found thee. Nowhere need I
run to seek thee, but within me where already thou art.
Thou art the treasure hidden within me: draw me therefore to thee that I may find thee and serve and possess thee
for ever.   *After Walter Hilton*

THE KNOWLEDGE OF GOD   198

O God, let me know thee and love thee so that I may
rejoice in thee. And if I cannot know thee, love thee,
rejoice in thee fully in this life, let me go forward from day
to day, until that knowledge, joy, and love at last may be
full. Let the knowledge of thee grow in me here, and there
be made full; so that my joy may here be great in hope and
there full in fruition.   *St. Anselm*

SERVICE   199

Inspire and strengthen us, O Lord God, by thy holy
Spirit, to seek thy will and uphold thine honour in all
things; in the purity and joy of our homes, in the trust and
fellowship of our common life, in daily service of the good;
after the pattern and in the power of thy Son our Lord and
Saviour Jesus Christ.   *E. Milner-White*

BIBLE-READING 200

O Lord, who hast given unto us thy word of truth: quicken within us an increasing love of thy revelation of thyself; and grant that, delighting daily to exercise ourselves therein, and bringing forth fruit as trees of thy planting, we may be nourished by the waters of thy grace and daily be ripening unto everlasting life.

Mozarabic

DEDICATION 201

Thanks be to thee, my Lord Jesus Christ, for all the benefits which thou hast given to me, for all the pains and insults which thou hast borne for me. O most merciful redeemer, friend, and brother, may I know thee more clearly, love thee more dearly, and follow thee more nearly.

St. Richard

THANKSGIVING: AGNUS DEI 202

O Lord God, Lamb of God, Son of the Father, that takest away the sins of the world: thou that sittest at the right hand of the Father: thou only art holy; thou only art the Lord; thou only, O Christ, with the Holy Ghost art most high in the glory of God the Father.

Thou art worthy to take the book, and to open the seals thereof: for thou wast slain, and hast redeemed us to God by thy blood out of every kindred, and tongue, and people, and nation.

Worthy is the lamb that was slain, to receive power, and riches, and wisdom, and strength, and honour, and glory, and blessing.

Praise our God, all ye his servants, and ye that fear him, both small and great. Let us be glad and rejoice, and give honour to him: for the marriage of the lamb is come.

Blessed are they who are called unto the marriage supper of the lamb.

Blessing, and honour, and glory, and power be unto him that sitteth upon the throne, and unto the lamb for ever and ever. *After Lancelot Andrewes*

E

GOD OUR SATISFACTION   203

O God, the true and only life, in whom and from whom
and by whom are all good things that are good indeed;
from whom to be turned is to fall, to whom to turn is to
rise again; in whom to abide is to dwell for ever, from whom
to depart is to die; to whom to come again is to revive, and
in whom to lodge is to live: take away from me whatsoever
thou wilt, so that thou give me only thyself.

Thomas Dekker

DAILY WORK   204

Almighty God, give us grace to do the work to which thou
hast called us with reverence and godly fear, not with eye-
service as pleasers of men, but in singleness of heart as in
thy sight.   Direct, we beseech thee, all our thoughts,
words, and deeds, with the help of thy Holy Spirit; that
we may set thy will ever before us, and turn away from
vanity and self-seeking, and give ourselves wholly unto
thee to spend and be spent in thy service; through Jesus
Christ, our only Lord and Saviour.

THE INWARD CHRIST   205

Lord, let it be my care so to behave myself, through the
help of Christ, that I may receive thee, my most holy
Lord, that thou may'st not only be my guest, but may'st
abide with me for ever.   *Archbishop Laud*

THANKSGIVING   206

Thanks be to thee, O God, thanks be to thee, O true and
undivided Trinity, O verity, one and three, O unity, three
and one.   Thanks be to thee, O God the Father, who hast
both manifested thy Son unto me, and given him to be my
teacher: O grant likewise that he may be so for ever,
according to thy mercies of old time.   *Archbishop Laud*

EVENING   207

O Lord, support us all the day long of this troublous life,
until the shades lengthen and the evening comes, and the
busy world is hushed, the fever of life is over, and our
work done. Then, Lord, in thy mercy, grant us safe
lodging, and holy rest, and peace at the last; through
Jesus Christ our Lord.   *Unknown*

ZEAL AND OBEDIENCE   208

Deliver me, O God, from a slothful mind, from all luke-
warmness, and all dejection of spirit. I know these cannot
but deaden my love to thee: mercifully free my heart from
them, and give me a lively, zealous, active, and cheerful
spirit; that I may vigorously perform whatever thou
commandest, thankfully suffer whatever thou choosest for
me, and be ever ardent to obey in all things thy holy love.
                                                John Wesley

LOVE OF CHRIST   209

Set our hearts on fire with love to thee, O Christ our God,
that in that flame we may love thee with all our heart, with
all our mind, with all our soul, and with all our strength,
and our neighbours as ourselves; so that, keeping thy
commandments, we may glorify thee, the giver of all good
gifts.   *Eastern Orthodox*

THANKSGIVING   210

O God, who hast given us life and all things good in this
world: thou hast created us for thy service, and when we
have forsaken thee in our wanderings thou hast sought us
out; thou hast vouchsafed to us the precious treasure of thy
Gospel; thou hast ordained that we should be born in the
bosom of thy Church; thou hast revealed to us thy
exceeding great mercies in Jesus Christ our Lord; thou
hast borne with us in our rebellions, raised us up from our
falls, comforted us in our sorrows. For all these gifts of
thy grace, and for thy benefits which we remember not, we
thine unworthy servants do give thee thanks, and bless thy
holy Name.   *Eugene Bersier*

INVOCATION　211

We pray thee, Lord, who art the author and giver of light,
that thou wouldest banish from us this day the shadows of
evil, and shed upon us the bright beams of thy loving-
kindness; through Jesus Christ our Lord.

Gelasian Sacramentary

LOVE OF GOD　212

My God, I desire to love thee perfectly: with all my heart
which thou madest for thyself, with all my mind which
only thou canst satisfy, with all my soul which fain would
soar to thee, with all my strength, my feeble strength,
which shrinks before so great a task, and yet can choose
naught else but spend itself in loving thee. Claim thou
my heart, fill thou my mind, uplift my soul, and reinforce
my strength, that where I fail thou mayest succeed in me,
and make me love thee perfectly.　　*Bishop Frere*

DAILY WORK　213

O Lord, renew our spirits and draw our hearts unto thyself, that our work may not be to us a burden, but a delight;
and give us such a mighty love to thee as may sweeten our
obedience. O let us not serve thee with the spirit of
bondage as slaves, but with cheerfulness and gladness,
delighting ourselves in thee and rejoicing in thy work.

Benjamin Jenks

LOYALTY TO CONVICTION　214

Heavenly Father, the Father of all wisdom, understanding, and true strength, we beseech thee look mercifully upon thy servants, and send thy Holy Spirit into
their hearts, that when they must join to fight in the field
for the glory of thy holy Name, then they, strengthened
with the defence of thy right hand, may manfully stand in
the confession of thy faith, and continue in the same unto
their lives' end.　　*Bishop Ridley*

215

Worthy is the lamb that hath been slain to receive the
power, and riches, and wisdom, and might, and honour,
and glory, and blessing.　　*Revelation 5. 12*

BIBLE-READING   216

O Lord and lover of men, let the pure light of the knowledge of thee shine forth in our hearts, and open the eyes of
our understanding that we may enter into the meaning of
the proclamation of thy Gospel.   Plant in us also the fear of
thy holy commandments, that we may trample underfoot
all carnal lusts, and seek our citizenship which is in heaven,
and think and do always such things as please thee.   For
thou, O Christ our God, art the enlightenment of our souls
and bodies, and to thee do we give glory, with thine
unbegotten Father and thine all-holy and good and life-
giving Spirit, now and for ever and ever.

Liturgy of St. Chrysostom

PEACE INWARD AND OUTWARD   217

We heartily beseech thee of thy goodness, O Lord, to
deliver us from adversity to the body and from all noxious
things which tempt and beset the soul: and as thou dost
mercifully ordain that we may dwell in outward tranquillity, so grant to us also thine inward peace; through
Jesus Christ our Lord.

EVENING   218

May the Almighty God take me, my family, my relations,
my friends, my benefactors, and my enemies, under his
gracious protection; give his holy angels charge concerning
us; preserve us from the prince and powers of darkness,
and from the dangers of the night; and keep us in perpetual peace and safety; through Jesus Christ our Lord.

Bishop Thomas Wilson

                                                219

To the holy and indivisible Trinity, to the humanity of
Jesus Christ crucified, glory infinitely be given of every
creature, world without end.   *The Primer*

INVOCATION   220

O eternal God, the great Father of spirits, the great lover
of souls, who didst send thy Holy Spirit upon thy Church
in the day of Pentecost, and hast promised that he shall
abide with thy Church for ever: let thy Holy Spirit lead us
into all truth, defend us from all sin, enrich us with his
gifts, refresh us with his comforts, rule in our hearts for
ever, conduct us with his truth, and lead us in the way
everlasting; that we living by thy Spirit, and walking in
him, may by him be sealed up to the day of our redemption.
O let thy Spirit witness to our spirits that we are the children of God, and make us to be so for ever, through Jesus
Christ our Lord; who liveth and reigneth with thee in the
unity of the same Spirit, one God, world without end.

Jeremy Taylor

DAILY WORK   221

Protect us, O Lord, and prosper us as we labour in our
vocations, that our work may be done with thy blessing and
be crowned with thine approval; through him who was
numbered among the craftsmen, Jesus Christ our Lord.

MORNING   222

O thou, who sendest forth light and createst the dawn,
making thy sun to shine upon the evil and on the good:
enlighten the blindness of our hearts by the knowledge of
thy truth, and lift up the light of thy countenance upon us;
that in thy light we may see light and behold at length in
the light of grace that light of glory everlasting; and save
us, good Lord.

                                                             223

To the only God invisible, the Father of truth, who sent
forth unto us the Saviour and Prince of immortality,
through whom also he made manifest unto us the truth and
the heavenly life, to him be the glory for ever and ever.

Early Christian Church

GOD OUR LIFE   224

Let me ever hold communion with thee, my hidden but
my living God. Thou art in my innermost heart: thou art
the life of my life: every breath I breathe, every thought of
my mind, every good desire of my heart, is from the
presence within me of the unseen God. By nature and by
grace thou art in me: I see thee not in the material world
except dimly, but I recognise thy voice in my own intimate
consciousness; I turn round and say, Rabboni. O be ever
thus with me; and if I am tempted to leave thee, do not
thou, O my God, leave me.   *Cardinal Newman*

THE KNOWLEDGE OF GOD   225

Almighty God, give us wisdom to perceive thee, intellect
to understand thee, diligence to seek thee, patience to wait
for thee, vision to behold thee, a heart to meditate upon
thee, and life to proclaim thee.   *St. Benedict*

DEPENDENCE UPON GOD   226

Preserve me thy servant from all evil, lead me into all
good; change my sorrows into comforts, my infirmity into
spiritual strength; take all iniquity from me, and let thy
servant never depart from thee. I am thine, O save me;
I am thine, sanctify me and preserve me for ever; that
neither life nor death, health nor sickness, prosperity nor
adversity, weakness within nor cross accidents without,
may ever separate me from the love of God which is in
Christ Jesus our Lord.   *Jeremy Taylor*

GOD AND OUR FRIENDS   227

The God of all love, who is the source of our affection for
each other formed here, take our friendships into his own
keeping, that they may continue and increase throughout
life and beyond it.   *William Temple*

INVOCATION 228

O heavenly King, O comforter, the Spirit of truth, who art
in all places, and fillest all things, the treasure of blessings,
and giver of life, come and abide in us. Cleanse us from all
impurity, and of thy goodness save our souls.

Eastern Orthodox

GOD TRANSCENDENT 229

O thou, who fillest heaven and earth, ever acting, ever at
rest, who art everywhere and everywhere art wholly
present, who art not absent even when far off, who with
thy whole being fillest yet transcendest all things, who
teachest the hearts of the faithful without the din of words;
teach us, we pray thee, through Jesus Christ our Lord.

St. Augustine

SEEKING GOD 230

Lord, I have sought thy face; thy face, Lord, will I seek;
O hide not thou thy face from me. Raise me up out of myself
unto thee. Cleanse, heal, quicken, enlighten the eye of my
mind that it may look unto thee. Grant that my soul may
collect its strength one more, and with all the power of my
understanding strive after thee, O Lord. Surely thou art
life and wisdom, and truth, and goodness, and blessedness,
and eternity, and everything that is truly good.

St. Anselm

DAILY WORK 231

O God, who movest in love unceasing, and dost give to
each man his appointed work: help us steadfastly, and as in
thy sight, to fulfil the duties of our calling; that when our
Lord shall take account of us, we may be found faithful in
that which is least, and enter into his eternal joy.

STRENGTH AND TASKS 232

O Lord, I do not pray for tasks equal to my strength: I ask
for strength equal to my tasks. *Phillips Brooks*

BIBLE-READING 233

Blessed Lord, by whose providence all Holy Scriptures were written and preserved for our instruction: give us grace to study them each day with patience and love; strengthen our souls with the fullness of their divine teaching; keep from us all pride and irreverence; guide us in the deep things of thy heavenly wisdom; and, of thy great mercy, lead us by thy word into everlasting life.

Bishop Westcott

THE INWARD CHRIST 234

O merciful Jesus, who when thou tookest upon thee to deliver man didst not abhor the Virgin's womb; vouchsafe evermore to dwell in the hearts of us thy servants; inspire us with thy purity; strengthen us with thy might; make us perfect in thy ways; guide us into thy truth; and unite us to thyself and to thy whole Church by thy holy mysteries; that we may conquer every adverse power, and be wholly devoted to thy service and conformed to thy will; to the glory of God the Father. *From the French*

PURITY 235

Almighty God, who hast made our bodies to be temples of thy Spirit: reveal, we beseech thee, in thy servants thy manifold gifts of grace; that living in thy love and fear, they may be purified from the corruption that is in the world, and attain to dwell in the blessed fellowship of thine eternal kingdom. *Unknown*

ENLIGHTENMENT 236

O Lord Jesus Christ, who knowest the Father, even as thou art known of him, lead us onward evermore in the knowledge of thee who art the truth, till at last we see thy face, and know thee as we are known of thee; who with the Father and the Holy Ghost livest and reignest, one God for ever and ever. *J. R. Illingworth*

MORNING   **237**

Give ear, O Lord, in this morning hour to the prayers of thy
servants, and mercifully uncover and heal the secret evils
of our hearts; that no dark desires may possess us whom
thou hast enlightened with thy heavenly grace; through
Jesus Christ our Lord.   *Gelasian Sacramentary*

INVOCATION   **238**

Help us, O Holy Spirit, giver of life and love, to be always
so mindful of the love from whence we came, that we may
learn more and more the love to which we go: and in this
love abounding, daily abide; through Jesus Christ our
Lord.   *E. Milner-White*

SERVICE   **239**

My God, my heart is set on serving thee. To serve the
world is hard, unsatisfying, but to serve thee is perfect joy
and liberty. My God, my heart is set on serving thee.
Here would I consecrate to thee and to thy cause each
faculty and power which thou hast given me: of intellect or
learning, of heart or sympathy, of spiritual fervour, of
influence or guidance: all come from thee, all shall revert
to thee: I only have the use of them and that I give to thee.
Take all and use it for thy holy purposes, use me to glorify
thee.   *Bishop Frere*

ALL SORTS AND CONDITIONS   **240**

God grant to the living, grace; to the departed, rest; to the
Church, the Queen, the Commonwealth, and to all mankind, peace and concord; and to us, and all his servants,
life everlasting.   *Elizabethan*

                                                      241

O Lord, forgive what I have been, sanctify what I am, and
order what I shall be.   *Unknown*

BIBLE-READING   242

O Lord, who hast given us thy holy Word that it may be to us a light upon the path of life: grant us after the example of thy saints so to search the Scriptures that we may daily increase in the knowledge of thy truth, and find in them the light that shineth more and more unto thy perfect day; through Jesus Christ our Lord.

CONSUMING LOVE   243

O God our Judge and Saviour, set before us the vision of thy purity, and let us see our sins in the light of thy countenance; pierce our self-contentment with the shafts of thy burning love, and let love consume in us all that hinders us from perfect service of thy cause; for as thy holiness is our judgement, so are thy wounds our salvation.

William Temple

THANKSGIVING   244

Most worthy art thou, O good and gracious God, of all praise, even for thine own sake which exceedeth all things in holiness. By thee only we are hallowed and made holy. As our duty continually bids us, we praise thee for our glorious redemption, purchased for us in thy dearly beloved Son, Jesus Christ. Give us therefore the Holy Spirit to givern us. And grant that all things that breathe with life may praise thee; through the same Jesus Christ our Lord, who reigneth with thee and the Holy Ghost, one God, for ever and ever.   *The Iona Books*

ENLARGEMENT   245

We beseech thee, O Lord, to set our feet in a large place, where hearts are made pure by faith in thee, and faces are turned to the light; where all are one in thee, and no narrow walls between man and man destroy the unity thou hast made in the Spirit of thy Son, Jesus Christ our Lord.

Unknown

DEDICATION   **246**

Lord, who hast given all for us: help us to give all for thee.
G. W. Briggs

AGAINST APATHY   **247**

O God, who art man's sovereign good, and dost seek the
love of thy children: deliver us from sloth in thy work and
coldness in thy cause; rekindle in us love by our looking
unto thee, and by our waiting upon thee renew our strength;
through Jesus Christ our Lord.

THANKSGIVING   **248**

O eternal and most blessed Saviour Jesus, thou art the
bright morning star, and the sun of righeousness; thou
dost enlighten our eyes with thy beauties, and our hearts
with thy comfort and with the joys of God; thou art the
fountain of health and life, of peace and truth, of rest and
holiness; thou givest to them that want, thou comfortest
them that suffer, thou forgivest them that repent, and
hearest the prayers of all them that call upon thee; we
adore thee and praise thy glories and rejoice in thy salvation, and give thee thanks for thy blessing and defending
us, from all the evils which we have deserved every day,
and from all the violences and snares by which the enemy
of mankind would have hurt us, or destroyed us, unless he
had been restrained by thy eternal goodness and thy
almighty power. Blessed be God.   *Jeremy Taylor*

FOR GRACE   **249**

May the grace of the Lord Jesus sanctify us and keep us
from all evil; may he drive far from us all hurtful things,
and purify both our souls and bodies; may he bind us to
himself by the bond of love, and may his peace abound in
our hearts.   *Gregorian Sacramentary*

THE CROSS   250

Fence me about, O Lord, with the power of thine honourable and life-giving cross, and preserve me from every evil.   *Eastern Orthodox*

UNSELFISHNESS   251

Grant us grace, O Father, not to pass by suffering or joy without eyes to see; give us understanding and sympathy, and guard us from selfishness, that we may enter into the joys and sufferings of others; use us to gladden and strengthen those who are weak and suffering; that by our lives we may help others to believe and serve thee, and shed forth thy light which is the light of life.

H. R. L. Sheppard

THANKSGIVING   252

O thou light of my heart, thou bread of my inmost soul, thanks be to thee, my joy and my glory, my confidence and my God, thanks be to thee for thy gifts. Preserve them to me, for so wilt thou preserve me myself, and those things shall be enlarged and perfected which thou hast given me, and I myself shall be with thee, who didst give me being. ... O Lord, my God, I lay my whole heart upon the altar of thy praise, a whole burnt-offering of praise I offer to thee. Let the flame of thy love set afire my whole heart; let nothing in me be left to myself, nothing wherein I may look to myself; but may I burn wholly before thee. Lord, let thy fire consume all that is mine: let all be thine.

St. Augustine

BEFORE ANY UNDERTAKING   253

O Lord Jesus Christ, only-begotten Son of thine eternal Father, thou hast said that without thee we can do nothing. O Lord, I embrace with faith and with my whole heart and soul what thou hast said. Help me, a sinner, to finish the work which I now undertake for thee; in the name of the Father, and of the Son, and of the Holy Spirit.

Eastern Orthodox

INVOCATION   **254**

Lord my God, call me, that I may come to thee: fix me,
that I may not leave thee.   *St. Augustine*

DEDICATION   **255**

Almighty and eternal God, so draw our hearts to thee,
so guide our minds, so fill our imaginations, so control
our wills, that we may be wholly thine, utterly dedicated
unto thee; and then use us, we pray thee, as thou wilt,
but always to thy glory and the welfare of thy people,
through our Lord and Saviour, Jesus Christ.
        William Temple

LOVE OF GOD   **256**

O God, which dost infuse the gifts of charity into the
hearts of the faithful through the grace of thy Holy Ghost:
grant unto thy servants, both men and women, for whom
we pray unto thy mercy, health of body and soul, that they
may love thee with all their power and perform with all
love the things that may be pleasing to thee; by Christ our
Lord.   *The Primer*

THANKSGIVING   **257**

Accept, O Lord God, our Father, the sacrifices of our
thanksgiving; this, of praise, for thy great mercies already
afforded to us; and this, of prayer, for the continuance and
enlargement of them; this, of penitence, for such only
recompense as our sinful nature can endeavour; and this,
of the love of our hearts, as the only gift thou dost ask or
desire; and all these, through the all-holy and atoning
sacrifice of Jesus Christ thy Son our saviour.
        Derived from John Donne

        258

Almighty and most merciful God, grant, we beseech thee,
that by the indwelling of thy Holy Spirit we may be
enlightened and strengthened for thy service; through
Jesus Christ our Lord.   *American Prayer Book*

THANKSGIVING 259

Thine own praise, O my God, thou thyself art; nor canst thou worthily be praised by any other than thyself; for of all things thou art the maker and ruler; and from thee do all things come, whose excellence and whose works declare the glory of thy Name. Ever therefore shouldst thou be praised and blessed by every creature. May then, O my God, thine own incomprehensible essence, thine own unspeakable almightiness, thine own unsearchable wisdom, thine own unutterable sweetness, thine own boundless tenderness, praise thee! Praise thee thy supreme goodness, thy surpassing mercy, thy eternal power also, and thy transcendent majesty! Praise thee thy infallible truth, thy unchangeable equity, thy inextinguishable light, thy knowledge from which no secrets are hid, thy own unapproachable substance! Praise thee thy unerring justice, thy all-wise providence, thy most calm governance, and thy unconquerable power! Praise thee thy infinite dignity, thy supreme loving-kindness, thy all-surpassing sweetness, thy peerless beauty, and thy all-excelling charity! May every name that can be used of thee, and every word that can be spoken of thee, praise thee and magnify thee for ever! *Thomas à Kempis*

AGAINST COLDNESS OF HEART 260

O my sweet saviour Christ, which in thine undeserved love towards mankind so kindly wouldst suffer the painful death of the cross, suffer not me to be cold nor lukewarm in love again towards thee. *Sir Thomas More*

PURITY 261

Lord Jesu Christ, whose property is ever to be merciful, which art alway pure and clean without spot of sin: grant us the grace to follow thee in mercifulness toward our neighbours, and always to bear a pure heart and a clean conscience toward thee, that we may after this life see thee in thy everlasting glory: which livest and reignest world without end. *The Primer*

262

Lord, let me not live to be useless.   *John Wesley*

INVOCATION   263

O Holy Spirit the comforter, spirit of Jesus, come thou
upon us and dwell within us. Not of ourselves, but of thee
is our life. Teach us that we may know; cleanse us and
purify us within; strengthen us to persevere, lest we fall
away from thee. Come into us, thou who art already there,
that by thine arrival again thou mayest enter into thy
possession anew. And out of wordly death in which we
languish create in us the life that shall make us as thou art,
through inward unity in which we are one with thee.
Come, then, eternal Spirit, who with the Father and the
Son art one God, and abide with us for ever.
                                        Frederick B. Macnutt

THANKSGIVING   264

For these thy most bounteous gifts, and for all other thy
benefits which thou daily givest unto us of thy great mercy
both for our body and soul; we most humbly thank thee,
most gentle and merciful Father, beseeching thee that thou
wilt give us grace through thy Holy Spirit not to be
unthankful, but to walk worthy of this thy kindness, and so
to behave ourselves all our lifetime in this world according
to thy holy will, that at the last day we may be found in the
number of them to whom thy only-begotten Son shall say:
Come, ye blessed of my Father, possess the kingdom which
was prepared for you from the beginning of the world;
through the same thy Son, Jesus Christ our Lord.
                                              Thomas Becon

FORBEARANCE   265

Lord, give me that grace that I may hold me still by thee,
and abide patiently upon thee; that I may not grieve
myself at the man whose way doth prosper, nor against
him that doth after evil counsels; that I may leave off from
wrath and let go displeasure, lest I fret myself, and be
moved to do evil.   *Archbishop Laud*

GOD WITHIN   266

God be in my head, and in my understanding; God be in
mine eyes, and in my looking; God be in my mouth, and in
my speaking; God be in my heart, and in my thinking;
God be at mine end, and at my departing.   *Sarum Primer*

BIBLE-READING   267

Almighty and most merciful God, who hast given the Bible
to be the revelation of thy great love to man, and of thy
power and will to save him: grant that our study of it may
not be made in vain by the callousness or carelessness of
our hearts, but that by it we may be confirmed in penitence,
lifted to hope, made strong for service, and, above all, filled
with the true knowledge of thee and of thy Son Jesus
Christ.   *George Adam Smith*

SEEKING GOD   268

Eternal God, who hast been the hope and joy of many
generations, and in all ages hast given men the power to
seek thee and in seeking to find thee: grant me, I pray thee,
a clearer vision of thy truth, a greater faith in thy power,
and a more confident assurance of thy love.   If I cannot
find thee, let me search my heart and know whether it is not
rather I that am blind—than thou who art obscure, and I
who am fleeing from thee rather than thou from me; and
let me confess these my sins before thee, and seek thy
pardon in Jesus Christ my Lord.   *John Baillie*

GLORIA   269

Glory be to thee, O God, the Father, the maker of the
world: Glory be to thee, O God, the Son, the redeemer of
mankind: Glory be to thee, O God, the Holy Ghost, the
sanctifier of thy people.   *Bishop Westcott*

F

MORNING　　　270

O good Christ, our most gracious redeemer, grant that as
thou dost mercifully raise up this my body, even so I
beseech thee, raise up my mind and heart to the true
knowledge and love of thee, that my conversation may be
in heaven, where thou art; to the glory of thy Name.

Henry Bull

SERVICE　　　271

Grant, O Lord, that this mind may be in us, which was
also in Christ Jesus, who left the heaven of thy holiness
and of thy glory that he might take upon him our sins and
our sorrows, and seek and save that which was lost. Stir
the hearts of thy people that they may multiply their
labours in the cause of charity and love, that they may
minister to the wants of others, and by their good works
lead many to glorify our Father who is in heaven; through
Jesus Christ our Lord. *C. J. Vaughan*

THANKSGIVING　　　272

O God, we thank thee for thy great mercies: for preserving
us, for our food and raiment, for our interests and comforts, for all that makes this present life to be desired, but
above all, for our place in thy family be redemption,
through Jesus Christ, thy Son. Praise be to thee for the
incarnation of Jesus: praise be to thee for the obedience of
Jesus: praise be to thee for the blood of Jesus; for he is
ours, and he is thine, and we are his. He is our sacrifice,
and thy satisfaction; our glorious head, and thine only-
begotten Son; our intercessor, and thy beloved; our
merciful high priest, and thine anointed King.

Henry Alford

273

Unto him that is able to do exceedingly abundantly above
all that we ask or think, according to the power that
worketh in us, unto him be the glory in the Church and in
Christ Jesus unto all generations for ever and ever. Amen.

Ephesians 3. 20-21

EVENING 274

Visit, O Lord, this dwelling, and drive far from it all the snares of the enemy; let thy holy angels dwell in it to preserve us in peace, and may thy blessing be upon us evermore; through Jesus Christ our Lord.

Office of Compline

DEDICATION 275

O Emmanuel, O Wisdom, I give myself to thee, I trust thee wholly. Thou art wiser than I, more loving to me than I myself: deign to fulfil thy high purposes in me, whatever they be. Work in and through me: I am born to serve thee, to be thine, to be thine instrument. Let me be thy blind instrument. I ask not to see, I ask not to know, I ask simply to be used. *Cardinal Newman*

THANKSGIVING 276

We give thee humble and hearty thanks, O most merciful Father, for all thy goodness and loving-kindness to us and to all men, for the blessings of this life and for the promise of everlasting happiness. And as we are bound, we specially thank thee for the mercies which we have received; for health and strength, for outward prosperity and well-being, for the manifold enjoyments of our daily life, and the hope of the future; for the opportunities of learning, for the knowledge of thy will, for the means of serving thee in thy holy Church, for the love which thou hast revealed to us in thy Son, our saviour; for every blessing of soul and body, we thank thee, O God. Add this, O Lord, to thy other mercies, that we may praise thee not with our lips only, but with our lives, always looking to thee as the author and giver of all good things; for Jesus Christ's sake.

Bishop Westcott

277

Save us, O Lord, waking; guard us sleeping; that awake we may watch with Christ, and asleep we may rest in peace.

Office of Compline

MORNING   278

O Lord Jesu Christ, be thou the beginning and the end of
all this day; the pattern whom I am to copy, the redeemer
in whom is my strength, the master whom I am to serve,
the friend to whom I may look for comfort and sympathy.
May I fix my eyes on thee as my help, my aim, the centre
of my being, my everlasting friend. O thou who hast so
looked on me that I may see thee, set thine eyes upon me,
I beseech thee.   Steady my unsteadfastness, unite me to
thyself, and guide me in whatever path thou seest fit to
lead me, till of thine infinite mercy thou wilt bring me to
thine eternal presence in paradise.

                                  Edward Bouverie Pusey

ADORATION   279

We praise thy divine power and glory, O God: the Father,
who createst all things from everlasting to everlasting; the
Son, our saviour and redeemer; the Holy Spirit, our helper
and comforter. We praise thee, that thou judgest the
earth in righteousness: we praise thee, that thou waitest for
us with thine eternity: we praise thee, who wilt bring all
things to an end: we praise thee, who wilt finish what thou
hast begun.   Help us, thy children, O Lord, and enlarge
our hope. We travel towards thee to meet thee, and we
wait for thy day. Thy kingdom come.

                                         From the German

SERVICE   280

Almighty God, who hast enabled thy faithful soldiers and
servants to play the man, to endure hardness, to love
mercy, to fight the good fight of faith, and to refuse no
service in the Name of Christ: grant unto us whom thou
hast called to serve under our saviour's banner a single
heart to spend and to be spent for thee and for those whom
he has loved even unto death; through the same Jesus
Christ our Lord.

EVENING   281

Look down, O Lord, from thy heavenly throne, and
illuminate the darkness of this night with thy celestial
brightness, and from the sons of light banish the deeds of
darkness; through Jesus Christ our Lord.

Office of Compline

BIBLE-READING   282

O gracious God and most merciful Father, which hast
vouchsafed us the rich and precious jewel of thy holy Word:
assist us with thy Spirit that it may be written in our hearts
to our everlasting comfort, to reform us, to renew us
according to thine own image, to build us up, and edify us
into the perfect building of thy Christ, sanctifying and
increasing in us all heavenly virtues.   Grant this, O
heavenly Father, for Jesus Christ's sake.   *Geneva Bible*

DEDICATION   283

Into thy hands, almighty Father, who dost will peace and
purpose loving-kindness, we commend our spirits: our
minds to know thee, our hearts to love thee, our wills to
serve thee, for we are thine.   Into thy hands, incarnate
saviour, who hast taught us that thou art the way, the
truth, and the life, do thou receive us and draw us after
thee, that we may follow thy steps: enlighten and guide us,
lest the night of sin and error overwhelm us; abide in us
and quicken us by the power of thine indwelling.   Into thy
hands, O Lord the Spirit, who createst good and des-
troyest evil, do thou take us and fashion us after thine
image; let thy comfort strengthen, thy grace renew, and
thy fire cleanse us.   Soul and body, in life and in death, in
this world of shadows and in thy changeless world of light
eternal, now and for ever, Father, Son, and Holy Spirit,
into thy hands.   *Frederick B. Macnutt*

INVOCATION   284

The God of peace and love vouchsafe alway to dwell with
us: and thou, Lord, have mercy upon us.   *The Primer*

DEDICATION   **285**

Into thy hands, O Lord, we commend ourselves and all
who are dear to us this day. Be with us in our going out
and in our coming in. Strengthen us for the work which
thou hast given us to do. And grant that, filled with thy
Holy Spirit, we may walk worthy of our high calling, and
cheerfully accomplish those things that thou wouldest
have done; through Jesus Christ our Lord.

Bishop F. T. Woods

SERVICE   **286**

O Lord, our heavenly Father, whose blessed Son came not
to be ministered unto but to minister: we beseech thee to
bless all those who follow in his steps and give themselves
to the service of their fellow-men. Endue them with
wisdom, patience, and courage, to strengthen the weak and
raise up those who fall; that being inspired by thy love,
they may worthily minister in thy Name to the suffering,
the friendless, and the needy; for the sake of him who laid
down his life for us, the same thy Son, our saviour Jesus
Christ.   *American Prayer Book*

VENI, CREATOR   **287**

Come, Holy Spirit of God, inspire the hearts of them that
believe in thee, and kindle in them the fire of thy love.

The Primer

ADORATION   **288**

Holy art thou, O God the Father, who hast made of one
blood all nations of the earth. Holy art thou, O God the
Son, who hast redeemed all mankind from the power of
darkness. Holy art thou, O God the Holy Spirit, giver of
life and light, by whom the whole Church is governed and
sanctified. Holy art thou, O God the eternal and adorable
Trinity, for whose glory man and all created things are,
and were created. Glory be to the Father, and to the Son,
and to the Holy Ghost: as it was in the beginning, is now,
and ever shall be, world without end.

PURE INTENTION 289

Grant me, gracious Lord, a pure intention of my heart, and a steadfast regard to thy glory in all my actions. Possess my mind continually with thy presence, and ravish it with thy love, that my only delight may be, to be embraced in the arms of thy protection. *Bishop Cosin*

KNOWLEDGE, LOVE, OBEDIENCE 290

O God our Father, who hast made us in thine own image, with a mind to understand thy works, a heart to love thee, and a will to serve thee: increase in us that knowledge, love, obedience, that we may grow daily in thy likeness; through Jesus Christ our Lord. *G. W. Briggs*

THANKSGIVING 291

It is meet and right, holy and becoming, and helpful to our souls, to worship thee who art the I AM, Lord God, Father Almighty; to hymn thee, to give thanks to thee, openly confess thee, by night and by day, with mouth unceasing, and lips that are never silent, and unresting heart: thee who hast made the heavens and all that is in them, the earth and all that is therein; thee who didst make man after thine own image and likeness, and freely gavest him the delights of paradise, and didst not reject nor forsake him when he transgressed, O good God; but thou didst recall him by the law and educate him by the prophets and reform him and renew him by thine aweful, and life-giving and heavenly mystery. All these things thou didst by thy wisdom, the true light, thine only-begotten Son, our Lord and God and Saviour, Jesus Christ, by whom we render thanks to thee with him and the Holy Spirit . . . from the rising of the sun unto the going down thereof, from the north and from the south, because thy Name is great among all peoples, and in every place incense and a pure sacrifice are offered to thy holy Name. *Liturgy of St. Mark*

PART TWO

PRAYERS FOR PUBLIC OR PRIVATE USE

OPENING AND CLOSING PRAYERS

FIRE OF LOVE 292

Almighty God, our heavenly Father, whose Son Jesus Christ came to cast fire upon the earth: grant that by the prayers of thy faithful people a fire of burning zeal may be kindled, and pass from heart to heart, till all our hardness is melted in the warmth of thy love; through him who loved us and gave himself for us, Jesus Christ our Lord.

G. C. Binyon

WORSHIP 293

High and holy Lord God Almighty, who art the fountain of all true thoughts and right resolves, be pleased to still the tumult of earthly cares within our breasts, and fill our minds with deep devotion; that for a little while we may rise above the jar and fret of daily life, and join with grateful hearts in that pure worship, which from spirits higher and holier than ours for ever ascends before thy throne, giving praise and thanks and honour unto the lamb that was slain, our Lord and Saviour Jesus Christ; to whom be glory both now and ever.

W. Gray Elmslie

PRAYER AND LIFE 294

O God, who art Spirit, and willest to be worshipped in spirit and in truth: grant to us that, loving thee in all things and above all things, we may please thee by our prayers and by our lives; through Jesus Christ our Lord.

William Bright

PRAYER AND SERVICE   **295**

Remember, O Lord, what thou hast wrought in us, and not
what we deserve; and, as thou hast called us to thy service,
make us worthy of our calling; through Jesus Christ our
Lord.   *J. Armitage Robinson*

THE SPIRIT OF PRAYER   **296**

Holy Jesus, give me the gift and spirit of prayer; and do
thou by thy gracious intercession supply my ignorances,
and passionate desires, and imperfect choices; procuring
and giving to me such returns of favour which may support
my needs, and serve the ends of religion and the Spirit,
which thy wisdom chooses, and thy passion hath purchased,
and thy grace loves to bestow upon all thy saints and
servants.   *Jeremy Taylor*

OPENING PRAYER   **297**

O God, the glory of thy saints, who being above all, and
through all, and in all, dost yet accept the sacrifice of the
contrite and the incense of their prayers: grant that we
may be hallowed in mind, fervent in spirit, and chaste in
body; and that mortifying within us all ungodly and worldly
lusts, we may offer to thee the pure sacrifice of hearts
uplifted in thy praise and lives devoted to thy service.
                                        Adapted from Gothic

                                                     298

God, our Father, who dost call us to prayer, and wilt grant
our petitions, if only, when we pray, we purpose in all
things amendment of life: hear us, as we cry to thee in our
darkness, and stretch forth thy right hand to help and
deliver us; hold out thy light before us; recall us from our
wanderings; guide us and restore us to ourselves and to
thee; through Jesus Christ our Lord.
                                        After St. Augustine

299

Blessed Jesu, lifting up holy hands perpetually for all mankind: breathe by thy Spirit such love into the prayers we offer, that they may be taken into thine, and prevail with thine; to the glory of thy holy Name.   *E. Milner-White*

300

Lord, we beseech thee, give ear to our prayers, and by thy gracious visitation lighten the darkness of our hearts; by our Lord Jesus Christ.   1549 *Prayer Book*

301

O Lord, my good God and Father, blessed be thy name for ever: dispose my heart, open my lips, and guide me by thy Holy Spirit to a truer acknowledgement of all my sins, that my prayer may be heard of thee, in the name of thy Son Jesus Christ.   So be it.   *Elizabethan*

302

O Lord our God, who hast given thy peace to men, and didst send down the gift of thy most Holy Spirit upon thy disciples and apostles, and by thy power didst open their lips with tongues of fire: open our sinful lips, and teach us how and for what we should pray; through Jesus Christ our Lord.   *Henry Vaughan*

303

O Almighty God, the searcher of all hearts, and from whom no secrets are hid, who hast declared that all such as shall draw nigh to thee with their lips, when their hearts are far from thee, are an abomination unto thee; cleanse, we beseech thee, the thoughts of our hearts, by the inspiration of the Holy Spirit, that no wandering, vain, nor idle thoughts may put out of our minds that reverence and godly fear that becomes all those who come in thy presence.
Dean Swift

304

Incline thine ear, O Lord, to our prayers, and enlighten the darkness of our minds by the grace of thy visitation: that in thy light we may see light and walk in thy truth without stumbling, and at last attain to the light of life everlasting; through Jesus Christ our Lord.   *Adapted from Sarum*

305

O Lord, take away from us all coldness, all wanderings of the thoughts, and fix our souls upon thee and thy love, O merciful Lord and Saviour, in this our hour of prayer.
Archbishop Benson

306

O Lord, open thou our lips, that we may bless thy holy Name; cleanse our hearts from all vain, evil, and wandering thoughts; enlighten our understandings, enkindle our affections, that we may worthily and devoutly offer up our prayers and praises to thee, and so be meet to be heard in the presence of thy divine majesty; through Jesus Christ our Lord.   *Anon.*

307

Give me, O God, the spirit of true devotion, such as may give life to all my prayers, so that they may find acceptance in thy sight. By thy Almighty power, O King of heaven, for the glory of thy Name, and for the love of a Father, grant me all those blessings which thy Son taught us to pray for.   *Bishop Thomas Wilson*

308

Give me grace, O my Father, to be utterly ashamed of my own reluctance. Rouse me from sloth and coldness, and make me desire thee with my whole heart. Teach me to love meditation, sacred reading, and prayer. Teach me to love that which must engage my mind for all eternity.
Cardinal Newman

309

Almighty God, who art ready at all times to hear the prayers of those who call upon thee, open our hearts and lips to bless and glorify thy name.   *Uppingham Prayer*

310

Look graciously upon us, O Holy Spirit, and give us for our hallowing thoughts that pass into prayer, prayers that pass into love, and love that passeth into life with thee for ever.   *E. Milner-White*

SUBMISSION IN PRAYER   **311**

Lord, I know not what I ought to ask of thee; thou only knowest what I need; thou lovest me better than I know how to love myself. Father, give thy child what he himself knows not how to ask; I presume not to ask either for crosses or consolations; in simplicity I present myself before thee and open my heart to thee. Regard thou the needs which I myself know not: behold and do according to thy tender mercy. Smite or heal: depress me or raise me up; I adore all thy purposes without knowing them. I keep silence, and offer myself as a sacrifice to thee: I yield myself to thee, and I would have no other desire than to accomplish thy will. Teach me to pray: pray thyself in me; through Jesus Christ our Lord.   *Fénelon*

CLOSING PRAYER   **312**

Almighty Father, well-spring of life to all things that have being, from amid the unwearied praises of Cherubin and Seraphin, who stand about thy throne of light which no man can approach unto: give ear, we humbly beseech thee, to the supplications of thy people who put their sure trust in thy mercy; through Jesus Christ our Lord.
    The Book of Deer

313

O God, the Father of our Lord Jesus Christ, incline thine ear, we beseech thee, to these our prayers which we offer in his Name; and grant that thy will may be done through us on earth as it is in heaven; through the same Christ our Lord.   *Unknown*

314

Lord, I humbly beseech thee to hear and accept my prayers for myself, and for thy people which call upon thee; and grant that we may perfectly know what things we ought to do and also have grace and power faithfully to fulfil the same.   *Archbishop Laud*

315

O gracious Lord, since thou hast promised that, where two or three are gathered together in thy Name, thou wilt be in the midst of them to grant their request, grant to us who are met in thy Name that those requests, which in the utmost sincerity and earnestness of our hearts we have now made (on behalf of this thy distressed servant, and of ourselves), may effectually be answered; through the merits of Jesus Christ our Lord.   *Dean Swift*

316

Good God, say amen to my prayers, if it be thy gracious will; but if in anything I have asked or done amiss, pardon mine infirmities, and answer my necessities, for Jesus and his mercies' sake.   *Bishop Thomas Wilson*

Section 2

GENERAL CONFESSION

CONFESSION   **317**

We confess to God Almighty, the Father, the Son, and the Holy Ghost, that we have sinned in thought, word, and deed, through our fault, our own fault, our own most grievous fault. Wherefore we pray God to have mercy upon us.   *Office of Compline*

318

Almighty Father, Lord of heaven and earth: we confess
that we have sinned against thee in thought, word, and
deed. Have mercy upon us, O Lord, have mercy upon us
after thy great goodness; according to the multitude of thy
mercies, do away our offences: wash us throughly from
our wickedness, and cleanse us from our sins; for Jesus
Christ's sake. *Canadian Prayer Book*

319

Father, Lord of heaven and earth, I confess to thee all the
hidden and open sins of my heart and mind, which I have
committed unto this day. Wherefore I beg of thee, the
merciful and righteous judge, forgiveness and grace to sin
no more. *Eastern Orthodox*

320

O thou who art the life of souls, having life in thyself: O
life of my soul, it is a good thing to make my confession
unto thee, O God of my heart, and say have mercy upon
me, heal my soul, for I have sinned against thee; and let
me never abuse thy mercy and take it for a licence to sin,
but remember thy words, Behold, thou art made whole, sin
no more lest a worse thing come unto thee. For who art
thou, O our God, but the very well-spring of righteousness, who renderest to every man according to his works;
and a broken and contrite heart thou wilt not despise.
St. Augustine

321

O Lord my God, thou judge of my conscience, before thee
is my heart and my remembrance: set my errors before my
face, that I may see and hate them. Behold, thou lovest
the truth and he that doeth truth cometh to the light; and I
would do this in my heart as I confess before thee. What
could be hidden in me from thee, O Lord, to whose eyes
the abyss of man's conscience is uncovered? For I would
hide thee from me, and not me from thee. To thee,

G

therefore, O Lord, I open whatever I am, and I confess unto thee, not with words of the flesh but with the words of my soul, and the cry of my thought, which thine ear knoweth. O Lord, have mercy upon me according to thy great mercy, for thine own Name's sake, and forsake not in any way what thou hast begun, but make perfect what is imperfect in me. Let me know thee, O Lord, who knowest me: let me know thee as I am known. O power of my soul, enter into it and fit it for thee, that without spot or wrinkle thou mayest have it and hold it. *St. Augustine*

322

O Lover of men, very tenderly pitiful, Father of mercies, rich in mercy toward all that call upon thee: I have sinned against heaven and before thee, neither am I worthy to be called a son, neither am I worthy to be made a hired servant, no, not the lowest of them all. But I repent, alas, I repent: help thou mine impenitence: be merciful to me a sinner.
Lancelot Andrewes

323

Almighty God, and most merciful Father, all merciful, mercy itself; I have erred willingly and strayed willingly, nay run from thy ways, more like an untamed heifer than a lost or wandering sheep. I have followed too much, even altogether, the absurd devices and brutish desires of my own heart, I have offended against, nay been offended at, thy holy, most holy, laws. I have left undone, not done at all, those things which I ought to have done. And I have done, done nothing else, but those things which I ought not to have done. And there is no health, no hope of health in me. But thou, Lord, have mercy upon me miserable, most miserable sinner, the greatest sinner, and most unthankful for so great grace. Spare me, and all them that confess their faults. Restore me, and all them that be penitent, that desire to be penitent, that wish they were, would be glad if they were; that fear that they are not enough, and are sorry they are not more.
Archbishop Laud

324

We confess unto thee, O heavenly Father, as thy children and thy people, our hardness, and indifference, and impenitence; our grievous failures in thy faith and in pure and holy living; our trust in riches, and our misuse of them, our confidence in self, whereby we daily multiply our own temptations. We confess our timorousness as thy Church and witness before the world, and the sin and bitterness that every man knoweth in his own heart. Give us all contrition and meekness of heart, O Father; grace to amend our sinful life, and the holy comfort of thy Spirit to overcome and heal all our evils; through Jesus Christ our Lord.   *Archbishop Benson*

325

Hear, O Lord, and have mercy, O Almighty God, heavenly Father, who forgivest iniquity and transgression; O Lord Jesus Christ, Lamb of God, who takest away the sin of the world; O Holy Spirit, who helpest the infirmities of those that pray: receive my humble confession. Give me true repentance and sincere faith in thee. Do away mine offences, and give me grace to live hereafter more worthily of our Christian calling, for the glory of thy great name.
                                    After Bishop Westcott

326

Almighty God, long-suffering and of great goodness: we confess to thee, we confess with our whole heart: our neglect and forgetfulness of thy commandments: our wrong-doing, speaking, and thinking: the hurts we have done to others: and the good we have left undone: O God, forgive thy people that have sinned against thee: and raise us to newness of life.   *E. Milner-White*

327

Almighty and most merciful God, we acknowledge and confess that we have sinned against thee in thought, word, and deed; that we have not loved thee with all our heart and soul, with all our mind and strength; and that we have

not loved our neighbour as ourselves. We beseech thee,
O God, to be forgiving to what we have been, to help us to
amend what we are, and of thy mercy to direct what we
shall be, so that the love of goodness may ever be first in
our hearts, that we may always walk in thy commandments
and ordinances blameless, and follow unto our life's end in
the footsteps of Jesus Christ our Lord.   *John Hunter*

328

O God our Father, from whom all fatherhood in heaven
and earth is named, graciously behold this thy family.
Thou art ever merciful and makest thy sun to rise on the
just and on the unjust: but we have misused thy gifts,
marred thy work, and robbed one another of our daily
bread. Help us to see and feel our share in the guilt of
the world, and grant us thy grace to bring forth fruits
worthy of repentance; through Jesus Christ our Lord.
Mrs. Reinhold Niebuhr

329

O God, most good, Father of mercies, be pleased to have
pity upon us, and pardon our sins for the love of Jesus
Christ our Saviour. Vouchsafe unto us also, and increase
continually within us, the gifts of thy Holy Spirit; that we
may ever more readily acknowledge our misdoings, and
being deeply affected by them, renounce them with our
whole heart, and bring forth fruits of righteousness and
holiness acceptable to thee; through Jesus Christ our Lord.
French Reformed Liturgy

330

O Lord, with heartfelt sorrow we repent and deplore our
offences. We condemn ourselves and our evil ways, with
true penitence entreating that thy grace may relieve our
distress. Be pleased to have compassion upon us, O most
gracious God, Father of all mercies, for the sake of thy
Son, Jesus Christ our Lord. And as thou dost remove our
guilt and our pollution, grant us the daily increase of the

grace of thy Holy Spirit, that acknowledging from our inmost hearts our own unrighteousness, we may be touched with sorrow that shall work true repentance, and that, mortifying all sins within us, thy Spirit may produce the fruits of holiness and righteousness well-pleasing in thy sight; through Jesus Christ our Lord. *Liturgy of Geneva*

331

Lord Jesus, merciful Saviour, who art touched with the feeling of our infirmities, and hast been at all points tempted even as we are, yet without sin: we have done amiss and dealt wickedly; we have sinned against thee in thought, word, and deed. Look with compassion upon our weakness, cleanse us from our sins, forgive us both what we have done and left undone; and give us grace to amend our lives, to thy glory who hast called us out of darkness into thy light and love; we ask it for thy sake and in thy Name.

332

Almighty God, rich in mercy and plenteous in loving-kindness, who searchest us out and knowest altogether the thoughts and inclinations of our hearts: we humbly acknowledge our sins and wickedness, and confess that we have done evil in thy sight. Have mercy upon us, O Lord, have mercy upon us, we beseech thee; cast us not away from thy presence, and do away our offences; cleanse us from the stains of our transgressions; break the power of evil within us; and give us grace to put away all hurtful things; that, being freed from the bondage of our sins, we may bring forth fruits worthy of repentance, and serve thee faithfully to our lives' end; through Jesus Christ our Lord.

333

O God, most gracious and merciful, slow to anger and of great kindness, who thinkest upon us for good and art ready to pardon those who truly repent: forgive, we beseech thee, us thy servants who so often and so grievously sin against thee, in thought, word, and deed; receive us who do truly acknowledge and confess our misdoings; renew within us the peace of thy salvation; and so make haste to help and deliver us, that we may henceforth walk before thee with a perfect heart, and, this life ended, may serve thee with thy saints for ever, where thou reignest in thy love and glory everlasting; for the sake of Jesus Christ our Lord.

REPENTANCE   **334**

Lover of mankind, since thou desirest to dwell within me, I make bold to draw near. Thou dost bid me open the door which thou thyself hast made, that when thou comest, as thou wilt, thou canst bring light into my darkened mind. Thou didst not reject the harlot when she came to thee in tears, neither refuse the publican when he repented, nor the robber when he sought entrance into thy kingdom, nor turn away the persecutor when he repented; but thou didst number all who came to thee in penitence among thy friends, for thou alone art blessed, now and for ever.

St. Chrysostom

335

O Lord and Master of my life, take from me the spirit of sloth, faint-heartedness, lust of power, and idle talk. Give rather to me thy servant the spirit of chastity, humility, patience, and love. Grant me, my Lord and King, to see my own errors and not to judge my brother, for thou art blessed for ever and ever.   *Ephraem of Edessa*

336

Lord, I bring thee my sorrows and miseries and sins, beseeching thee to clothe me with some portion of thy holiness, and to give me of thy joy. I bring thee of my emptiness; do thou give me of thy fullness. I bring thee a broken heart; do thou remake it, and bind it up, that it may be remade, as vessel of thy glory to contain thee. Feed me with thy body, which thou didst take that it might be broken for us. Wash me with thy blood, which thou sheddest for the remission of our sins. Gladden me with the new wine of thy Spirit, so that I may go forth out of myself new-born as a little child in thy childhood: dying in thy death: living by thy life in me, to rise again through thy resurrection, who art our resurrection and our life, on that glorious morrow which setteth not. To which do thou of thy mercy bring me, a sinner, thou, our only Saviour and redeemer. *Edward Bouverie Pusey*

337

O merciful God, make me to lift up my heart oft-times to thee, and, when I fall, make me to think on thee, and be sorry with a steadfast purpose of amendment. My God, make me humble without feigning, merry without lightness, sad without mistrust, sober without dullness, true without doubleness, fearing thee without desperation, trusting in thee without presumption, telling my neighbour's faults without dissimulation, teaching them with words and examples without mockings, obedient without arguing, patient without grudging, and pure without corruption.
St. Thomas Aquinas

338

O merciful God, full of compassion, long-suffering, and of great pity, who sparest when we deserve punishment, and in thy wrath thinkest upon mercy: make me earnestly to repent, and heartily to be sorry for all my misdoings; make the remembrance so burdensome and painful, that I may flee to thee with a troubled spirit and a contrite heart; and, O merciful Lord, visit, comfort, and relieve me; cast me not out from thy presence, and take not thy Holy Spirit from me, but excite in me true repentance; give me in this world knowledge of thy truth, and confidence in thy mercy, and in the world to come life everlasting, for the sake of our Lord and Saviour, thy Son Jesus Christ. *Dr. Johnson*

339

Almighty God, who by thy grace and providence hast brought my great and crying sins to light, I most humbly beseech thee to continue thy grace and mercy to me, that my conscience being now awakened, I may call my ways to remembrance, and confess, and bewail and abhor all the sins of my life past. And, O merciful God, give me true repentance for them, even that repentance to which thou hast promised mercy and pardon, that even the consequences of my wrongdoing may bring a blessing to me, and that in all I may find mercy at thy hands, through the merits and mediation of our Lord Jesus Christ.

Bishop Thomas Wilson

340

Grant, I beseech thee, merciful Lord, that the designs of a new and better life, which by thy grace I have now formed, may not pass away without effect. Incite and enable me, by thy Holy Spirit, to improve the time which thou shalt grant me; to avoid all evil thoughts, words, and actions; and to do all the duties which thou shalt set before me. Hear my prayer, O Lord, for the sake of Jesus Christ.

Dr. Johnson

FORGIVENESS   **341**

May the almighty and merciful Lord grant unto me pardon and remission of all my sins, time for amendment of life, and the grace and comfort of the Holy Spirit.

342

Lord, for thy tender mercies' sake, lay not our sins to our charge, but forgive that is past, and give us grace to amend our lives; to decline from sin and incline to virtue, that we may walk with a perfect heart before thee, now and evermore.

John Lydney

343

We make our prayer unto thee, O God of our life. So long as we live will we magnify thee, and lift up our hands in thy Name. Let our prayer be set forth in thy sight as the incense. Blessed art thou, O Lord our God, the God of our fathers, who hast created the changes of day and night. Deal not with us after our sins, neither reward us after our iniquities: and look mercifully upon our infirmities for the glory of thy Name; through Jesus Christ our Lord.

Lancelot Andrewes

344

Lord, of thy great goodness I beseech thee give me true repentance, and forgive me all my sins, negligences, and ignorances, and endue me with the grace of thy Holy Spirit, that I may amend my life according to thy holy Word.

Archbishop Laud

345

Forgive me my sins, O Lord; the sins of my present and the sins of my past, the sins of my soul and the sins of my body, the sins which I have done to please myself and the sins which I have done to please others. Forgive me my casual sins and my deliberate sins, and those which I have laboured so to hide that I have hidden them even from myself. Forgive me them, O Lord, forgive them all; for Jesus Christ's sake.   *Bishop Thomas Wilson*

346

O Lord our God, our creator and our judge, provoked every day, yet strong and patient: forgive, we beseech thee, our rebellion against thy will, our forgetfulness of thy law, our complacent apathy, our culpable ignorance, our tolerance of intolerable wrongs. Have mercy upon us, O Lord, and turn our hearts, through Jesus Christ, our blessed Lord and saviour.   *Unknown*

347

Blot out, we humbly beseech thee, O Lord, our past transgression; forgive our negligence and ignorance; help us to amend our mistakes and to repair our misunderstanding; and so uplift our hearts in new love and dedication, that we may be unburdened from the grief and shame of past faithlessness, and go forth to serve thee with renewed courage and devotion; through Jesus Christ our Lord.   *Anon.*

348

O Lord, the house of my soul is narrow; enlarge it that thou mayest enter in.   It is ruinous, O repair it!   It displeases thy sight; I confess it, I know. But who shall cleanse it, or to whom shall I cry but unto thee? Cleanse me from my secret faults, O Lord, and spare thy servant from strange sins.   *St. Augustine*

349

O God, the glory of thy saints and the rewarder of the faithful, who despisest not the sacrifice of a contrite heart and acceptest the prayer of the humble: grant that we, and all for whom we pray, may mortify our wordly lusts, and with pure hearts and minds offer unto thee the incense of our praise and thanksgiving; through Jesus Christ our Lord.

Section 3

THE CHRISTIAN YEAR

EVE OF ADVENT   **350**

Stir up, we beseech thee, O Lord, the wills of thy faithful people; that they, plenteously bringing forth the fruit of good works, may of thee be plenteously rewarded; through Jesus Christ our Lord.   *Gregorian Sacramentary*

ADVENT 351

Stir up thy power, we pray thee, O Lord, and come: that
through thy protection we may be delivered from the
dangers which overhang us by reason of our sins, and
through thy liberation of us we may be saved; who livest
and reignest with the Father in the unity of the Holy
Spirit, God for evermore. *Sarum*

352

O Lord, raise up, we pray thee, thy power, and come
among us, and with great might succour us; that whereas,
through our sins and wickedness, we are sore let and
hindered in running the race that is set before us, thy
bountiful grace and mercy may speedily help and deliver
us; through the satisfaction of thy Son our Lord, to whom
with thee and the Holy Ghost be honour and glory, world
without end. *1549 Prayer Book*

353

Stir up our hearts, we beseech thee, O Lord, to make
ready the ways of thine only-begotten Son: that, when he
cometh he may find us watching; and attentive to meet
him with minds that wait for his presence; through Christ
our Lord.

354

Stir up thy power, O Lord, and come, and mercifully fulfil
thy promise to thy Church unto the end of the world;
through Jesus Christ our Lord. *Gelasian Sacramentary*

355

O thou, who hast foretold that thou wilt return to judgement in an hour that we are not aware of: grant us grace to
watch and pray always; that whether thou shalt come at
even, or at midnight, or in the morning, we may be found
among the number of those servants who shall be blessed
in watching for their Lord; to whom be all glory now and
for evermore. *Non-Jurors' Prayer Book*

356

O God, who didst send thy messengers and prophets to prepare the way of thy Son before him: grant that our Lord when he cometh may find in us a dwelling prepared for himself; through the same Jesus Christ our Lord, who came to take our nature upon him that he might bring many sons unto glory; who now liveth and reigneth with thee and the Holy Spirit, ever one God, world without end.   *Anon.*

357

O thou who when thou comest wilt take account of thy servants: remember for good thine eternal pact and promise in thy cross and resurrection; in judgement forget not mercy; take not from us the help and comfort of thy Holy Spirit; and suffer us not at that last hour to fall from thee; who livest and reignest with the Father and the Holy Spirit, one God, world without end.

Frederick B. Macnutt

358

O great and glorious God, holy and immortal, who searchest out the policies of nations and triest the hearts of men: come, we pray thee, in judgement, upon the nations of the world; come and bring to destruction all that is contrary to thy holy will for mankind, and cause the counsels of the wicked to perish. Come, O Lord, into our hearts, and root out from them all that thou seest, and we cannot see, to be unlike the spirit of thy Son, Jesus Christ our Lord.   *Harold Anson*

359

O Lord Jesus Christ, let the love of thine appearing so continually dwell within us that our hearts may never depart from thee; and so number us now with those for whom thou dost intercede in heaven, that in the last day we may not be ashamed before thee when thou comest to judge the world; who livest and reignest with thy Father and the Holy Spirit, world without end.   *Mozarabic*

360

Almighty Father, whose blessed Son at his coming amongst us brought redemption unto his people and peace to men of goodwill: grant that, when he shall come again in glory to judge the world and to make all things new, we may be found ready to receive him, and enter into his joy; through the same our Lord Jesus Christ.

Frederick B. Macnutt

THE GREAT ACCOUNT **361**

O Lord Jesus Christ, before whose judgement seat we must all appear and give account of the things done in the body: grant, we beseech thee, that, when the books are opened in that day, the faces of thy servants may not be ashamed; through thy merits, O blessed saviour, who live stand reignest with the Father and the Holy Spirit, one God, world without end. *Altus of St. Columba*

ADVENT AND CHRISTMAS **362**

O day-spring, splendour of the light eternal, sun of righteousness: come, enlighten those who sit in darkness and the shadow of death. O King of nations, whom they long for, corner-stone who makest all one, come and save mankind, whom thou didst fashion out of the dust. O Emmanuel, our King and Law-giver, desire of all nations and their saviour: come and save us, O Lord our God.

CHRISTMAS EVE **363**

O Lord God Almighty, who by the incarnation of thy only-begotten Son hast banished the darkness of this world, and by his glorious birth didst enlighten this most holy night: drive away from us, we beseech thee, the darkness of sin, and continue ever to enlighten our hearts with the glory of thy grace, which thou hast given unto us in the same, our saviour Jesus Christ.

364

O God, who hast hallowed this sacred night with the joyful
tidings of the word made flesh: grant that we, beholding
here on earth as through a veil the mystery of his glory who
was born among us, at last may see him face to face, where
there is no more need of light from lamp or sun, in the
fullness of thine eternal glory in heaven; through Jesus
Christ our Lord.   *Frederick B. Macnutt*

365

O Lord, we beseech thee, incline thine ear to our prayers,
and lighten the darkness of our hearts by thy gracious
visitation; through Jesus Christ our Lord.
                                        Gregorian Sacramentary

366

Almighty Father, who hast given thine only-begotten Son
to take our nature upon him and as at this time to be born
of the Virgin Mary, his mother; grant that he may be born
in our hearts; that as by his most glorious incarnation he
became the firstborn of many brethren, so by his renewing
presence he may give us the right to become the sons of
God; through the same thy Son Jesus Christ our Lord, to
whom with thee and the Holy Spirit be given all praise and
love, all loyalty and adoration, for ever and ever.   *Anon.*

CHRISTMAS   **367**

Almighty God, who didst wonderfully create man in thine
own image, and didst yet more wonderfully restore him:
grant, we beseech thee, that, as thy Son our Lord Jesus
Christ was made in the likeness of men, so we may be made
partakers of the divine nature; through the same thy Son,
who with thee and the Holy Ghost liveth and reigneth, one
God, world without end.

368

O God, whose blessed Son Jesus Christ became man that we might become the sons of God: grant, we beseech thee, that being made partakers of the divine nature of thy Son, we may be conformed to his likeness; who liveth and reigneth with thee and the Holy Ghost, now and ever.

Scottish Prayer Book

369

We pray thee, O Lord, to purify our hearts that they may be worthy to become thy dwelling place. Let us never fail to find room for thee, but come and abide in us that we also may abide in thee, who as at this time wast born into the world for us, and dost live and reign, King of kings and Lord of lords, now and for evermore. *William Temple*

370

Lord Jesus, child of Bethlehem, for love of men made man: create in us love so pure and perfect that whatsoever our heart loveth may be after thy will, in thy Name and for thy sake. *E. Milner-White*

371

O God, who makest us glad with the yearly remembrance of the birth of thine only Son Jesus Christ: grant, that as we joyfully receive him as our redeemer, so we may with sure confidence behold him, when he shall come to be our judge; who liveth and reigneth with thee and the Holy Spirit, one God, world without end.

Gelasian Sacramentary

372

O God, to whom glory is sung in the highest, while on earth peace is proclaimed among men of goodwill: grant that goodwill to us thy servants; cleanse us from evil, and give peace to all thy people; through thy mercy, O blessed Lord God, who dost live and govern all things, world without end. *Mozarabic*

373

O Father, who hast declared thy love to men by the birth of the holy child at Bethlehem: help us to welcome him with gladness and to make room for him in our common days; so that we may live at peace with one another, and in goodwill with all thy family; through the same thy Son Jesus Christ our Lord.   *Anon.*

374

Good Jesu, who didst empty thyself of thine eternal glory and become a little child for love of me: empty me wholly of myself, and make me a little child, that I may love thee wholly, as thou didst love me infinitely.
                                        Edward Bouverie Pusey

NEW YEAR'S EVE   **375**

Most gracious God, who hast been merciful unto us in the year that is past, and hast guided and upheld us through all the years of our life on earth: we beseech thee to pardon our sins and to make us abound in faith and love; fashion in us those virtues which are acceptable unto thee, and grant that we may serve thee more faithfully in the year that is to come; through Jesus Christ our Lord.

NEW YEAR   **376**

O eternal Lord God, who inhabitest eternity, and hast brought thy servants to the beginning of another year: pardon, we beseech thee, our sins in the past; graciously abide with us all the days of our life; direct our goings in thy ways, and guard us from evil in the years that are to come; that we may finish our course with joy and at last become partakers of the inheritance of thy saints in light; through Jesus Christ our Lord.

377

Almighty God, who alone art without variableness or shadow of turning, and hast safely brought us through the changes of time to the beginning of another year: we beseech thee to pardon the sins that we have committed in the year which is past; and give us grace that we may spend the remainder of our days to thy honour and glory; through Jesus Christ our Lord.   *Church of Ireland Prayer Book*

378

O God, who art the beginning and the end of all things, grant us so faithfully to pass through the coming year, that we may think and do always such things as shall please thee; through Jesus Christ our Lord.

379

Eternal God, who makest all things new, and abidest for ever the same: grant us to begin this year in thy faith, and to continue it in thy favour; that, being guided in all our doings, and guarded all our days, we may spend our lives in thy service, and finally, by thy grace, attain the glory of everlasting life; through Jesus Christ our Lord.

W. E. Orchard

THE NAME OF JESUS   380

O almighty God, who hast given unto thy Son Jesus Christ the Name which is above every name, and hast taught us that there is none other whereby we may be saved: mercifully grant that as thy faithful people have comfort and peace in his Name, so they may ever labour to proclaim it unto all nations; through the same Jesus Christ our Lord.

Scottish Prayer Book

381

O God, who hast made the glorious Name of thine only-begotten Son, our Lord Jesus Christ, to be exceeding lovable to thy faithful servants: mercifully grant that all who devoutly venerate the Name of Jesus on earth may in this life receive thy holy comfort, and at the last attain to thine unending joy; through the same Jesus Christ our Lord.   *Sarum*

H

382

O God, who didst send forth thine only-begotten Son to be the saviour of mankind, and didst ordain that he should be called Jesus: mercifully grant that as we love and honour his holy Name on earth, we may also enjoy the vision of his glory in heaven; through the same thy Son Jesus Christ our Lord. *Anon.*

FORGETTING THINGS BEHIND **383**

Eternal Father, who alone canst control the days that are gone and the deeds that are done: remove from my burdened memory the weight of past years, that being set free from the glamour of complacency and the palsy of remorse, I may reach forth unto those things which are before, and press towards the mark for the prize of the high calling of God in Christ Jesus. *Bishop Brent*

CHILDREN OF TIME **384**

Almighty Father, who dwellest eternal in the heavens, and hast appointed unto us our habitation in this world of change and time: stir up our wills, we beseech thee, so to number our days that we may apply our hearts unto wisdom; grant that our lives may be filled with thy praise and service, and make us to be numbered at last with thy saints in glory everlasting; through Jesus Christ our Lord. *Frederick B. Macnutt*

IN THE MIDST OF THE YEARS **385**

Grant, almighty God, that, since the dullness and harshness of our flesh is so great that it is needful for us in various ways to be afflicted, we may patiently bear thy chastisement, and under a deep feeling of sorrow flee to thy mercy displayed to us in Christ; and that not depending upon the earthly blessings of this perishable life, but relying only upon thy Word, we may go forward in the course of our calling; until at length we be gathered to that blessed rest which is laid up for us in heaven; through Jesus Christ our Lord. *John Calvin*

EPIPHANY   386

O God, who by the leading of a star didst manifest thy
only-begotten Son to the nations: mercifully grant that we
who know thee now by faith may so follow the light of thy
truth revealed in him that we may attain at last to the vision
of thy glory in heaven; through Jesus Christ our Lord.

387

Almighty God, who at the baptism of thy blessed Son
Jesus Christ in the river Jordan didst manifest his glorious
Godhead: grant, we beseech thee, that the brightness of
his presence may shine in our hearts, and his glory be set
forth in our lives; through the same Jesus Christ our Lord.
Bishop John Dowden

388

O Father everlasting, the light of faithful souls, who didst
bring the nations to thy light and kings to the brightness of
thy rising: fill the world with thy glory, we beseech thee,
and show thyself unto all the nations; through him who is
the true light and the bright and morning star, Jesus
Christ, thy Son our Lord.   *Gothic Missal*

389

Almighty God, who to wise men who sought him didst
manifest the incarnation of thy Son by the bright shining
of a star: grant that, as they presented unto him gifts, gold
and frankincense and myrrh, so we also out of our
treasures may offer to him ourselves, a living sacrifice
acceptable in thy sight; through him who for our sakes was
born on earth a little child, Jesus Christ our Lord.
Frederick B. Macnutt

390

Lord Jesus, our master, go with us while we travel to the
heavenly country: that, following thy star, we may not
wander in the darkness of this world's night, while thou,
who art our way, and truth, and life, dost shine within us to
our journey's end; for thy mercy's sake.

391

Almighty and everlasting God, who didst make known the incarnation of thy Son by the bright shining of a star, and when the wise men beheld it they adored thy majesty and presented costly gifts: grant that the star of righteousness may always shine in our hearts; and that we may freely give ourselves and all that we possess to thy service; through Jesus Christ our Lord.

ASH WEDNESDAY   392

O God, who through thy blessed Son hast gloriously reconciled mankind to thyself; grant us to keep such a fast as he has chosen; that following the example of our Lord, we may obey thee with faithful hearts, and serve one another in holy love; through the same Jesus Christ our Lord.   *Gelasian Sacramentary*

LENT   393

O God, who by thy care and counsel for mankind hast moved thy Church to appoint this holy season wherein the hearts of those who seek thee may receive thy help and healing: we beseech thee, saviour of our souls and bodies, to purify us by thy discipline, that, abiding in thee and thou in us, we may grow in grace and in the faith and knowledge of thee; through Jesus Christ our Lord.

394

Grant, we beseech thee, O Lord, that by the observance of this Lent we may advance in the knowledge of the mystery of Christ, and show forth his mind in conduct worthy of our calling; through Jesus Christ our Lord.
                                              Gelasian Sacramentary

395

Into thy hands, O Lord our God, we commend our souls and bodies this Lent. Draw nigh to us as we draw nigh to thee, and enlighten us by thy Holy Spirit. Be present with us in our worship, and abide with us amidst the cares and duties of our daily lives; and draw us after thee to follow withersoever thou wilt lead us in thy way of faith and love; through Jesus Christ our Lord.   *Frederick B. Macnutt*

396

O Lord Jesus Christ, who didst take upon thyself the form of a servant, humbling thyself and accepting death for us, even the death of the cross: grant that this mind may be also in us; so that we may gladly take upon ourselves the life of humility and service, and taking up our cross daily may follow thee in thy cross-bearing in thy suffering and death, that with thee we may attain unto the power of thy endless life. Grant this, O Christ, our saviour and our king.   *Harold Anson*

397

O God, who art spirit, the spirit in us prays to thee for mastery of the flesh, that living without fear for ourselves, we may abound in help to others; so shall we quicken the hope and increase the knowledge of thy heaven, where spirit is lord of matter, as love is lord of spirit, now and for ever.   *A. Clutton Brock*

398

O Lord and heavenly Father, who hast given unto us thy people the true bread that cometh down from heaven, even thy Son Jesus Christ: grant that throughout this Lent our souls may so be fed by him that we may continually live in him and he in us; and that day by day we may be renewed in spirit by the power of his endless life, who gave himself for us, and now liveth and reigneth with thee and the Holy Spirit, one God, for ever and ever.   *Frederick B. Macnutt*

HOLY WEEK   **399**

O God, who didst send thy Son Jesus Christ into the world for our salvation, that he might humble himself to our estate and call us back to thee: grant, we beseech thee, that we may prepare a way of faith for him in our hearts and minds, and daily follow the example of his self-giving love; through the same Jesus Christ our Lord.

400

O God, whose blessed Son for our sake endured the cross that thou mightest liberate us from the power of our enemy: grant to us thy servants grace that we may attain unto the glory of his resurrection; through the same Jesus Christ our Lord. *After Sarum*

THE MAUNDY **401**

Lord Jesus Christ, who when thou wast able to institute thy Holy Sacrament at the Last Supper, didst wash the feet of the Apostles, and teach us by thy example the grace of humility: cleanse us, we beseech thee, from all stain of sin, that we may be worthy partakers of thy holy mysteries: who livest and reignest with the Father and the Holy Ghost, one God, world without end. *The Royal Maundy*

THE THIRD HOUR **402**

O Lord Jesus Christ, Son of the living God, who at the third hour of the day wast led forth to the pain of the cross for the salvation of the world: we humbly beseech thee, that by the virtue of thy most sacred passion thou wouldest blot out all our sins, and mercifully bring us to the glory of thy blessedness; who livest and reignest, God, world without end. *Sarum: Terce*

THE ASCENT OF CALVARY **403**

Lord, thou goest forth alone to thy sacrifice: thou dost offer thyself to death, whom thou art come to destroy. What can we miserable sinners plead, who know that for the deeds that we have done thou dost atone? Ours is the guilt, Lord: why then must thou suffer torture for our sins? Make our hearts so to share in thy passion, that our fellow-suffering may invite thy mercy. This is that night of tears, and the three days' eventide of sadness, until the day break with the risen Christ, and with joy to those that mourn. May we so suffer with thee, Lord, that we may be partners of thy glory, and our three days' mourning shall pass away and become thine Easter joy. *Peter Abelard*

THE CRUCIFIXION **404**

O Lord Jesus Christ! Son of the living God! Who for the redemption of mankind didst vouchsafe to ascend the wood of the cross, that the whole world which lay in darkness might be enlightened: we beseech thee, pour such light into our souls and bodies, that we may be enabled to attain to that light which is eternal, and through the merits of thy passion, may after death joyfully enter within the gates of paradise; who with the Father and the Holy Ghost livest and reignest, one God, world without end. *Sarum*

BEFORE THE CROSS **405**

O my redeemer, deliverer, and saviour, draw me to thee, that being always mindful of thy death, trusting always in thy goodness, and being always thankful for thine unspeakable benefits, I may be made partaker of so great bountifulness, and not be separated from thee through my own unthankfulness, so that thou shouldest not have been born in vain, in respect of me, and in vain have suffered so many torments, yea, and even most bitter death, of thine own accord, for my sake. *Ludovicus Vives*

TO CHRIST CRUCIFIED **406**

O Loving wisdom of the living God, O living word and power of the Father everlasting: grant what thou hast promised, and give us, unworthy though we are, what we most earnestly desire; that thy passion may be our deliverance, thy death our life, thy cross our redemption, and thy wounds our healing; and that, being crucified with thee, thy grace may lift us up on high to thy Father; with whom thou livest and reignest, one God, world without end.

THE CROSS **407**

O Lord Jesu Christ, take us to thyself, draw us with cords to the foot of thy cross; for we have not strength to come, and we know not the way. Thou art mighty to save, and none can separate us from thy love: bring us home to

thyself; for we are gone astray. We have wandered; do
thou seek us. Under the shadow of thy cross let us live all
the rest of our lives, and there we shall be safe.

Archbishop Frederick Temple

408

Lord Jesus, who on this holy day of thy passion didst
stretch out thine arms upon the hard wood of the cross, that
all men might be brought within their saving embrace;
draw us unto thyself with the bands of thy love, that we
may be found of thee and find thee; and grant that,
evermore being bound unto thee as thy faithful servants,
we may take up our cross daily and follow thee, and at last
attain to thine eternal joy; who livest and reignest with the
Father and the Holy Spirit, world without end.

Unknown

409

Grant, O Lord, that in thy wounds I may find my safety, in
thy stripes my cure, in thy pain my peace, in thy cross my
victory, in thy resurrection my triumph, and a crown of
righteousness in the glories of thy eternal kingdom.

Jeremy Taylor

410

O Christ, our God, who for us sinners didst endure the
cross, and so didst enlighten the world's darkness: visit
our hearts, we beseech thee, with thy heavenly light, and
open the eyes of our minds to know thee as thou art, thou
lover of souls; who through death didst destroy death and
ever livest to make intercession for us; and with the Father
and the Holy Spirit art one God, for ever and ever.

411

O Lord, who for our sake didst endure the bitterness of
death and despise the shame, and in thy cross and passion
dost draw all men unto thyself: kindle in our hearts the
vision of thy love, and shed abroad the light of thy victory

in the darkness of the world; who now livest and reignest with the Father and the Holy Spirit, and art loved, worshipped, and adored, world without end.

Frederick B. Macnutt

EASTER EVEN 412

O Lord Jesus Christ, Son of the living God, who at this evening hour didst rest in the sepulchre and didst thereby sanctify the grave to be a bed of hope to thy people: make us so to abound in sorrow for our sins, which were the cause of thy passion, that when our bodies lie in the dust, our souls may live with thee; who livest and reignest with the Father and the Holy Spirit, one God, world without end.

Office of Compline

413

O God, whose loving-kindness is infinite, mercifully hear our prayers: that, as in this life we are united in the mystical body of thy Church; and in death are laid in holy ground with hope of resurrection, so at the last day we may rise again with all thy blessed saints; through him who died and rose again for us, Jesus Christ our Lord.

414

My God, my lover, I thirst after thee, I hunger after thee. As I can, not as I ought, having in mind thy passion, thy buffetings, thy scourgings, thy wounds, remembering how thou wast slain for my sake, how thou wast embalmed, how and where thou wast buried, I sit with Mary at the sepulchre in my heart weeping. Where faith hath laid thee, hope seeketh to find thee, love to anoint thee. Come now, O Lord, reveal thy face to me, show thy mercy to those that implore it. We know that thy resurrection is accomplished: manifest to our eyes thy blessed incorruption. Abide with us, abide with us until the morning. Let us enjoy thy presence; let us be glad and rejoice in thy resurrection. The darkness thickens, the evening cometh fast. May our sun, the light eternal, Christ our God, show us the light of his countenance!

St. Anselm

415

Abide with us, O Lord, for it is toward evening and the day is far spent: abide with us, and with thy whole Church. Abide with us in the evening of the day, in the evening of life, in the evening of the world. Abide with us in thy grace and mercy, in holy Word and sacrament, in thy comfort and thy blessing. Abide with us in the night of distress and fear, in the night of doubt and temptation, in the night of bitter death, when these shall overtake us. Abide with us and with all thy faithful ones, O Lord, in time and in eternity. *Lutheran Manual of Prayer*

EASTER: BENEDICTUS **416**

Blessed be thou, O God and Father of our Lord Jesus Christ, who according to thine abundant mercy didst beget us again unto a living hope by the resurrection of Jesus Christ from the dead; to an inheritance incorruptible and undefiled and that fadeth not away, reserved in heaven for us who are kept by thy power through faith unto salvation ready to be revealed in the last time; through Jesus Christ our Lord, whom having not seen, we love; to whom with thee, O Father, and the Holy Spirit, be all honour and glory, praise and dominion, for ever and ever.

After St. Peter

EASTER **417**

O God of peace, who didst bring again from the dead the great Shepherd of the sheep with the blood of the eternal covenant, even our Lord Jesus: make us perfect in every good thing to do thy will, working in us that which is well-pleasing in thy sight through Jesus Christ; to whom be glory for ever and ever. *After Hebrews 13*

418

O God, who for our redemption didst give thine only-begotten Son to the death of the cross, and by his glorious resurrection hast delivered us from the power of the enemy: grant us so to die daily unto sin, that we may evermore live with him in the joy of his resurrection; through the same Jesus Christ our Lord.

1549 Prayer Book

419

Almighty God, who art worshipped by the heavenly host with hymns that are never silent and thanksgivings that never cease: fill our mouths with thy praise that we may worthily magnify thy holy Name for all the wonderful blessings of thy love, and chiefly on this day for the resurrection of thy Son. Grant us, with all those that fear thee and keep thy commandments, to be partakers of the inheritance of the saints in light; through the same Jesus Christ our Lord, to whom with thee and the Holy Ghost may praise from all the world be given, now and for evermore. *Unknown*

420

O risen Lord, who after thy passion didst show thyself alive unto thine Apostles by many infallible proofs, and didst speak unto them the things that concern the kingdom of God: speak unto us also who wait upon thee, and fill us with joy and peace in believing; that we may abound in hope, and knowing thy will may faithfully perform it, even unto the end; through thy grace, who livest and reignest, Lord of the dead and of the living. *Unknown*

421

Almighty God, who didst bring again from the dead our Lord Jesus, and hast brought life and immortality to light with him through the Gospel: grant that we, who are raised together with him and are partakers of the joy and hope of his resurrection, may daily die unto sin and walk on earth in the power of his endless life in heaven; to whom with thee and the Holy Spirit be praise and thanksgiving, dominion and power, both now and for evermore. *Frederick B. Macnutt*

422

O God, who through thine only-begotten Son Jesus Christ hast overcome death and opened unto us the gate of everlasting life: grant that, as he was raised from the dead by the glory of the Father, so we may walk in newness of life, and seek those things which are above; where with thee, O Father, and the Holy Spirit, he liveth and reigneth for ever and ever.

423

Grant to us, Lord, we beseech thee, that as we joyfully celebrate the mysteries of the resurrection of our Lord Jesus, so at his coming we may rejoice before thee with all thy saints; through the love of him who died for us and rose again.

424

We give thee thanks, almighty Father, who hast delivered us from the power of darkness, and translated us into the kingdom of thy Son: grant, we beseech thee, that as by his death he has restored to us hope and peace, he may raise us up with him to life eternal; through the same Jesus Christ our Lord.

425

O thou, who didst manifest thyself in the breaking of bread to thy disciples at Emmaus, grant us ever through the same blessed sacrament of thy presence to know thee, and to love thee more and more with all our hearts. Abide with us, abide in us, that we may ever abide in thee; dwell in us that we may ever dwell in thee, O good Jesu, thou God of our salvation. *Edward Bouverie Pusey*

426

Lord Jesus, I beseech thee by thy glorious resurrection, raise me up from the sepulchre of my sins and vices, and daily give me a part in thy resurrection by grace, that I may be made a partner also in thy resurrection of glory. *St. Augustine*

427

Pour upon us, O Lord, thy heavenly benediction, that we may be armed with the faith of the resurrection not to fear any army of men set against us. *Archbishop Parker*

428

O Lord Jesus Christ, who when thou hadst conquered death didst bless those who have not seen thee and yet have believed: forgive us who, like thy disciples, are slow of heart to believe, and pour into our hearts the joy of faith unspeakable and full of glory; that being risen with thee in heart and mind, we may seek those things which are above, where thou sittest on the right hand of God, and livest and reignest with the Father and the Holy Spirit, world without end.   *Frederick B. Macnutt*

429

O Christ, the light of men, who on the third day didst arise from the grave and shed thy bright beams upon the darkness of the world; grant, we beseech thee, that, enlightened by thy presence, we may walk as children of the day, to the glory of thy Name who livest and reignest, world without end.

430

O God, who by thine only-begotten Son hast destroyed the reign of death, and hast made us partakers of the kingdom of thy love: grant, we beseech thee, that as thou hast begotten us again unto a living hope by his resurrection, so also we may be kept by his power through faith unto salvation, ready to be revealed in him, where he reigneth with thee and the Holy Spirit, one God, world without end.   *Frederick B. Macnutt*

ASCENSION   **431**

O almighty God who by thy holy Apostle hast taught us to set our affection on things above: grant us so to labour in this life as ever to be mindful of our citizenship in those heavenly places whither our saviour Christ is gone before; to whom with thee, O Father and thee, O Holy Ghost, be all honour and glory world without end.

South African Prayer Book

432

Almighty God, whose blessed Son, our saviour Jesus Christ, ascended far above all heavens that he might fill all things: mercifully give us faith to perceive that according to his promise he abideth with his Church on earth, even unto the end of the world; through the same Jesus Christ our Lord. *Scottish Prayer Book*

433

O Lord Jesus Christ, who hast gone up on high that thou mayest fill all things, and didst fulfil thy promise to thy Church and send gifts unto men: we beseech thee to dwell continually with us by thy Spirit, that we may seek those things which are above, where thou sittest on the right hand of God, from henceforth expecting till thine enemies be made thy footstool, world without end.

434

Almighty God, who after thy Son had ascended on high didst send forth thy Spirit in the Church to draw all men unto thee: fulfil, we beseech thee, this thy gracious purpose, and in the fullness of time gather together in one all things in Christ, both which are in heaven, and which are on earth; even in him, who is the head over all things in the Church which is his body, Jesus Christ our Lord.

435

O God, who hast exalted the crucified, thy Son, by a triumphant resurrection and ascension into heaven: may his triumphs and glories so shine in the eyes of our hearts and minds, that we may more clearly comprehend his sufferings, and more courageously pass through our own; for his sake who with thee and the Holy Ghost liveth and reigneth, one God, for ever and ever. *E. Milner-White*

436

Almighty and merciful God, into whose gracious presence we ascend, not by the frailty of the flesh, but by the activite of the soul: make us ever by thine inspiration to seek thy

courts of the heavenly city, whither our saviour Christ
hath ascended, that by thy mercy we may confidently enter
them both now and hereafter; through the same Jesus
Christ our Lord.   *Leonine Sacramentary*

437

Grant us, Lord, we beseech thee, not to mind earthly
things, but to seek things heavenly; so that though we are
set among scenes that pass away, our heart and affection
may steadfastly cleave to the things that endure for ever;
through Jesus Christ our Lord.   *Leonine Sacramentary*

438

O Lord Jesus Christ, who didst gloriously ascend into
heaven after thy resurrection: grant us the help of thy
grace, that as thou hast promised to dwell with us always
on earth, so in heart and mind we may never cease to dwell
with thee in heaven; where with the Father and the Holy
Spirit thou livest and reignest, one God, world without
end.   *Frederick B. Macnutt*

439

O Christ, the King of glory, who through the eternal doors
didst ascend to the throne of thy Father, and open the
kingdom of heaven to all believers: grant that, while thou
dost reign in heaven, our hearts may not be bowed down
by the things of earth, but rather be lifted up whither thou,
our redemption, hast gone before; who with the Father and
the Holy Spirit livest and reignest, one God, world without
end.   *Mozarabic*

440

O Lord Jesus Christ, who after thy resurrection didst
manifestly appear to thine Apostles, and in their sight
didst ascend into heaven to prepare a place for us: grant
that, being risen with thee, we may lift up our hearts continually to seek thee where thou art, and never cease to
serve thee faithfully here on earth; until at last, when thou
comest again, thou shalt receive us unto thyself; who livest
and reignest with the Father and the Holy Spirit, one God,
world without end.   *Frederick B. Macnutt*

441

O King of glory, Lord of might, who in triumph didst
ascend this day above all heavens: leave us not bereaved, but
send upon us the promise of the Father, even the Spirit of
truth. *Sarum*

442

O Lord, the only joy and comfort of our souls, show us thy
loving countenance; embrace us with the arms of thy
mercy; pour thy Holy Spirit into our hearts; pluck us up
from the earth and things earthly; open our eyes and lift
them up unto thee; open thy mouth, and call us unto thee;
open our ears, that we may hear thee: so that, whatsoever
we do speak or think, it may be directed unto thee alone, our
redeemer, mediator, and advocate. *Ludovicus Vives*

WHITSUNDAY **443**

O almighty God, who on the day of Pentecost didst send
the Holy Ghost the comforter to abide in thy Church unto
the end: bestow upon us and upon all thy faithful people
his manifold gifts of grace, that with minds enlightened by
his truth, and hearts purified by his presence, we may day
by day be strengthened with power in the inward man;
through Jesus Christ our Lord, who with thee and the
same Spirit liveth and reigneth, one God, world without
end. *Bishop John Dowden*

444

O God, who in all ages hast sent forth thy power to
sanctify the faithful: let the flame of thy Spirit so kindle
and cleanse thy Church that in purity and strength we may
present unto thee the glad oblation of our lives; through
Jesus Christ our Lord. *J. W. Suter*

445

O God, who didst graciously send to thy disciples the
Holy Ghost, the comforter, in the likeness of fiery flame:
grant to thy people that they may be united in fervent faith,

and that abiding ever in thy love, they may be found stead-fast in faith and active in serving thee; through Jesus Christ our Lord. *Gelasian Sacramentary*

446

O God, who on the day of Pentecost didst fulfil thy pro-mise to pour out thy Spirit upon all flesh: we beseech thee to shed abroad upon thy Church in every race and nation the gifts of the same Spirit; that through the preaching of the Gospel thy glory may be manifested unto all mankind; through Jesus Christ our Lord.

447

O God, the Father of our Lord Jesus Christ, who after his ascension didst send upon the first disciples thy promised gift of the Holy Spirit: regard, we pray thee, the need of thy Church, and grant us by the same Spirit to be endued with power from on high, that we may bear effectual wit-ness to the truth of thy holy Gospel, and be strengthened to serve thee with fervent hearts; through Jesus Christ our Lord. *Unknown*

TRINITY SUNDAY **448**

O Lord God almighty, immortal, invisible, the mysteries of whose being are unsearchable: accept, we beseech thee, our praises for the revelation which thou hast made of thyself, Father, Son, and Holy Ghost, three persons and One God; and mercifully grant that, ever holding fast this faith, we may magnify thy glorious Name; who livest and reignest, one God, world without end. *Bishop John Dowden*

THE TRANSFIGURATION **449**

O God, who before the passion of thine only-begotten Son didst reveal his glory upon the holy mount: grant unto us thy servants, that in faith beholding the light of his countenance, we may be strengthened to bear the cross, and be changed into his likeness from glory to glory; through the same Jesus Christ our Lord.

1928 Prayer Book

I

450

O almighty and everlasting God, whose blessed Son revealed himself to his chosen Apostles when he was transfigured on the holy mount, and amidst the excellent glory spake with Moses and Elijah of his decease which he should accomplish at Jerusalem: grant to us thy servants that beholding the brightness of thy countenance we may be strengthened to bear the cross; through the same Jesus Christ our Lord. *Scottish Prayer Book*

451

O God, who on the mount didst reveal to chosen witnesses thine only-begotten Son wonderfully transfigured, in raiment white and glistering: mercifully grant that we, being delivered from the disquietude of this world, may be permitted to behold the King in his beauty; who with thee, O Father, and thee, O Holy Ghost, liveth and reigneth, one God, world without end. *American Prayer Book*

452

O God, who on the holy mount didst reveal to chosen witnesses thy well-beloved Son wonderfully transfigured: mercifully grant unto us such a vision of his divine majesty, that we, being purified and strengthened by thy grace, may be transformed into his likeness from glory to glory; through the same thy Son Jesus Christ our Lord. *Canadian Prayer Book*

453

Christ our God, who wast transfigured upon the mountain, and didst manifest thy glory to thy disciples as they were able to bear it: shed forth thine everlasting light upon us, thy servants, that we may behold thy glory and enter into thy sufferings, and proclaim thee to the world, O thou who givest light in the darkness and art thyself the light of men, Jesus Christ our Lord. *Eastern Orthodox*

ALL SAINTS   454

O God, we give thee most high praise and hearty thanks
for the wonderful grace and virtue declared in all thy saints,
who have been the choice vessels of thy grace, and lights of
the world in their several generations; most humbly
beseeching thee to give us grace so to follow the example of
their steadfastness, that we, with all those who are of the
mystical body of thy Son, may be set on his right hand,
who reigneth with thee and the Holy Spirit, one God,
world without end.   *The English Liturgy*

455

Almighty God, who dost choose thine elect out of every
nation, and dost show forth thy glory in their lives: grant,
we pray thee, that, following the example of thy saints, we
may be fruitful in good works to the praise of thy holy
Name; through Jesus Christ our Lord.
                                   Scottish Prayer Book

456

O almighty God, who willest to be glorified in thy saints
and hast raised them up to shine as lights in the world:
shine, we pray thee, in our hearts, that we also in our
generation may show forth thy praises, who hast called us
out of darkness into marvellous light; through Jesus Christ
our Lord.   *South African Prayer Book*

457

O Lord most high, who in the righteousness of thy saints
hast given us an ensample of godly living, and in their
blessedness a glorious pledge of the hope of our calling:
grant, we beseech thee, that being compassed about with so
great a cloud of witnesses, we may run with patience the
race that is set before us, and with them receive the crown
of glory that fadeth not away; through Jesus Christ our
Lord.

458

O God, who hast brought us near to an innumerable company of angels and to the spirits of just men made perfect: grant us in our pilgrimage on earth to continue in their fellowship, and in our heavenly country to become partakers of their joy; through Jesus Christ our Lord.

William Bright

459

Almighty and everlasting God, who dost kindle the flame of thy love in the hearts of thy saints: grant to our minds the same faith and power of love; that as we rejoice in their triumph, we may also follow the example of their patience; through Jesus Christ our Lord. *Gothic Missal*

460

Grant, O Lord, that the example of thy saints may incline our hearts to holiness of living; and that always having in remembrance their faith and patience, we may steadfastly dedicate ourselves to follow with them in the following of thee; through Jesus Christ our Lord.

THE SAINTS OF ENGLAND **461**

We beseech thee, O Lord, to multiply thy grace upon us who commemorate the saints of our nation; that, as we rejoice to be their fellow-citizens on earth, so we may have fellowship also with them in heaven; through Jesus Christ our Lord. *1928 Prayer Book*

462

God, whom all the saints adore, assembled in thy glorious presence from all times and places of thy dominion; who gathered us far dwellers of the islands of the sea into the kingdom of thy Son; and hast adorned our country with many splendid lamps of holiness: grant us worthily to celebrate the saints of England by following their footsteps throughout the world, whithersoever thou shalt send us, each in his office lowly serving, till all nations confess thy Name and all mankind know and fulfil its destiny in Christ; to whom with thee and the Holy Spirit be all honour and glory, world without end.   *Alexander Nairne*

A MARTYR'S WITNESS

St. Thomas of Canterbury   **463**

Almighty God, who didst suffer thy martyr Thomas to be cruelly slain by the swords of wicked men, and yet madest him in his death to become a flaming sword of witness to the might of things unseen: grant unto us that we may be ever mindful of his example, and show forth our thankfulness in loyalty to thy Church, and in strong confidence and faith in thee; through Jesus Christ our Lord.

Frederick B. Macnutt

THE MARTYRS   **464**

Almighty God, by whose grace and power thy holy martyrs triumphed over suffering and despised death: grant, we beseech thee, that, enduring hardness and waxing valiant in fight, we may receive with them the crown of everlasting life; through Jesus Christ our Lord.

Unknown

ALL SOULS   **465**

Almighty, eternal God, who wouldest have all men to be saved: be merciful, we beseech thee, to the souls of thy servants who have departed from this world in the confession of thy Name, that they may be joined to the company of thy saints; through Jesus Christ thy Son our Lord, who liveth and reigneth with thee in the unity of the Holy Ghost, ever one God, world without end.

Church Union Prayer

ROGATION: HARVEST   **466**

O gracious Father, who openest thine hands and fillest all things living with plenteousness: vouchsafe to bless the lands and multiply the harvests of the world; let thy breath go forth to renew the face of the earth; show thy loving-kindness, that our land may give her increase; and so fill us with good things that the poor and needy may give thanks unto thy Name through Jesus Christ our Lord.

Adapted from American Prayer Book

467

O almighty God, who hast created the earth for man, and man for thy glory: mercifully hear the supplications of thy people, and be mindful of thy covenant, that both the earth may yield her increase, and the good seed of thy Word may bring forth abundantly, to the glory of thy holy Name; through Jesus Christ our Lord.   *Canadian Prayer Book*

468

O almighty God, who in thine unfailing providence givest food to all flesh: vouchsafe, we beseech thee, to bless the seed sown in our fields, and to grant that, having received thy good gifts in due season, we may ever with thankful hearts offer up our praises unto thee; through Jesus Christ our Lord.

469

O Lord, who alone givest seed to the sower and bread to the eater, and hast taught us to seek from thee our daily bread: bless the sowing of the seed, and grant fertility to the soil that receives it; and accept the labours of thy servants, for thy glory and the well-being of thy people; through Jesus Christ our Lord.   *Unknown*

470

Almighty God, Lord of heaven and earth, in whom we live and move and have our being; who doest good unto all men, making thy sun to rise on the evil and on the good, and sending rain on the just and on the unjust; favourably behold us thy servants, who call upon thy Name, and send us thy blessing from heaven, in giving us fruitful seasons, and filling our hearts with food and gladness; that both our hearts and mouths may be continually filled with thy praise, giving thanks to thee in thy holy Church, through Jesus Christ our Lord.   *Bishop Cosin*

471

Almighty God, who crownest the year with thy goodness, we beseech thee to bless with thy bounty the farmers and workers on the land, that as they sow in hope so in due time they may gather in the sheaves with joy; through Jesus Christ our Lord. *Unknown*

472

Almighty Father, Lord of heaven and earth; of thy great goodness, we beseech thee to give and preserve to our use the kindly fruits of the earth, the treasures of mines, and the harvest of the sea, so as in due time we may enjoy them with thanksgiving. *Archbishop Benson*

HARVEST THANKSGIVING **473**

O almighty and everlasting God, who hast given unto us the fruits of the earth in their season, and hast crowned the year with thy goodness: give us grateful hearts, that we may unfeignedly thank thee for all thy loving-kindness, and worthily magnify thy holy Name; through Jesus Christ our Lord. *Bishop John Dowden*

474

O most merciful Father, who hast blessed the labours of the husbandman and given unto us the fruits of the earth in their season: we give thee humble and hearty thanks for this thy bounty; and we beseech thee to continue this thy loving-kindness toward us, that year by year our land may yield her increase, to thy glory and our comfort; through Jesus Christ our Lord. *American Prayer Book*

475

O almighty and everlasting God, who hast given unto us the fruits of the earth in their season: grant us grace to use the same to thy glory, the relief of those that need, and our own comfort, through Jesus Christ, who is the living bread which cometh down from heaven and giveth life unto the world; to whom, with thee and the Holy Ghost, be all honour and glory, world without end. *Anon.*

476

O most merciful Father, who of thy gracious goodness hast heard the devout prayers of thy Church, and hast granted us to gather in the kindly fruits of the earth in their season: we give thee humble thanks for this thy bounty, beseeching thee to continue thy loving-kindness towards us, that our land may yield her increase; through Jesus Christ our Lord. *Anon.*

SPIRITUAL HARVEST **477**

O God, who by the voice of holy prophets hast made manifest in the children of thy Church in every place of thy dominion that thou dost sow good seed and cultivate the branches of thy vine: grant to thy people, from whom thou wilt gather in thy harvest, that they may be freed from the evil growths of thorns and briars, and abundantly bring forth good fruit to the glory of thy Name; through Jesus Christ our Lord.

478

O Lord, we pray thee, sow the seed of thy Word in our hearts, and send down upon us thy heavenly grace; that we may bring forth the fruit of the Spirit, and at the great day may be gathered by thy holy angels into thy garner, through Jesus Christ our Lord. *Anon.*

479

Most mighty Lord and merciful Father, we yield thee hearty thanks for our bodily sustenance, requiring also most entirely thy gracious goodness, so to feed us with the food of thy heavenly grace that we may worthily glorify thy holy Name in this life, and after be partakers of the life everlasting, through our Lord Jesus Christ. *The Primer*

Section 4

THE HOLY COMMUNION

PREPARATION   480

O Lord, who in a wonderful sacrament didst leave us a
memorial of thy cross and passion: grant us so to venerate
the sacred mysteries of thy body and blood, that we may
always receive within ourselves the fruits of thy redemption; who livest and reignest with the Father and the Holy
Spirit, one God, world without end.

St. Thomas Aquinas

481

Most gracious God, incline thy merciful ears to our prayers,
and enlighten our hearts by the grace of thy Holy Spirit,
that we may worthily celebrate these holy mysteries, and
love thee with an everlasting love; through Jesus Christ our
Lord.

482

Cleanse us, O Lord, from our secret faults, and mercifully
absolve us from our presumptuous sins; that we may receive
these holy mysteries with pure minds; through Jesus
Christ our Lord.   *Leonine Sacramentary*

483

May the sacred feast of thy table, O Lord, always strengthen
and renew us, guide and protect our weakness amid the
storms of the world, and bring us into the haven of everlasting salvation.   *Leonine Sacramentary*

484

We beseech thee, O Lord, to visit and purify our souls and
bodies, that thy Son, our Lord Jesus Christ, when he
cometh may find in us a mansion prepared for himself;
through the same Jesus Christ our Lord.

Gelasian Sacramentary

485

O God, who didst wonderfully create the glory of our human nature, and hast yet more wonderfully restored it: grant that as thy Son, our Lord Jesus Christ, has deigned to take upon him our flesh, so also, through the mysteries of his body and blood, we may become partakers of his divine nature, who was made in our likeness; through the same Jesus Christ, our Lord.

486

Grant, O Lord, that we who shall receive the blessed sacrament of the body and blood of Christ, may come to that holy mystery with faith, charity, and true repentance; that being filled with thy grace and heavenly benediction, we may obtain remission of our sins and all other benefits of his passion, to our great and endless comfort; through him who died and rose again and ascended for us, that he might fill all things, Jesus Christ our Lord.

487

O God, who in our baptism hast made us partakers of thy grace: grant, we beseech thee, that as we have been made members of the body of thy Son, so by the sacrament of his cross and passion we may be strengthened to grow up in all things unto him who is the head, even Jesus Christ; to whom with thee and the Holy Spirit be honour and glory, world without end.

488

O Lord and heavenly Father, who hast given unto us thy people the true bread that cometh down from heaven, even thy Son Jesus Christ: grant that our souls may so be fed by him who giveth life unto the world, that we may abide in him and he in us, and thy Church be filled with the power of his unending life; through Jesus Christ our Lord.

489

O Lord our God, bread of heaven, life of the world, I have sinned against heaven and before thee, and I am not worthy to partake of thine immaculate mysteries. But thou art

God, full of compassion; deem me worthy, I beseech thee,
by thy grace to partake of thy holy body and thy precious
blood without condemnation, unto remission of sins and
eternal life.   *Liturgy of St. James*

490

I am not worthy, Lord and Master, that thou shouldest
come under the roof of my soul; but since thou desirest to
dwell within me, O lover of mankind, I am bold to draw
near. Thou dost bid me to open the door which thou
alone hast made, that thou mayest enter and bring light
into my darkened mind. I believe that thou wilt do this,
for thou didst not cast out the harlot when she came to
thee in tears, nor reject the publican when he repented, nor
cast out the robber when he confessed thy kingdom, nor
forsake the persecutor when he repented; but thou didst
number among thy friends all who came to thee in penitence, O thou who alone art blessed, now and world without end.   *St. Chrysostom*

491

O Lord Jesus Christ, my God, let not my partaking of thy
most pure and life-giving mysteries bring me into judgement, and let me not become weak in soul and body by
reason of unworthy partaking of them. Grant me, even
unto my last breath, to receive uncondemned my share of
thy holy things, and to receive thereby my portion in the
fellowship of the Holy Spirit, provision for the journey of
eternal life, and an account acceptable at thy dread
judgement-seat; that with all thine elect I also may be
partaker of those good things undefiled which thou hast
prepared for them that love thee, O Lord; amongst whom
thou abidest and art glorified for ever.
                                          St. Basil the Great

492

Lord, thou hast prepared a table for me against them that
trouble me: let that holy sacrament of the Eucharist be to
me a defence and shield, a nourishment and medicine, life
and health, a means of sanctification and spiritual growth;

that I, receiving the body of my dearest Lord, may be one with his mystical body, and of the same spirit, united with indissoluble bonds of a strong faith, and a holy hope, and a never-failing charity, that from this veil I may pass into the visions of eternal clarity, from eating thy body to beholding thy face in the glories of thy everlasting kingdom, O blessed and eternal Jesus. *Jeremy Taylor*

493

O Lord, into a clean, charitable, and thankful heart, give me grace to receive the blessed body and blood of thy Son, my most blessed saviour, that it may more perfectly cleanse me from all dregs of sin; that being made clean, it may nourish me in faith, hope, charity, and obedience, with all other fruits of spiritual life and growth in thee; that in all the future course of my life, I may show myself such an ingrafted member into the body of thy Son, that I may never be drawn to do anything that may dishonour his Name. Grant this, O Lord, I beseech thee, even for his merit's and mercy's sake. *Archbishop Laud*

494

Behold, O God, I am now coming to thee, O thou fountain of purgation. Thou well of living waters, wash me clean; be unto me the bread of life to strengthen me in my pilgrimage toward heaven. Thy flesh is meat indeed, and thy blood is drink indeed: O give me grace to receive both worthily. Lord Jesus Christ, I believe all that thou hast said, and all that thou hast promised; help thou mine unbelief. Thou art the author, be thou the finisher of my faith; and for thy glory's sake, for thine own Name's sake, lead me in the right way to this great mercy and mystery. *Henry Vaughan*

BEFORE RECEPTION **495**

O Lord Jesus Christ, who hast taught us that man doth not live by bread alone: feed us, we humbly beseech thee, with the true bread that cometh down from heaven, even thyself, O blessed saviour; who livest and reignest, with the father and the Holy Spirit, one God, world without end.

Bishop John Dowden

496

Come, Lord Jesus, in the fullness of thy grace, and dwell in the hearts of us thy servants; that, adoring thee by faith, we may with joy receive thee, and with love and thankfulness abide in thee, our guide, our bread of pilgrims, our comrade by the way. *E. D. Sedding, S.S.J.E.*

497

O Lord Jesus Christ, who by the sacrifice of thyself didst break the power of sin and death and open unto us the gate of life eternal: mercifully look upon us thy servants, and feed us with thyself, the living bread; that, established in thy grace and strengthened by thy Spirit, we may walk before thee in faith and holiness, and serve thee unto our lives' end. *Frederick B. Macnutt*

498

O merciful Jesus, who in this holy sacrament dost vouchsafe to us the immortal food which is thyself: grant to our weak and languishing souls new supplies of grace, new life, new love, new vigour, and new resolution; that we may nevermore fail in our duty, nor faint in our service; to the glory of thy Name.

499

Lord, I believe and confess that thou art the Christ, the Son of the living God, who didst come into the world to save sinners, of whom I am chief. I believe also that this is thine undefiled body, and that this is indeed thy precious blood. I pray thee, therefore, have mercy upon me and forgive me my offences, willing and unwilling, in word or in deed, knowing or unknowing; and account me worthy to partake uncondemned of thine undefiled mysteries, unto remission of sins and life eternal.
Liturgy of St. Chrysostom

500

Thanks be unto thee, good Jesus, eternal Shepherd, for that thou hast vouchsafed to refresh us exiles with thy precious body and blood. O Lord, I draw near, a sick man to the saviour, hungry and thirsty to the fountain of life, a poor vagabond to the King of heaven, a servant to his Lord, a creature to the creator, a desolate soul to my tender comforter. Behold, in thee is all that I can desire; thou art my salvation and my redemption, my hope and my strength, my honour and glory. Rejoice, therefore, this day the soul of thy servant, for unto thee, Lord Jesus, do I lift up my soul. Receive me for the honour and glory of thy Name: thou who hast prepared thy body and blood to be my meat and drink. Grant, O Lord God of my salvation, that with the frequenting of thy mystery the zeal of my devotion may increase. *Thomas à Kempis*

501

We pray thee, Lord, let thy Spirit purify our hearts, lest we come unworthily to this heavenly feast; that thou mayest be shed abroad in our hearts, and we may grow strong in spirit to persevere in the blessed society of thy mystical body, which thou willest to be one with thee as thou art one with the Father in the unity of the Holy Spirit; to whom be praise and thanksgiving for ever. *Erasmus*

502

Glory be to thee, O God our Father, who hast vouchsafed to make us at this time partakers of the body and blood of thy holy Son: we offer unto thee, O God, ourselves, our souls and bodies, to be a reasonable, holy, and living sacrifice unto thee: keep us under the shadow of thy wings, and defend us from all evil, and conduct us by the Holy Spirit of grace into all good: for thou who hast given thy holy Son unto us, how shalt not thou with him give us all things else? Blessed be the Name of our God for ever and ever. *Jeremy Taylor*

503

Lord, I am not worthy of the least of all the mercies, and of all the truth, which thou hast showed unto thy servant, all my life long unto this very day; much less am I worthy that thou shouldest come under my roof. But seeing it is thy free institution and free mercy that will have it so, be jealous, O God, of the place of thine honour; cause me to remember whose temple I am, and suffer not my last state to be worse than the first. Even so, Lord Jesus, come quickly. *Henry Vaughan*

504

Let the remembrance of thy death, O blessed Jesus, be ever present with me when temptations assault me. Let thy good Spirit preserve my body evermore a fit temple for the Lord God to dwell in. Give me desires as great as my necessities, that all who are partakers of this one bread may be united and of one heart and soul, at peace with God and one with another. *Bishop Thomas Wilson*

505

O blessed Jesus, saviour, who didst agonize for us: God Almighty, who didst make thyself weak for the love of us: stir us up to offer to thee our bodies, our souls, our spirits; and in all we love and all we learn, in all we plan and all we do, to offer ourselves, our labours, our pleasures, our sorrows, to thee; to work for thy kingdom, to live as those who are not their own, but bought with thy blood, fed with thy body. And enable us now, in thy most holy sacrament, to offer to thee our repentance, our prayers, our praises, living, reasonable, and spiritual sacrifices—thine from our birth-hour, thine now, and thine for ever. *Charles Kingsley*

AT THE SANCTUS 506

In world of worlds without ending thanked be thou, Jesu, my King. All my heart I give it thee, great right it is that it so be; with all my will I worship thee, Jesu, blessed might thou be. With all my heart I thanke thee the good that thou hast done to me; sweet Jesu, grant me now this, that I may come unto thy bliss, there with angels for to sing the sweet song of thy praising: Sanctus, Sanctus, Sanctus. Jesu, grant that it be thus. *Twelfth Century*

AFTER RECEPTION   **507**

O Lord, my God, Father, Son, and Holy Spirit, make me
ever to seek and love thee, and, by this holy communion
which I have received, never to depart from thee; for thou
art God, and beside thee there is none else, for ever and
ever.   *Mozarabic*

508

We thank thee, loving Master, benefactor of our souls,
because thou hast admitted us this day to thy heavenly
mysteries.   Guide our path aright, we beseech thee;
stablish us in thy fear; watch over our lives; and make safe
our goings in thy way.   *Liturgy of St. James*

509

We give thee thanks, O Lord, holy Father, almighty everlasting God, who not for any merit of ours, but of the
condescension of thy mercy only, hast vouchsafed to feed
us sinners, thy unworthy servants, with the precious body
and blood of thy Son our Lord Jesus Christ.   And we
humbly entreat thy boundless mercy, almighty and merciful Lord, that this holy communion may not bring guilt
upon us to condemnation, but may be unto us for pardon
and salvation.   Let it be to us an armour of faith and a
shield of good resolution.   Let it be to us a riddance of all
vices, an extermination of all evil desires and lusts, and an
increase of love and patience, of humility and obedience,
and of all virtues; a sure defence against the wiles of our
enemies, visible or invisible; a perfect quietening of all
sinful impulses, fleshly or spiritual; a firm adherence to
thee, the one true God, and a blessed consummation of our
end.   And we pray thee that thou wouldest vouchsafe to
bring us sinners to that ineffable feast, where thou, with
thy Son and the Holy Spirit, art to thy saints true light,
abundant fulfilment, and everlasting joy, and perfect
happiness; through the same Jesus Christ our Lord.
                                        St. Thomas Aquinas

510

Give unto me, O God, and unto all that have communicated this day in the divine mysteries a portion of all the good prayers which are made in heaven and earth; the intercession of our Lord, and the supplications of all thy servants; and unite us in the bands of the common faith and a holy charity; that no interests or partialities, no sects or opinions, may keep us any longer in darkness and division. *Jeremy Taylor*

CONCLUSION **511**

From glory to glory going onward, we hymn thee, saviour of our souls. Glory be to the Father, and to the Son, and to the Holy Ghost, now and for ever, world without end: we hymn thee, saviour of our souls. From strength to strength going onward, and having accomplished the divine celebration in thy temple, now also we pray thee, O Lord our God, mercifully to grant to us thy perfect love. Order our way aright, root us in thy fear, and account us worthy of thy heavenly kingdom, in Jesus Christ our Lord, with whom and with thine all-holy and good and life-giving Spirit thou art blessed now and for ever, world without end. *Liturgy of St. James*

512

Visit, we beseech thee, O Lord, thy family, and guard with watchful tenderness the hearts which have been hallowed by sacred mysteries; that as by thy mercy we have received the healing gifts of eternal salvation, so by thy protection we may retain them unto life eternal; through Jesus Christ our Lord. *Leonine Sacramentary*

513

Glory be to thee, O Jesus, my Lord and my God, for thus feeding my soul with thy most blessed body and blood. O let thy heavenly food transfuse new life and new vigour into my soul, and into the souls of all that communicate

K

with me, that our faith may increase: that we may all grow more humble and contrite for our sins, that we may all love thee, and serve thee, and delight in thee, and praise thee more fervently, more incessantly, than ever we have done heretofore.   *Thomas Ken*

514

Lord, I have received this sacrament of the body and blood of my dear saviour. His mercy hath given it, and my faith received it into my soul. I humbly beseech thee speak mercy and peace unto my conscience, and enrich me with all those graces which come from that precious body and blood, even till I be possessed of eternal life in Christ.
                                                     Archbishop Laud

Section 5

OTHER SACRAMENTS

THE BAPTIZED   515

O God, by whose Spirit the whole body of the Church is multiplied and governed: preserve in the new-born children of thy family the fullness of thy grace; that, being renewed in body and soul, they may be fervent in the unity of the faith, and be counted worthy, O Lord, to serve thee; through Jesus Christ our Lord.   *Gelasian Sacramentary*

516

O God, who hast united men of every nation in the confession of thy Name, and dost continually multiply thy Church with new offspring: grant that those who have been born again, of water and of the Spirit, may be one both in inward faith and in outward devotion, and with thankful hearts may show forth in their lives the grace of that sacrament which they have received; through Jesus Christ our Lord.   *Scottish Prayer Book*

THANKSGIVING FOR HOLY BAPTISM 517

Almighty God, our heavenly Father, who hast given unto us the sacrament of holy baptism that souls thereby being born again may be heirs of everlasting salvation: we yield thee hearty thanks for this thy gift, and humbly we beseech thee to grant that we who have thus been made partakers of the death of thy Son may also be partakers of his resurrection; through the same Jesus Christ, our Lord.

1928 Prayer Book

CANDIDATES FOR CONFIRMATION 518

Merciful Lord, we pray thee abundantly to strengthen these thy servants with the sevenfold gifts of thy Holy Spirit; that they who are admitted by thine ordinance to the perfection of Christian grace may grow unto the perfection of Christian life in the exercise of the power which thou hast given to us; through thy Son Jesus Christ, our mediator and redeemer. *Richard Meux Benson*

519

O God, who through the teaching of thy Son Jesus Christ didst prepare the disciples for the coming of the comforter: make ready, we beseech thee, the hearts and minds of thy servants who at this time are seeking the gift of the Holy Spirit through the laying on of hands, that, drawing near with penitent and faithful hearts, they may be filled with the power of his divine indwelling; through the same Jesus Christ our Lord. *1928 Prayer Book*

MINISTRY TO THE SICK 520

Grant, we beseech thee, O merciful God, to all who minister healing and comfort to the sick and suffering thy protection in the way of duty, strength and patience, tenderness and love for men, and that they may faithfully serve thee in their office for the love of thee; through Jesus Christ our Lord. *Anon.*

LOVE AND HEALING 521

Almighty God, who didst inspire thy servant Saint Luke the physician to set forth in the Gospel the love and healing power of thy Son: manifest in thy Church the like power and love, to the healing of our bodies and our souls; through the same Jesus Christ our Lord.

American Prayer Book

522

O Lord and Master, Jesus Christ, Word of the everlasting Father, who hast borne our griefs and carried the burdens of our infirmities: renew by thy Holy Spirit in thy Church, we beseech thee, thy gifts of healing, and send forth thy disciples again to preach the Gospel of thy kingdom, and to cure the sick and relieve thy suffering children, to the praise and glory of thy holy name. *Liturgy of St. Mark*

RECOVERY OF THE SICK 523

Almighty and immortal God, giver of life and health, we beseech thee to hear our prayers for thy servant . . . that by thy gifts of faith and healing and the use of thy provided means he (she) may be restored to health of body and mind; through Jesus Christ our Lord.

DEDICATION BEFORE ORDINATION 524

O love, I give myself to thee, thine ever, only thine to be. This day I consecrate all that I have or hope to be to thy service. All that I have been I lay at the foot of thy cross. O crucified Lord, forgive the sins of my past life: fold me in the embrace of thy all-prevailing sacrifice: purify me by thy passion: raise me by thy perfect submission. Son of man, hallow all my emotions and affections; gather them to thyself and make them strong only for thy service, enduring through thy presence. Eternal word, sanctify my thoughts; make them free with the freedom of thy Spirit. Son of God, consecrate my will to thyself: unite it with thine: and so fill me with thine own abundant life. King of glory, my Lord and Master, take my whole being:

redeem it by thy blood: engird it with thy power: use it in thy service: and draw it ever closer to thyself. From this day forth, O Master, take my life and let it be ever, only, all for thee. *Archbishop Lang*

CANDIDATES FOR ORDINATION 525

O thou true light, that lightenest every man that cometh into the world: do thou in thy mercy touch the hearts and enlighten the understandings of all who are being prepared for the ministry of thy Church; that they may readily acknowledge, and cheerfully obey, all that thou wouldest have them believe and practise, to the benefit of those to whom they shall minister; through Jesus Christ our Lord.

526

O God, who dost ever hallow and protect thy Church: raise up from among us, we beseech thee, through thy Spirit a good and faithful succession of the stewards of the mysteries of Christ; that by their ministry and example the Christian people under thy defence may be sustained and guided in the way of truth; through Jesus Christ our Lord. *Unknown*

527

O thou good shepherd, who didst lay down thy life for thy sheep, and dost ever nourish them with the spiritual food of thy most precious body and blood: we pray thee to quicken with thy divine charity the hearts of those whom thou dost choose to be pastors of thy flock, that they may resolve gladly to spend whatsoever thou hast given them, in ministering to the salvation of thine elect servants, and to thine own eternal praise and glory, who livest and reignest with the Father and the Holy Ghost, ever one God, world without end. *Anon.*

Section 6

THE WORK OF THE CHURCH

THE CHURCH OF ENGLAND 528

O merciful God, bless this particular Church in which I live; make it, and all the members of it, sound in faith, and holy in life, that they may serve thee, and thou bless them; through Jesus Christ our Lord. *Archbishop Laud*

THANKSGIVING FOR ST. AUGUSTINE
First Archbishop of Canterbury 529

Almighty God and heavenly Father, who, of thine infinite love and goodness towards us, hast given to us thine only Son, Jesus Christ, to be our redeemer and the author of everlasting life; we render unto thee most hearty thanks that thou didst send thy servant Augustine, to call us out of darkness into light, and to be the first archbishop of thy Church in this land. We humbly beseech thee to grant that we may continue to show ourselves thankful to thee for these thy so great benefits, and that with him, and with all who in every age have truly and godly served thee in this life, we may live with thee in life everlasting; through the same Jesus Christ our Lord. *The Ordinal, adapted*

THE CHURCH 530

Almighty and merciful God, who in days of old didst give to this realm and people the benediction of thy holy church: withdraw not, we pray thee, thy favour from us; and so set right what is amiss and supply what is lacking, that more and more we may bring forth fruit to thy glory and the welfare of this land; through Jesus Christ our Lord.
Unknown

531

Almighty Father, who dost from age to age revive and inspire thy Church; look now upon that branch of it which thou hast planted in this land; that being fulfilled with thy Holy Spirit, we may be worthy of the freedom which thou hast given to us, and in zeal and courage, faithfulness and love, may manifest thy glory in service of our nation and the world; through Jesus Christ our Lord. *Anon.*

532

Lord, for thy holy Catholic Church we pray: for the Churches throughout the world, for their truth, unity, and stability, that in all charity may thrive and truth live: for our own Church, that the things that are wanting therein may be supplied, and those things set in order that are not right: that all heresies, schisms, and scandals, as well public and private, may be put out of the way: for the clergy, that they may rightly divide the word of truth, that they may walk uprightly, and that while they are teaching others they may learn themselves: and for the people, that they may not think of themselves more highly than they ought, but be persuaded by reason to walk in the ways of truth and peace. *After Lancelot Andrewes*

533

We give thee thanks, almighty Father, for thy gifts to this nation in past times through thy Church. Grant that we may be worthy of our inheritance; quicken our faith and inspire us with thy Spirit that we may walk together in fellowship and peace; draw all men unto thee and one to another by the bands of thy love; and unite us in a sacred brotherhood, wherein justice, mercy, and faith, truth and freedom, may flourish, to the glory of thy Name; through Jesus Christ our Lord. *Anon.*

534

Almighty and everlasting God, who hast revealed thy glory in Christ to all the nations: protect, we beseech thee, what thy compassion has created, that thy Church which is spread abroad throughout the world may persevere with steadfast faith in the confession of thy Name; through Jesus Christ our Lord. *Gelasian Sacramentary*

535

O Lord, who blessest them that bless thee and hallowest
them that put their trust in thee, save thy people and bless
thine inheritance: guard the fullness of thy Church; hallow
them that love the beauty of thine house; lift them up in
glory and reward them by thy divine power; and forsake us
not whose hope is in thee. Give thy peace to thy world, to
thy Churches, to priests, to the forces, and to all thy
people; for every good gift and every perfect gift is from
above and cometh down from thee, the Father of lights:
and to thee do we give glory, thanksgiving, and worship,
Father, Son, and Holy Spirit, now and for ever and ever.
Liturgy of St. Chrysostom

536

We pray thee, Lord, to guide and uphold thy Church with
thine unfailing goodness; that it may walk warily in times
of quiet, and in troublous times with faith and courage;
through Jesus Christ our Lord. *After St. Francis*

537

Remember, O Lord, thy Church, to deliver it from all evil
and to perfect it in thy love. Strengthen and preserve it by
thy Word and sacraments. Enlarge its borders, that so thy
Gospel may be preached to all nations; and gather the
faithful from all the ends of the earth into the kingdom
which thou hast prepared. *Swedish Liturgy*

538

Preserve, O God, the Catholic Church in holiness and
truth, in unity and peace, free from persecution, or glorious
under it; that she may advance the honour of her Lord
Jesus, for ever represent his sacrifice, and glorify his person,
and advance his religion, and be accepted of thee in her
blessed Lord, that being filled with his spirit she may partake of his glory. *Jeremy Taylor*

539

O thou gracious Father of mercy, Father of our Lord Jesus Christ, have mercy upon thy servants, who bow our heads, and our knees, and our hearts to thee; pardon and forgive us all our sins; give us the grace of holy repentance, and a strict obedience to thy holy Word; strengthen us in the inner man with the power of the Holy Ghost for all parts and duties of our calling and holy living; preserve us for ever in the unity of the holy Catholic Church, and in the integrity of the Christian Faith, and in the love of God and of our neighbours, and in hope of life eternal.

Jeremy Taylor

540

Gracious Father, we humbly beseech thee, for thy holy Catholic Church; fill it with all truth, in all truth with all peace. Where it is corrupt, purge it; where it is in error, direct it; where it is superstitious, rectify it; where anything is amiss, reform it; where it is right, strengthen and confirm it; where it is in want, furnish it; where it is divided and rent asunder, make up the breaches of it; O thou Holy One of Israel.

Archbishop Laud

541

O God, we pray for thy Church which is set to-day amid the perplexities of a changing order, and is face to face with new tasks: fill us afresh with the Spirit of Pentecost; help us to bear witness boldly to the coming of thy kingdom; and hasten the time when the knowledge of thyself shall fill the earth as the waters cover the sea.

Unknown

542

God, our shepherd, give to the Church a new vision and a new charity, new wisdon and fresh understanding, the revival of her brightness and the renewal of her unity; that the eternal message of thy Son, undefiled by the traditions of men, may be hailed as the good news of the new age; through him who maketh all things new, Jesus Christ our Lord.

Percy Dearmer

UNITY **543**

O Lord, the God of patience and consolation, grant us to be like-minded one towards another according to Jesus Christ; that with one mind and one mouth we may glorify thee, the Father of our Lord Jesus Christ. *Romans 15. 5-6*

544

O God, the Father of our Lord Jesus Christ, our only saviour, the prince of peace: give us grace seriously to lay to heart the great dangers we are in by our unhappy divisions. Take away all hatred and prejudice, and whatsoever else may hinder us from godly union and concord: that, as there is but one body, and one Spirit, and one hope of our calling, one Lord, one faith, one baptism, one God and Father of us all, so we may henceforth be all of one heart, and of one soul, united in one holy bond of truth and peace, of faith and charity, and may with one mind and one mouth glorify thee; through Jesus Christ our Lord.
Accession Service, 1714

545

O sovereign Lord, almighty God, look upon thy Church and upon all thy people, and all thy flock, and save us all, thine unworthy servants, the sheep of thy flock. Give us thy peace, and thy love, and thy help, and send down upon us the free gift of thine all-holy Spirit; that with pure heart and good conscience we may be united blameless and spotless in one spirit in the bond of peace and of love, one body and one spirit, in one faith as we have been called in one hope of our calling; so that we all may attain to the divine and boundless love, in Christ Jesus our Lord; with whom, and with thy all-holy and good and life-giving Spirit, thou art blessed for evermore. *Liturgy of St. Mark*

546

Gracious Lord, who art the God of concord and peace; unite our hearts and affections in such sort together, that we may walk as brethren in thy house, in brotherly love and charity, and as members of the body of Christ. Let the

sanctifying oil of thy Holy Spirit inflame us, and the dew of
thy blessing continually fall upon us, that we may enter
into life eternal; through the same Jesus Christ our Lord.
After Scottish Psalter, 1595

547

Lord, we beseech thee: let the whole christian folk be made
one; bring together those whom thou hast called and
chosen; break down the walls of division; and frustrate the
enemies of peace.   Lord, we beseech thee, bring in the day
when there shall be one flock and one shepherd.
From the German

548

Vouchsafe, we beseech thee, almighty God, to grant unto
the whole Christian people unity, peace, and true concord,
both visible and invisible; through Jesus Christ our Lord.
Anon.

549

O Lord Jesu Christ, who didst pray for thy disciples that
they might be one, even as thou art one with the Father:
draw us to thyself, that in common love and obedience to
thee we may be united to one another, in the fellowship of
the one Spirit, that the world may believe that thou art
Lord, to the glory of God the Father.   *William Temple*

550

O Lord, we pray thee to set our feet in a large room, where
hearts are made pure from sin by faith in thee, and faces
are turned to the light; grant that we may be one in thee,
and that no narrow walls of division between man and man
may destroy the unity which thou hast made in the Spirit
of thy Son, Jesus Christ our Lord.

551

Grant, O Lord, that as there is one Spirit, one Lord, one faith, and one hope of our calling; so thy Church, as one body, may draw all nations into peace and unity; through him in whom all men are one, our saviour Jesus Christ.
Unknown

THE CONFESSION OF FAITH   **552**

O Lord Christ, who judgest the earth, and hast laid the sure foundation upon which thy Church has upraised its confession of faith: grant that we may not build our faith upon the sand, where storms may overthrow it; and establish us upon the rock which is steadfast in thee; to the glory of thy Name.   *Mozarabic*

THE CHURCH IN PERSECUTION   **553**

O God, our refuge and strength, who art a very present help in time of trouble: have mercy upon thy Church in its hour of persecution; deliver thy people by thy mighty protection from tyranny and oppression; save them from the dangers that beset them; and restore to them the blessings of freedom and peace; through Jesus Christ our Lord.   *Unknown*

554

Blessed Lord, who thyself didst undergo the pain and suffering of the cross: uphold, we beseech thee, with thy promised gift of strength all those of our brethren who are suffering for their faith in thee.   Grant that in the midst of their persecutions they may hold fast by this faith, and that from their steadfastness thy Church may grow in grace, and we ourselves increase in perseverance, to the honour of thy Name; who with the Father and the Holy Spirit art ever one God.   *Anon.*

555

O Lord, grant, we beseech thee, liberty to the captives, and the opening of the prison to them that are in bondage for thy truth; that thy people may rejoice in the freedom which thy mercy giveth, both in this world and that which is to come.   *Gothic Missal*

A CONFERENCE OF BISHOPS   556

Eternal Father, who wouldest make the Church of thy dear
Son a city great and fair, the joy of the whole earth; we
beseech thee, by the sending of thy Holy Spirit to direct its
counsels in all manner of wisdom, love, and might;
remove perplexity, establish concord, kindle flame; and
gather a people single and strong of faith, to the praise of
him who with thee and the same spirit liveth and reigneth,
one God, world without end.

Lambeth Conference, 1930

THE ARCHBISHOP   557

Almighty God, giver of all good things, who by thy Holy
Spirit hast appointed divers orders of ministers in thy
Church: mercifully behold thy servant *N* . . ., enthroned
into the high office and dignity of archbishop and metro-
politan of this province; and replenish him so with the
truth of thy doctrine, and adorn him with innocency of
life, that both by word and deed he may faithfully serve
thee in this office, to the glory of thy Name, and the edifying
and well governing of thy Church; through Jesus Christ
our Lord.   *Book of Common Prayer*

THE BISHOPS   558

Almighty God, who by thy Son Jesus Christ didst give to
thy holy Apostles many excellent gifts, and didst charge
them to feed thy flock: give grace, we beseech thee, to all
bishops, the pastors of thy Church, that they may diligently
preach thy Word, and duly administer the godly discipline
thereof; and grant to the people, that they may obediently
follow the same; that all may receive the crown of everlasting glory; through Jesus Christ our Lord.

Book of Common Prayer

THE BISHOP   559

O God, the pastor and ruler of thy faithful servants, look
down in thy mercy upon thy servant, our bishop, *N* . . ., to
whom thou hast given charge over this diocese; evermore

guide, defend, comfort, and save him; and grant that he, with the flock committed to his charge, may attain to everlasting life; through Jesus Christ our Lord.

Ambrosian Use

560

O God, who art the pastor and ruler of thy holy Church: look graciously upon this diocese, and especially upon thy servant *N . . .,* our bishop. Endue him plentifully with thy manifold gifts of grace; and guide him continually in thy paths, that he may lead aright the flock committed to him. Grant this for his sake, who is the chief shepherd, Jesus Christ our Lord.   *After Ambrosian Use*

561

Grant, we beseech thee, O Lord, to thy servant *N . . .,* our bishop, that by preaching and doing those things that be godly, he may set forth the example of good works, and teach and strengthen the souls of the people committed to his government; and that finally he may receive the everlasting recompense of the reward from thee, the most merciful pastor; through Jesus Christ our Lord.

As used in St. Paul's

A BISHOP'S PRAYER   **562**

O God, the pastor and governor all thy faithful people, look down in mercy upon me thy servant whom thou hast been pleased to appoint chief pastor of thy Church of Canterbury: grant, I most humbly beseech thee, that I may profit those whom I am set over, both by doctrine and example; that I, together with my flock committed to my charge, may come to eternal life.   *Archbishop Laud*

BISHOPS AND CLERGY   **563**

O almighty God, who by thy Son Jesus Christ didst give to thy Apostle Saint Peter many excellent gifts, and commandedst him earnestly to feed thy flock: make, we beseech thee, all bishops and pastors of thy Church diligently to preach thy holy Word, and the people obediently to follow the same, that when the chief shepherd shall appear, they may together receive the crown of everlasting glory; through Jesus Christ our Lord.

Canadian Prayer Book

THE DIOCESE 564

O God, who hast called us to be members together of thy Church, which is the body of thy Son, pour out, we beseech thee, thy Spirit upon this diocese. Endue with strength and love and wisdom all who bear authority and serve thee therein. Accept our gifts, our labours, and our love, and use them for the advancement of thy kingdom and the glory of thy Name. Lead us in all our work for thee, and unite us in the joyful service of thy Son, our saviour Jesus Christ.

Bishop A. A. David

565

O God, who hast graciously united us in a goodly fellow-ship, we pray for thy Church in this diocese and for thy people in our parishes, that comeliness of worship, preaching of the faith, and holiness of living may always abound and everywhere be spread abroad amongst us; through Jesus Christ our Lord.

After A. J. Mason

566

Almighty and everlasting God, we beseech thee to look down with mercy upon this diocese. Remember for good its bishop, priests, and deacons, and all thy faithful people therein; bless, we beseech thee, the ministration of thy holy Word and sacraments, and the preaching of thy Gospel to those that are without; that thy holy Name may be glorified and thy blessed kingdom enlarged; through Jesus Christ our Lord.

Oremus, adapted

567

O Lord God, our ruler and guide, who from generation to generation dost lead thy people, and givest to those who seek it the guidance of thy wise and loving Spirit: be present, we pray thee, with us to whom thou givest in trust

the welfare of this diocese. Unite us ever more closely in
the fellowship of faith and devotion; that we may perceive
and know what things we ought to do, and have grace and
power to fulfil the same. Guide us in all our works and
ways, that thy people may faithfully serve thee, to the glory
of thy Name, the extension of thy Church, and the coming
of thy kingdom. Grant this, O Lord, for the sake of thy
Son, Jesus Christ our Lord.   *A. E. Daldy*

568

O Lord God, the Father of lights, from whom cometh
every good and perfect gift: pour out, we beseech thee, thy
heavenly blessing upon thy people in this diocese; that
through their faith and fellowship thy holy Name may be
glorified and thy Church be strengthened in thy service;
through Jesus Christ our Lord.   *Frederick B. Macnutt*

569

O Lord Jesus Christ, who didst charge thine Apostles that
they should preach the Gospel to every creature: prosper,
we pray thee, the work of thy Church in this diocese; and
so guide the minds of *N* . . ., our bishop, and those who
work with him, that thy people may be moved to extend to
others the means of grace, and to share with them the
blessings of thy redeeming love; who livest and reignest
with the Father and the Holy Spirit, for ever and ever.
                                              Unknown

THE CLERGY   570

O Lord Jesus Christ, whose servants Simon Peter and
Andrew his brother did at thy word straightway leave their
nets to become fishers of men: give thy grace, we humbly
beseech thee, to those whom thou dost call to the sacred
ministry of thy Church, that they may hear thy voice, and
with glad hearts obey thy call; who livest and reignest with
the Father and the Holy Spirit, one God, world without
end.   *South African Prayer Book*

571

O Lord our God, fill, we beseech thee, all those whom thou hast set as pastors over thy flock with righteousness and true holiness; that by their faith and devotion they may overcome evil and deliver us in time of danger and adversity. *Gothic Missal*

572

O thou good shepherd, who didst lay down thy life for thy sheep, and dost ever nourish them with the spiritual food of thy most precious body and blood: we pray thee to quicken with thy divine charity the hearts of those whom thou dost choose to be pastors of thy flock, that they may resolve gladly to spend whatsoever thou hast given them in ministering to the salvation of thine elect servants, and to thine own eternal praise and glory; who with the Father, and the Holy Ghost, livest and reignest, one God, world without end. *Oremus*

573

O God, who makest thine angels spirits, and thy ministers a flame of fire: vouchsafe, we beseech thee, to stir up and confirm the sacred grace of orders in all stewards of thy mysteries; that as ministering spirits they may gather out of thy kingdom all things that offend, and may kindle in the hearts of all that fire which thou camest to send upon the earth; who livest and reignest with the Father and the Holy Ghost, ever one God, world without end.
Henry Parry Liddon

574

Remember, O gracious Lord, for good these thy ministering servants: pour out upon them evermore thy Holy Spirit, to strengthen, deepen, chasten, and purify them; that, giving themselves up to thy service, they may do and suffer all that thou willest, and finally may reign with thee in life everlasting; through Jesus Christ our Lord.
J. Armitage Robinson

L

575

O Lord, who delightest to effect by grace what the weakness of our nature cannot attain: illuminate the stewards of thy mysteries with thy indwelling purity, that in the work of the ministry their word may go forth as fire to purify the unclean, to enlighten the ignorant, and to quicken the dead. *Richard Meux Benson*

576

Almighty God, grant, we beseech thee, to all whom thou hast called to the sacred ministry of thy Church, such a sense of their high calling that they may count no sacrifice too great to make in thy service; and that, so bringing a blessing to their people, they may themselves be blessed of thee; for the sake of Jesus Christ our Lord. *Peter Green*

577

O Lord, we beseech thee to support, guide, and bless the clergy who are called to labour in this diocese: give them grace to witness to the faith, endue them with burning zeal and love, make them patient under disappointments and meekly submissive under provocations; that they may turn many to righteousness, and themselves obtain a crown of everlasting joy; through Jesus Christ our Lord.
Wells Office Book

INCREASE OF THE MINISTRY   **578**

O Lord, we beseech thee to raise up for the work of the ministry faithful and able men, counting it all joy to spend and be spent for the sake of thy dear Son, and for the souls for which he shed his most precious blood upon the cross; and we pray thee to fit them for their holy function by thy bountiful grace and heavenly benediction.
Archbishop Benson

DURING A VACANCY IN A PARISH 579

O merciful God, who knowest the needs of thy Church and
people in this place: look favourably upon us at this time,
and of thy great goodness grant unto us a parish priest
according to thy heart, who shall perform all thy will;
through our Lord Jesus Christ, the shepherd and bishop
of our souls.

A RETREAT 580

O Lord Jesus Christ, who didst say to thy disciples, come
ye apart into a desert place and rest awhile: grant, we
beseech thee, to thy servants now gathered together, so to
seek thee whom our souls desire to love, that we may both
find thee and be found of thee; and grant such love and
such wisdom to accompany the words which shall be spoken
in thy Name, that they may not fall to the ground, but may
be helpful in leading us onward through the toils of our
pilgrimage to that rest which remaineth; where, nevertheless, they rest not day nor night from thy perfect service; who livest and reignest God for ever and ever.

Richard Meux Benson

BEFORE A RETREAT 581

O Lord Jesu Christ, who didst say to thine apostles,
'Come ye apart into a desert place and rest awhile,' for
there were many coming and going: grant, we beseech
thee, to thy servants, here gathered together, that they may
rest awhile at this present time with thee. May they so
seek thee, whom their souls desire to love, that they may
both find thee and be found of thee. And grant such love,
and such wisdom to accompany the words which shall be
spoken in thy Name, that they may not fall to the ground,
but may be helpful in leading us onward through the toils
of our pilgrimage to that rest, which remaineth to the
people of God; where, nevertheless, they rest not day and
night from thy perfect service; who with the Father and
the Holy Ghost livest and reignest ever one God, world
without end. *Richard Meux Benson*

READERS 582

Look, we beseech thee, merciful Father, upon those whom thou hast called to be readers in thy Church; and grant that they may be so filled with thy Holy Spirit that, seeking only thy glory and the salvation of souls, they may preach thy Word with steadfast devotion, and by the constancy of their faith and the innocency of their lives may adorn the doctrine of Christ our saviour in all things; through the same Jesus Christ our Lord. *Frederick B. Macnutt*

DEACONESSES 583

Almighty God, who hast committed to men and women the ministry of the Gospel: pour thy grace upon thy servants called to the order of deaconesses; that in all they do and teach they may love and serve thee, to the glory of thy Name and the benefit of thy Church; through thy Son our saviour Jesus Christ. *Prayer of the Order*

A DEACONESS 584

Almighty God, who hast called this thy servant to the office and ministry of a deaconess in thy Church: mercifully grant unto her grace and power to perform the work which thou givest her to do; that through her service thou mayest forward thy purposes of love; through Jesus Christ our Lord. *Convocation*

CHURCH EXTENSION 585

O Lord Jesus Christ, who hast taught us that it is more blessed to give than to receive, and that to whom much is given, of them shall much be required: pour out upon us the spirit of thine own abundant giving; that as we have received the Churches in which we worship, we also may freely give, that others may enjoy a like inheritance, and become partakers with us in the fellowship of thy Church; who livest and reignest with the Father and the Holy Spirit, ever one God, world without end. *Frederick B. Macnutt*

BUILDING A NEW CHURCH   **586**

Almighty Father, who dwellest not in temples made with
hands, and yet willest that thy children shall worship thee
in houses set apart to thine honour: look graciously, we
beseech thee, upon us whom thou hast called to build a
Church for this parish, that thou mayest put thy Name there
and hallow it as a witness to generations that are yet to
come.   Inspire us by thy Spirit, that we may lay its foundations in love and set up its pillars with sacrifice.   Move
the hearts of thy people to give willingly and to work
patiently that this thy house may be brought to fulfilment
in beauty, and that we ourselves may be built up a spiritual
temple acceptable unto thee; through Jesus Christ our
Lord.   *Frederick B. Macnutt*

A PARISH CHURCH AND CONGREGATION   **587**

O everlasting God, who art ever adored by the holy angels,
and yet dost choose us to be stewards of thy mysteries:
bless, we beseech thee, the work of this Church and
congregation, that we may serve before thee in purity and
love; through Jesus Christ our Lord.
                              Office of Compline, adapted

BEAUTY IN WORSHIP   **588**

O God, who hast chosen material things to be the instruments of divine grace: grant us so to realize the glory of
that heavenly fellowship wherein thou callest us to worship
thee, that we may the better show our reverence for thy
majesty by our care for thy holy house; and, rejoicing in
the outward beauty of thy sacred functions, may gain fuller
experience of their inward power; to the glory of thy great
name through Christ our Lord.   *Richard Meux Benson*

CHURCH INSTITUTIONS   **589**

Vouchsafe, we beseech thee, merciful Lord, to prosper
with thy blessing all institutions designed for the promotion of thy glory and the good of souls.   Grant that those
who serve thee in religious houses, hospitals, and schools,
may set thy holy will ever before them, and do that which
is well-pleasing in thy sight, and persevere in thy service
unto the end.   *Richard Meux Benson*

CHURCH CHOIRS   **590**

O Lord Jesus Christ, who before thy passion didst join
with thy disciples in a hymn of praise: grant, we beseech
thee, to those who offer the sacrifice of song in thy Church
that they may be admitted hereafter to have their part in
the music of thy Church in heaven, and adore thee for
ever; to whom with the Father and the Holy Spirit be all
honour and glory, world without end.

As used at Salisbury

591

Almighty God, who hast given unto men power to invent
for themselves instruments of music, and skill to use them
in sounding forth thy praise: grant that the music heard in
this thy holy and beautiful house may kindle a spirit of
devotion in us thy servants; and that we, taking our part in
prayer and praise to thee here on earth, may hereafter be
admitted into thy heavenly temple, and join in the everlasting song of the redeemed around thy throne; through
Jesus Christ our Lord.   *As used at Salisbury*

592

O Lord God almighty, behold and hallow thy servants
who bear office in the choirs of thy Church; and grant that
in purity of heart and mind they may sing thy praises and
offer unto thee true and acceptable worship. Keep them
we beseech thee, in the fellowship of thy saints; through
the grace of thine only-begotten Son, who liveth and
reigneth with thee in the unity of the Holy Spirit, Jesus
Christ our Lord.   *Unknown*

593

O Lord our God, before whom the heavens do bow and
adore, who dost give ear to the praises of thy Church on
earth: look, we beseech thee, upon those who sing in this
choir; give them reverence in worship, sincerity of purpose, and purity of life; that what they sing with their lips
may be the sacrifice of their hearts; to the honour and
glory of thy holy Name.

CHOIRS AND CHORAL FESTIVALS 594

Almighty God, who hast ordained that the hearts of men are moved by sacred harmonies, and their minds attuned thereby to the understanding of thy divine mysteries: grant, we pray thee, that all who in this holy house unite in making unto thee an offering of music may know themselves to be thy ministers, and that the hearts of those who hear may be uplifted and strengthened in their faith and hope in thee; through Jesus Christ our Lord.   *Anon.*

MUSIC 595

O God, who in the gift of music hast given unto us a revelation of thy divine beauty: teach us to love thee in all thy gifts, and so to devote ourselves in all our work to thy glory, that through music we may raise men from the sorrows of this world to the enjoyment of thy divine loveliness.   *Harold Anson*

THE PARISH 596

Almighty and everlasting God, who dost govern all things in heaven and earth, mercifully hear the supplications of us thy servants, and grant unto this parish all things that are needful for its spiritual welfare: schools wherein to bring up the young in thy faith and fear, ministers to labour in this portion of thy vineyard, a church restored to the beauty of holiness. Strengthen and increase the faithful: visit and relieve the sick: turn and soften the wicked: rouse the careless: recover the fallen: restore the penitent: remove all hindrances to the advancement of thy truth: bring us all to be of one heart and mind within the fold of thy holy Church, to the honour and glory of thy Name.

W. J. Butler

A PAROCHIAL CHURCH COUNCIL 597

Almighty God, who hast united us in thy service as members of one body: grant that we may walk worthy of the vocation wherewith thou hast called us; may brotherly kindness abound amongst us, thy blessing rest upon our work, thy Name be hallowed in our midst, and thy peace guard our hearts; through Jesus Christ our Lord.

Unknown

598

O Lord and heavenly Father, strengthen us, we beseech thee, in love one to another, and increase in us the love of thyself. Deliver us from self-seeking in the work that we undertake for thee; and grant us grace so faithfully to serve thee with one heart and soul in the fellowship of thy Church on earth, that hereafter we may be united in the communion of thy saints in heaven; through Jesus Christ our Lord.

CHURCHWORKERS   **599**

Almighty Father, from whom every family in heaven and earth is named, who hast called us into the fellowship of thy Church: grant, we beseech thee, that in all our parishes we may fulfil the duties and enjoy the privileges of our spiritual home. And upon those who offer themselves for thy service bestow the fullness of thy grace; that, united in love to thee and to one another, we may show forth thy glory and hasten the coming of thy kingdom.   *Unknown*

600

O thou true light that lightest every man, coming into the world: we pray thee in thy mercy to inflame the heart and enlighten the understanding of all whom thou dost call to the service of thy Church; that they may cheerfully acknowledge and readily obey thy call, to the benefit of thy people and the glory of thy holy Name; who with the Father and the Holy Spirit livest and reignest, world without end.   *Henry Parry Liddon*

601

Grant, O Lord, that those whom thou dost choose to work for thee may labour in union with thy holy purposes, and in living unity with thy dear Son Jesus Christ; that by the power of thy Holy Spirit we may accomplish far more than we ever know, and work not for results but for the single love of thee; through Jesus Christ our Lord.
                              Bishop G. H. Wilkinson

602

O Lord, without whom our labour is but lost, and with whom thy little ones go forth as the mighty: be present to all works in thy Church which are undertaken according to thy will; and grant to thy labourers a pure intention, patient faith, sufficient success upon earth, and the bliss of serving thee in heaven; through Jesus Christ our Lord.
William Bright

603

O God, who hast delivered us from the power of darkness and admitted us into the fellowship of thy saints; grant we beseech thee, that as by baptism we are made members of the body of Christ, so by thy grace we may grow up in all things into him who is the head, even Jesus Christ our Lord.

604

O Almighty God, who makest us to will and to do of thy good pleasure: give thy servants grace that they may be faithful to the charge committed to them, and that they may be a godly example to the people among whom they are called to work; so that, this life ended, they may come to thy heavenly kingdom; through Christ our Lord.
As used in Southwark Diocese

INCREASE OF LAY WORKERS **605**

Blessed Jesus, Lord of the harvest, send forth, we pray thee, labourers into thy harvest, and by thy Holy Spirit stir the hearts of many, that they may be ready to spend and be spent in thy service; and, if it please thee, so to lose their life in this world that they may gather fruit unto life eternal, O Lord, thou lover of souls. *Bishop Milman*

BELL-RINGERS **606**

Grant, O Lord, that those who are appointed to ring the bells of thy church may serve thee faithfully in this their calling; and being ever mindful that thy house is holy, may put away from them light behaviour and evil thoughts, and so continue in purity of life that they may be accounted worthy at last to praise thee in thy heavenly temple; through Jesus Christ our Lord. *Unknown*

CHURCH BELLS 607

Incline thine ear, O Lord, to our prayers, and grant that whensoever the bells of thy Church shall sound in this parish, they may awaken in the hearts of those who hear them the desire to worship thee with thy Church, that faith and devotion may be increased in all Christian people among us; through Jesus Christ our Lord. *Unknown*

GUIDANCE IN FINANCE 608

O Lord our God, who art the supreme owner of all that we possess: grant us grace to use our stewardship of money in accordance with thy will, and wisdom that we may prudently administer that which has been committed to our trust, to the glory of thy name; through Jesus Christ our Lord.

LIBERAL GIVING 609

Stir up, we beseech thee, O Lord, the wills of thy faithful people: that they who have freely received of thy bounty, may of thy bounty freely give; through Jesus Christ our Lord. *Bishop John Dowden*

Section 7

EVANGELISM

CHRIST THE KING 610

Almighty and everlasting God, who hast willed to restore all things in thy well-beloved Son, the King and Lord of all: mercifully grant that all peoples and nations, divided and wounded by sin, may be brought under the gentle yoke of his most loving rule; who with thee and the Holy Spirit liveth and reigneth, ever one God, world without end. *Sarum*

THE KINGDOM OF GOD   **611**

O Lord, who hast set before us the great hope that thy
kingdom shall come, and hast taught us to pray for its
coming: give us grace to discern the signs of its dawning,
and to work for the perfect day when thy will shall be done
on earth as it is in heaven; through Jesus Christ our Lord.
Percy Dearmer

612

O God and Father of all, whom the whole heavens adore:
let the whole earth also worship thee, all kingdoms obey
thee, all tongues confess and bless thee, and the sons of
men love thee and serve thee in peace; through Jesus
Christ our Lord.   *E. Milner-White*

613

Enlarge thy kingdom, O God, and deliver the world from
the tyranny of Satan.   Hasten the time, which thy Spirit
hath foretold, when all nations whom thou hast made shall
worship thee and glorify thy Name.   Bless the good
endeavours of those who strive to propagate the truth, and
prepare the hearts of all men to receive it; to the honour of
thy Name.   *Bishop Thomas Wilson*

THE ETERNAL GOAL   **614**

O God, the Father of our Lord Jesus Christ, from whom
every family in heaven and on earth is named: grant, we
beseech thee, that the earth may be filled with the knowledge of thy Son, and that we may behold him coming into
his kingdom.   Grant that thy Church may carry his light to
those who wait in the darkness for its shining, and that
with one heart and mind we may labour to build up the
fellowship of men in the family of Christ through the one
Spirit; so that thou, O Father, mayest gather together into
one all things in Christ; to whom with thee and the Holy
Spirit be all honour and glory, dominion, and power,
world without end.

EVANGELISM   **615**

O Lord Jesus Christ, thou good shepherd of the sheep,
who didst come to seek and to save that which was lost:
we beseech thee to be present in thy power with the
missions of thy Church in this our land. Show forth thy
compassion to the helpless, enlighten the ignorant, succour
those in peril, and bring home the wanderers in safety to
thy fold; who livest and reignest with the Father and the
Holy Spirit, one God, world without end.

Irish Prayer Book

616

Almighty God, whose Son Jesus Christ came to cast fire
upon the earth: grant that by the prayers of thy faithful
people a fire of burning zeal may be kindled and pass from
heart to heart, that the light of thy Church may shine forth
bright and clear to all mankind; through the same thy Son
Jesus Christ our Lord.

617

Almighty God, our heavenly Father, to forget whom is to
stumble and fall, to remember whom is to rise again: we
pray thee to draw the people of this country to thyself;
prosper all efforts to make known to them thy truth; and
grant that many may learn their need of thee and thy love
for them; that thy Church and kingdom may be established
among us to the glory of thy Name; through Jesus Christ
our Lord.   *Unknown*

618

O God, who by the coming of thy Spirit didst hallow the
universal Church for the fulfilment of its mission to
mankind: grant, we beseech thee, his manifold gifts to thy
faithful people in our land and nation; that those who by
the blindness of ignorance and sin are at variance with one
another may be united at last in the one confession of thy
Name; through Jesus Christ our Lord.

619

O Lord Jesus Christ, great shepherd of the sheep, who seekest those that are gone astray, bindest up those that are broken, and healest those that are sick: bless, we beseech thee, all efforts that are made to convert souls unto thee. Open the deaf ears of the wandering, that they may hear the words which belong unto their peace; and grant that those whom thou dost raise to newness of life may through thy grace persevere unto the end, of thy mercy, who art blessed, and livest and reignest with the Father and the Holy Spirit, one God, world without end.

After Richard Meux Benson

620

O Lord our God, who through the preaching of the Gospel didst call our fathers into the fellowship of thy true religion, and dost summon us their children to return to thee: give us grace to hear and to obey thy call; release us from the bondage of ignorance and fear; restore unto us the joy of thy salvation; and so inspire and strengthen us by thy Holy Spirit that by word and good example we may devote ourselves wholly to thy service, for the glory of thy Name; through Jesus Christ our Lord. *Frederick B. Macnutt*

621

O Lord Jesus Christ, who hast called those who believe on thee to be evangelists of thy kingdom and to carry thy Gospel to the souls of men: renew in us the spirit of faith and service; enlighten our minds to understand thy message; and inflame our hearts with such love toward thee that thy word upon our lips may be mighty to overthrow the powers of darkness, and to turn the feet of many into thy way of light and peace, to the glory of thy name.

Frederick B. Macnutt

OBEDIENCE AND CONFESSION **622**

O God, who hast deigned to reveal thyself to us by thy Son, and hast committed to us the previous treasure of thy Gospel: grant that we may humbly obey thy Word, faithfully confess thy Name, and live and die in thy faith; through Jesus Christ our Lord. *Eugène Bersier*

PERSONAL WITNESS   **623**

O God, who hast made known to us in Jesus Christ the love with which thou lovest us and all mankind: help us to be faithful witnesses for thee, and to spread the knowledge of thy kingdom in all the world; through Jesus Christ our Lord.   *S.P.G.*

624

O Lord, who hast called us to be thy witnesses to all the nations: have mercy upon us, who have known thy will but have failed to do it. Cleanse us from unbelief and sloth, and fill us with hope and zeal, that we may do thy work, and bear thy cross, and bide thy time, and see thy glory; who with the Father and the Holy Spirit art one God, world without end.   *Unknown*

625

I pray thee, Lord Jesus Christ, make those whom thou lovest, and who return thy love, mirrors of thee unto their unloving brethren; that these too becoming enamoured of thine image may reproduce it, light reflecting light, and ardour kindling ardour, until God be all and in all.
       Christina Rossetti

MISSIONS   **626**

O God, who hast made of one blood all nations of men for to dwell on the face of the earth, and didst send thy blessed Son, Jesus Christ, to preach peace to them that are afar off, and to them that are nigh: grant that all the peoples of the world may feel after thee and find thee; and hasten, O heavenly Father, the fulfilment of thy promise to pour out thy Spirit upon all flesh; through Jesus Christ our Saviour.   *Bishop Cotton*

627

Almighty God, who hast given unto thy Son Jesus Christ the Name which is above every name, and hast taught us that there is salvation in none other: mercifully grant that as thy faithful people have comfort and peace in his Name, they may ever labour to publish it unto all nations; through the same Jesus Christ our Lord.   *Unknown*

628

O thou, who art the light of the world, the desire of all nations, and the shepherd of our souls: let thy light shine in the darkness, that all the ends of the earth may see the salvation of our God.   By the lifting up of thy cross gather the peoples to thine obedience; let thy sheep hear thy voice, and be brought home to thy fold; so that there may be one flock, one shepherd, one holy kingdom of righteousness and peace, one God and Father of all, above all, and in all, and through all.   *W. E. Orchard*

629

Almighty and everlasting God, who in days of old didst cause thy word to grow mightily and to prevail: we praise and magnify thy holy name for the manifestation of thy presence in this our day; and we pray thee to pour out thy Spirit upon thy Church, that thy way may be known upon earth and thy saving health among all nations; through Jesus Christ our Lord.   *Anon.*

630

Almighty and everlasting God, who hast revealed thy glory in Christ to all nations: grant, we beseech thee, to those whom thou hast called into thy Church, that they may continue faithful in the confession of thy Name; through Jesus Christ our Lord.

631

O Almighty and everlasting God, who didst give to thine Apostles grace truly to believe and to preach thy Word: grant, we beseech thee, unto thy Church to love the Word which they believed, and both to preach and receive the same: through Jesus Christ thy Son our Lord, who liveth and reigneth with thee in the unity of the Holy Ghost, ever one God, world without end.   *Church Union Prayer*

632

O Lord, who hast charged thy Church to preach the Gospel to the whole creation, and to make disciples of all nations: inspire us with thy Spirit and empower us by thy presence, that we may not fail thee in the fulfilment of thy purpose.   *Frederick B. Macnutt*

633

O God, who in the exaltation of thy Son Jesus Christ dost sanctify thy universal Church: we beseech thee to shed abroad in every race and nation the gift of thy Spirit; that his work begun at the first preaching of the Gospel may be extended by thy power throughout the whole world; through him who liveth and reigneth with thee in the unity of the same Spirit, now and ever.   *Anon.*

634

Almighty God, who by the power of thy Holy Spirit didst send forth thine Apostles to make disciples of all nations, and to baptize them into thy Church: quicken, we beseech thee, by the same Spirit the Church of these latter days, that with wisdom and fervent zeal we may preach thy Gospel to those who dwell in darkness, till all men everywhere are brought into the clear light and true knowledge of thee and of thy Son, Jesus Christ our Lord.

635

O Lord, make bare thy holy arm in the eyes of all men that the uttermost ends of the world may see thy salvation. Show forth thy righteousness openly in the sight of the nations, that the kingdom of thy Christ may be established over all mankind; hasten the coming of the end when he shall deliver up the kingdom unto thee; and having put down all rule and authority and power, and put all things under his feet, he himself shall be subject unto thee, and with thee in the unity of the Holy Ghost, three Persons in one God, shall be our all in all.

636

O Lord, who hast warned us that thou wilt require much of those to whom much is given: grant that we, whose lot thou hast cast in so goodly a heritage, may strive the more earnestly to extend the blessings of thy kingdom; and as we have entered into the labours of others, so to labour that in their turn other men may enter into ours; to thy glory and the fulfilling of thy holy will; who with the Father and the Holy Spirit livest and reignest, ever one God, world without end. *Anon.*

637

Remember for good, we beseech thee, O Lord, the missionary work of thy Church in every land: protect and provide for thy servants in the mission fields, and preserve them in danger and in all their need. Give to the Churches abroad and to us at home such an increased spirit of faith, sacrifice, and service that thy work may not be hindered but rather advanced, so that thy kingdom may come and the powers of evil be driven back and overthrown; through Jesus Christ our Lord.
Bishop C. C. B. Bardsley

638

O blessed Jesus, Lord of the harvest, we pray thee to send forth labourers into thy harvest: stir by thy Holy Spirit the hearts of many that they may be ready to spend and be spent in thy service, and if it please thee, so to lose their life in this world, that they may gather fruit unto life eternal, O Lord, thou lover of souls. *Bishop Milman*

639

O thou who didst command thy Apostles to go into all the world and to preach the Gospel to every creature: let thy Name be great among the nations, from the rising up of the sun unto the going down of the same, O Lord our light and our salvation. *Unknown*

M

THE MINISTRY OF WOMEN   640

Gracious Lord, who wast born of a woman, and didst
accept the ministry of women, and take into thine arms
little children to bless them: be present, we pray thee, with
the women of thy Church who have gone forth as thy
messengers to people overseas. Grant that they may teach
the mothers of all the lands to bring up their children in
thy faith and love; and so bless their ministry that many
who have not known thee may receive the blessing and
honour which thou hast purposed for women.

Church Missionary Society

THE HARVEST OF MISSIONS   641

O almighty God, whose dearly beloved Son, after his
resurrection from the dead, did send his Apostles into all
the world to preach the Gospel to every creature: hear us,
we beseech thee, O Lord, and look upon the fields now
white unto harvest; bless those who are labouring for thee
in distant lands, and prosper thou their handiwork; send
forth more labourers into thy harvest to gather fruit unto
life eternal; and grant us grace to labour with them in
prayers and offerings, that we, together with them, may
rejoice before thee; through Jesus Christ our Lord.

Convocation, 1862

ALL MANKIND   642

O Son of God, our redeemer, we beseech thee by the
mystery of thy holy Incarnation, by thy precious sacrifice,
oblation, and satisfaction for the sins of all mankind, by the
kindness and love of thy blessed appearing, by thy prayers
and supplications, by thy strong crying and tears, by thy
lifting up upon the cross for us lost and helpless sinners:
draw all men unto thee, O thou healer of souls.

Oxford Mission to Calcutta

NON-CHRISTIANS   643

Merciful God, who hast made all men for love, and willest
that all should be saved and come to the knowledge of thy
truth; have mercy upon those who know thee not; and so
fetch them home, blessed Lord, to thy Son who was lifted

up to draw all men unto him, that they may be numbered among thy faithful servants, and be made one flock under one Shepherd, our Lord and Saviour Jesus Christ.

A MISSIONARY CONFERENCE 644

O almighty God, pour forth, we beseech thee, thy Holy Spirit upon thy servants who shall come together from many lands for counsel and mutual help in the work of thy holy Church. Grant unto them and unto us both wisdom and zeal, that we may know thy will and fulfil it with all our powers to thy honour and glory, through our Lord and Saviour Jesus Christ. *J. Armitage Robinson*

MEDICAL MISSIONS 645

Almighty God, who in thy great love towards mankind didst send thy Son to be the physician both of the body and of the soul: bless, we pray thee, the ministry of thy missionary servants now working in the hospitals and dispensaries of countries overseas; and so prosper them that thy way may be known upon earth, thy saving health among all nations; through Jesus Christ our Lord.
Unknown

MISSIONS TO THE JEWS 646

O Lord Jesus Christ, Son of David, King of Israel; who hast in all ages an elect remnant among thine ancient people, and art ever hastening the time when all Israel shall be saved: grant, we beseech thee, that we may share thy compassion for them; show us what thou wouldest have us attempt for their ingathering into thy Catholic Church, and help us to bring them to thee, their true Messiah; who livest and reignest with the Father and the Holy Spirit, one God, for ever and ever. *Anon.*

647

O God, the God of Abraham: look upon thine everlasting covenant, and cause the captivity of Judah and Israel to return. They are thy people, O be thou their Saviour; that all who love Jerusalem and mourn for her may rejoice with her; for Jesus Christ's sake, their Saviour and ours.
Bishop Thomas Wilson

THE MINISTRY 648

We pray thee, Lord, for all who minister in thy Name in thy Church throughout all the world. In time of weakness strengthen them, in trial uphold them, and in perplexity direct them. Increase in them the spirit of power and love, and of a sound mind, that they may diligently preach thy Word, and set forth thy glory, to the building up of thy Church and the salvation of souls; that so the nations may become thine inheritance, and the uttermost parts of the earth thy possession; through Jesus Christ our Lord.

S.P.G.

MISSIONARIES 649

O God our Saviour, who willest that all men should be saved and come to the knowledge of the truth: prosper, we pray thee, our brethren who labour in distant lands (especially *those* for whom our prayers are desired). Protect them in all perils; support them in loneliness and in the hour of trial; give them grace to bear faithful witness unto thee; and endue them with burning zeal and love, that they may turn many to righteousness, and finally obtain a crown of glory; through Jesus Christ our Lord.

Scottish Prayer Book

650

O Lord Jesus Christ, who callest to thee whom thou willest, and sendest them whither thou dost choose: we give thee thanks for thy servants whom thou hast called to serve thee in other lands, and especially for those who have laid down their lives for thy sake; and we beseech thee to raise up in thy Church men and women from among us who shall go forth to publish thy Gospel and to build up thy Church among the peoples beyond the seas; who livest and reignest with the Father and the Holy Spirit, one God, world without end.

Section 8

WISE GOVERNMENT AND PEACE

THE QUEEN   651

O God, who providest for thy people by thy power and
rulest over them in love: grant unto thy servant Elizabeth,
our Queen, the spirit of wisdom and government, that
being devoted unto thee with all her heart, she may so
wisely govern, that in her time thy Church and people may
continue in safety and prosperity; and that, persevering in
good works unto the end, she may through thy mercy come
to thine everlasting kingdom; through Jesus Christ our
Lord, who liveth and reigneth with thee and the Holy
Ghost, ever one God, world without end.

Coronation Service

652

O God, the King of glory, who hast set thy servant
Elizabeth, our Queen. upon the throne of her fathers:
establish her, we beseech thee, in thy grace, endue her with
the manifold gifts of thy Spirit, and grant that we her
people may dedicate ourselves with her to thy service;
through Jesus Christ our Lord.   *Frederick B. Macnutt*

653

Almighty God, the fountain of all goodness: give ear, we
beseech thee, to our prayers, and multiply thy blessings
upon thy servant Elizabeth, our Queen; defend her evermore from all dangers, ghostly and bodily; make her a
great example of virtue and piety, and a blessing to this
kingdom; through Jesus Christ our Lord, who liveth and
reigneth with thee, O Father, in the unity of the Holy
Spirit, world without end.   *Coronation Service*

THE ROYAL FAMILY   654

Grant, O Lord, we beseech thee, to our Sovereign Lady
Elizabeth, and Philip, Duke of Edinburgh, that they may
ever know thee to be their shield and deliverer; and that

casting all their care upon thee, they may be supported in all trials and succoured in time of danger and temptation; through Jesus Christ our Lord. *Frederick B. Macnutt*

655

O Lord our God, who upholdest and governest all things by the word of thy power: receive our humble prayers for our Sovereign Lady Elizabeth, set over us by thy grace and providence to be our Queen; and together with her, bless, we beseech thee, our gracious Elizabeth, the Queen Mother, Philip, Duke of Edinburgh, Charles, Prince of Wales, and all the Royal Family; that they, ever trusting in thy goodness, protected by thy power, and crowned with thy gracious and endless favour, may long continue before thee in peace and safety, joy and honour, and after death may obtain everlasting life and glory; by the merits and mediation of Christ Jesus our Saviour, who with thee and the Holy Ghost liveth and reigneth, ever one God, world without end. *Accession Service*

THE BRITISH COMMONWEALTH **656**

Almighty God, Father of all men, who hast given to our nation a great dominion in all parts of the earth: help us ever to remember that we are stewards of thy gifts. Bless our countrymen who are scattered afar in many lands; give to us the spirit of wisdom and understanding, and of the fear of the Lord; make us just and fair in our dealings with other peoples; and keep the nations of our Commonwealth united in one bond of faith and fellowship; to the glory of thy Name. *Unknown*

657

O Lord God of our fathers, who in thy goodness hast led this people hitherto by wondrous ways; who makest the nations to praise thee, and knittest them together in the unity of peace; we beseech thee to pour thine abundant blessing upon the dominions over which thou hast called thy servant Elizabeth to be Queen. Grant that all, of whatever race or tongue, may be united in the bond of brotherhood, and in the one fellowship of the faith; so that we may be found a people acceptable unto thee; through Jesus Christ our Lord.

658

Look down, O Lord, upon our own countrymen who are scattered abroad, and quicken in them the fire of thy love; that realizing the blessedness of the true faith, they may be living witnesses for thee, in word and deed, unto the heathen amongst whom they dwell; who livest and reignest with the Father and the Holy Spirit, one God for ever and ever.

659

Almighty God, Father of all men, under whose providence we are become members of a great Commonwealth of Nations, and have in our keeping the government and protection of many peoples: give us such a spirit of wisdom and understanding, of justice and truth, of knowledge and of the fear of the Lord, that all the nations and peoples of this Empire may ever abide in one bond of fellowship and service; to the glory of thy Name.   *G. W. Briggs*

660

Almighty God, who dost raise up nations and empires to fulfil thy purposes: we pray thee to bind together in the faith of Christ our Lord the peoples of the British Commonwealth of Nations; that, inspired by a common loyalty, they may be strong to further thy holy will; through the same Jesus Christ our Lord.   *Unknown*

THE QUEEN'S FORCES   **661**

Lord God of Hosts, stretch forth, we pray thee, thine almighty arm to strengthen and protect the sailors and soldiers of the Queen in every peril of sea and land and air: give them victory in the day of battle, and in the time of peace keep them safe from all evil; endue them with loyalty and courage; and grant that in all things they may serve as seeing thee who art invisible; through Jesus Christ our Lord.

THE NATION **662**

O Lord Jesus Christ, who wast lifted up on the cross to draw all men unto thee, look in mercy, we beseech thee, upon this nation. Send out thy light and thy truth that they may lead us into paths of fellowship and peace; break down all barriers of contention and strife; and grant that, seeking first thy kingdom and righteousness, we may live together in brotherly unity and concord, to thy glory and the welfare of this realm. Hear us, blessed Lord, to whom, with the Father and the Holy Spirit, be all honour and glory, world without end. *Bishop Woods*

663

Into thy hands, O Lord God of our fathers, we commend our nation and people this day. Forgive our selfish aims and our blind forgetfulness of thee. Purge out from among us the sins that displease thee; give us true religion; crown our faith with righteousness; renew our hope and courage; deliver us from weakness and fear; and lift us up, a holy people, to thy praise and honour, O God, thou king of earth and heaven; through Jesus Christ our Lord.

664

Almighty God, who hast given us this good land for our heritage: we humbly beseech thee to bless us with honourable industry, sound learning, and pure manners. Save us from violence, discord, and confusion, from pride and arrogance and every evil way. Defend our liberties, preserve our unity, endue with the spirit of wisdom and fortitude all those to whom is entrusted the authority of government; and grant that there may be justice and peace at home, and obedience to thy laws among the nations of the earth; to thy honour and glory, who livest and reignest, God over all.

665

We beseech thee, merciful Father, to look upon thy people, and lead us in paths of righteousness and peace; that we may forsake whatsoever things are false and hurtful, and follow all such things as be good and wholesome, to the glory of thy Name and the well-being of this realm; through Jesus Christ our Lord.   *Frederick B. Macnutt*

666

Lord, bless this kingdom and commonwealth, that religion and virtue may season all sorts of men, that there may be peace within our gates and prosperity in all our borders. In time of trouble guide us, and in peace may we not forget thee; and whether in plenty or in want may all things be so ordered, that we may patiently and peaceably seek thy kingdom and its righteousness, the only full supply and sure foundation both of men and states; so that we may continue a place and people to do thee service to the end of time; through Jesus Christ our only saviour and redeemer.   *After Archbishop Laud*

667

O Lord God Almighty, who hast made for thy glory all nations over the face of the earth, that they may do thee service in the joy of freedom: give to this people of England the passion of righteousness, and the strength of self-control; that they may exercise their liberty with a single desire to fulfil thy gracious will; through Jesus Christ, our master, redeemer, and king.

Henry Scott Holland

LEADERS   **668**

O God most high, who alone rulest in the kingdoms of men: grant, we beseech thee, to all Members of Parliament the light and guidance of thy Holy Spirit; that they may wisely take counsel together, and come to such decisions as shall promote thy glory and the well-being of this nation; through Jesus Christ our Lord.

669

Almighty God, by whom alone kings reign, and princes decree justice; and from whom alone cometh all counsel, wisdom, and understanding; we, thine unworthy servants, here gathered together in thy Name, do most humbly

beseech thee to send down thy heavenly wisdom from
above, to direct and guide us in all our consultations: and
grant that, we having thy fear always before our eyes, and
laying aside all private interests, prejudices, and partial
affections, the result of all our counsels may be to the glory
of thy blessed Name, the maintenance of true religion and
justice, the safety, honour, and happiness of the Queen, the
public wealth, peace, and tranquillity of the realm, and the
uniting and knitting together of the hearts of all persons
and estates within the same, in true Christian love and
charity one towards another; through Jesus Christ our
Lord and saviour.   *'Prayer for the Parliament'*

670

O God, the Lord of all kings and kingdoms, let thy strong
hand control the nations and order their doings unto the
fulfilment of thy purposes upon earth. Strengthen, we
pray thee, those who strive after fellowship and brotherhood, and labour to establish righteousness and peace;
guide the hearts and minds of rulers and statesmen, that
they may seek first thy kingdom of justice and freedom for
all peoples, both great and small; for the sake of Jesus
Christ our Lord.   *After Hugh Johnston*

671

Almighty God, who alone givest wisdom and understanding: inspire, we pray thee, the hearts of all to whom
thou hast committed the government of the nations. Give
them the vision of truth and justice, and guide them so to
temper justice with mercy that by their counsels the nations
may work together in fellowship and brotherhood, and thy
holy Church throughout the world may be free to serve
thee in unity and peace; through Jesus Christ our Lord.
                               Anon.

672

O Lord, we pray thee to raise up leaders of the people who
will fear thee and thee alone, whose delight shall be to do
thy will and work thy work: that the heart of this people
may be wise, its mind sound, and its will righteous;
through Christ our Lord.   *Unknown*

673

O God, almighty Father, King of kings and Lord of all our rulers, grant that the hearts and minds of all who go out as leaders before us, the statesmen, the judges, the men of learning, and the men of wealth, may be so filled with the love of thy laws, and of that which is righteous and life-giving, that they may serve as a wholesome salt unto the earth, and be worthy stewards of thy good and perfect gifts; through Jesus Christ our Lord.

Prayer of the Order of the Garter

AT A GENERAL ELECTION   **674**

O Lord, we beseech thee to govern the minds of all who are called at this time to choose faithful men into the great council of the nation; that they may exercise their choice as in thy sight, for the welfare of all our people; through Jesus Christ our Lord.   *Bishop Gore*

FREEDOM   **675**

O eternal God, through whose mighty power our fathers won their liberties of old: grant, we beseech thee, that we and all the people of this land may have grace to maintain these liberties in righteousness and peace; through Jesus Christ our Lord.   *Bishop E. L. Parsons*

676

Almighty God, who hast created man in thine own image: grant us grace fearlessly to contend against evil, and to make no peace with oppression; and, that we may reverently use our freedom, help us to employ it in the maintenance of justice among men and nations, to the glory of thy holy Name; through Jesus Christ our Lord.

American Prayer Book

677

Grant, O Lord God, that laying aside the sins that hinder the coming of thy kingdom, the nations of the world may be assured of the right which thou hast given them to live in freedom; freedom from want and fear, freedom of thought and speech, and freedom to worship thee according to thy will; through Jesus Christ our Lord.

Frederick B. Macnutt

PEACE **678**

O almighty God, the Father of all mankind, we pray thee to turn to thyself the hearts of all peoples and their rulers, that by the power of thy Holy Spirit peace may be established on the foundation of justice, righteousness, and truth; through him who was lifted up on the cross to draw all men unto himself, even thy Son Jesus Christ our Lord.

William Temple

679

Almighty God, whose kingdom alone bringeth true peace to the earth: reveal again thy law, that all nations may bow before it; and thine everlasting love, that they may dwell together in unity; through Jesus Christ our Lord.

After Archbishop Garbett

680

O God, who wouldest fold both heaven and earth in a single peace: let the design of thy great love lighten upon the waste of our wraths and sorrows; and give peace to thy Church, peace among nations, peace in our dwellings, and peace in our hearts; through thy Son our saviour Jesus Christ.

E. Milner-White

681

Almighty God, who canst bring good out of evil, and makest even the wrath of man to turn to thy praise; teach thy children to live together in charity and peace, and grant that the nations of the world may be united in a firmer fellowship for the promotion of thy glory and the good of all mankind; through Jesus Christ our Lord.

J. Armitage Robinson

682

O God and Father of all, whom the whole heavens adore:
let the whole earth also worship thee, all kingdoms obey
thee, all tongues confess and bless thee, and the sons of
men love thee and serve thee in peace; through Jesus
Christ our Lord.   *E. Milner-White*

683

Inspire, we beseech thee, O Lord, the hearts of all men
everywhere with the spirit of love and justice; and enlighten
the leaders of the nations with the wisdom which is from
above, that they may seek first the coming of thy kingdom
and the fellowship of thy children: deliver us, thy people,
from faithlessness and fear, save us from the sins and
cruelties of war, and guide our feet into thy way of peace;
through Jesus Christ our Lord.   *Frederick B. Macnutt*

684

O almighty and most merciful God, Father of us all, who
in thy holy Word hast taught us that the kingdoms of this
world shall become the kingdom of thy Son: send thy
blessing, we beseech thee, upon the rulers and governors
of the peoples, and especially upon those who are seeking
to kindle the desire for righteousness and peace among the
nations of the earth. Guide their counsels with the light of
thy Holy Spirit of truth and wisdom, so that in all their
work they may glorify thy holy Name; through Jesus Christ
our Lord.

685

Almighty and everlasting God, who healest us by discipline
and by forgiveness dost preserve us: graciously fulfil the
desires of thy servants, and grant that in tranquillity we
may rejoice in the comfort of thy gift of peace, and show
forth our thankfulness by the amendment of our lives;
through Jesus Christ our Lord.

                          After Leonine Sacramentary

686

O Lord of peace, who by thy coming unto us hast bound earth to heaven and made of all men one family in the kingdom of thy love: we beseech thee to unite the nations in obedience to thyself; suffer not thy Church to fail thee in this time of stress and crisis; and strengthen our faith in thine eternal purpose to establish the dominion of righteousness and peace. *Frederick B. Macnutt*

687

Grant thy people rest, O God, we beseech thee, each in his own place and over all the world; deliverance from suspicion, injustice, discord, and despair, relief from want, and salvation from evil; and gather them, O Father, by one holy faith into one family of peace; through Jesus Christ our Lord.

AN INTERNATIONAL CONFERENCE   **688**

O God, who art the lover of justice and peace: direct, we beseech thee, the minds and wills of those who are called to deliberate for the welfare of the nations and the peace of the world; that as faithful stewards of the things which belong unto righteousness, they may have regard to thy laws and the true welfare of mankind. And so guide them by thy Holy Spirit, that by word and deed they may promote thy glory, and set forward peace and mutual goodwill among men; through Jesus Christ our Lord.

INSTRUMENTS OF PEACE   **689**

Lord, make us instruments of thy peace. Where there is hatred, let us sow love; where there is injury, pardon; where there is discord, union; where there is doubt, faith; where there is despair, hope; where there is darkness, light; where there is sadness, joy; for thy mercy and for thy truth's sake.   *St. Francis of Assisi*

ATOMIC POWER   **690**

Almighty and merciful God, without whom all things hasten to destruction and fall into nothingness: look, we beseech thee, upon thy family of nations and men, to which thou hast committed power in trust for their mutual health and comfort. Save us and help us, O Lord, lest we abuse thy gift and make it our misery and ruin; draw all men unto thee in thy kingdom of righteousness and truth; uproot our enmities, heal our divisions, cast out our fears; and renew our faith in thine unchanging purpose of goodwill and peace on earth; for the love of Jesus Christ our Lord. *Frederick B. Macnutt*

IN TIME OF CRISIS **691**

Look in compassion, O heavenly Father, upon this troubled and divided world. Though we cannot trace thy footsteps or understand thy working, give us grace to trust thee with an undoubting faith; and when thine own time is come, reveal, O Lord, that new heaven and new earth wherein dwelleth righteousness, where the prince of peace ruleth, thy Son our saviour Jesus Christ. *C. J. Vaughan*

692

Grant, we beseech thee, almighty God, that we who in our tribulation are yet of good cheer because of thy loving kindness may find thee mighty to save us in all dangers and adversities; through Jesus Christ our Lord. *Roman Breviary*

693

O God, who hast knit together in one family all the nations of the earth: remove far from us, we beseech thee, the menace of war; pour out upon the rulers of the peoples thy spirit of peace; restrain the passions of such as plan aggression; and hasten the time when the kingdoms of this world shall become the kingdom of thy Son, our saviour Jesus Christ.

AN INTERCESSION **694**

Lord God, we beseech thee, glorify thy Name, bring in thy kingdom, fulfil thy purpose; revive our faith, renew thy Church, convert the nations; defend the right, preserve freedom, defeat aggression; deliver the oppressed, comfort the sorrowful, relieve the suffering. God save mankind, draw all men unto thee, and give peace to the world; through Jesus Christ our Lord. *Frederick B. Macnutt*

UNITY **695**

God of our fathers, who from generation to generation hast watched over us in love: hear us now in hours of perplexity and need; save us from the dangers of disunion and strife; remove all hindrances to brotherly concord; and grant that we may serve thee in all godly quietness; through Jesus Christ our Lord.

696

O God, the creator of the ends of the earth, with whom there is no distinction of race or habitation, but all are one in thee: break down, we beseech thee, the barriers which divide us; that we may work together in one accord with each other and with thee; through him who is the saviour of all, Jesus Christ thy Son our Lord. *G. W. Briggs*

CIVIC AUTHORITIES **697**

O Lord our God, we beseech thee to enlighten and guide those who bear authority in our towns and cities; that there may be open ways and noble streets therein, and that everywhere the wisdom of science and the skill of art may be devoted to the service of the common weal, for thy glory and for the health and delight of men. Give us courage, O Lord, to remove mean streets and unworthy dwellings, that thy people may live together in decency and honour, as citizens of that heavenly city, to which we pray thee to bring us all at last; for the sake of Jesus Christ our Lord.

698

O Lord God, the Father of lights, from whom cometh every good and perfect gift: we beseech thee to send forth upon thy servants who bear office in this city (*or* town) the spirit of prudence, charity, and justice; that in all things they may walk before thee with steadfast purpose and single heart, and faithfully serve thy people committed to their charge; through Jesus Christ our Lord.

Frederick B. Macnutt

699

O God, who hast taught us to live in the towns and cities of this world as those who know that their citizenship is in heaven: guide, we pray thee, with thy heavenly wisdom those who bear office in the government of this city (*or* town), that they may keep ever before them the vision of that city which hath foundations, whose builder and maker is God; through Jesus Christ our Lord.

A CIVIC ELECTION **700**

Guide, O Lord, we pray thee, the mayor and corporation with all, from the greatest to the least, who share in the ordering of this town (*or* city), and give strength, honour, and charity to us and to our fellow-citizens; that we may exercise our votes as in thy sight, and seeking not our own, may see ever before us the vision of that free city, perfect in the heavens, whose builder and maker is God; through Jesus Christ our Lord. *After Percy Dearmer*

ADMINISTRATION OF JUSTICE **701**

O God, the just and merciful judge of all mankind: look down from heaven, we beseech thee, on these thy servants, who are set by thy appointment to minister justice between man and man, to clear the innocent, and to convict and punish the guilty. Grant unto them thy Holy Spirit, the spirit of uprightness, the spirit of discernment, and the spirit of love; that they may boldly, discreetly, and mercifully fulfil their sacred duties, to the good of thy people and the glory of thy Name; through Jesus Christ our Lord.

Westminster Abbey

N

702

O God, mighty and merciful, the judge of all men: grant to those who minister justice the spirit of wisdom and discernment; and that they may be strong and patient, upright and compassionate, fill them, we beseech thee, with the spirit of thy holy fear; through Jesus Christ our Lord.

J. Armitage Robinson

CITIZENS OF HEAVEN **703**

O God of truth, who hast taught us that we are the light of the world, a city set on a hill that cannot be hid, and hast bidden us to let our light shine before men: uncover in us, we pray thee, the hidden works of darkness, and reveal the falsehood of selfishness and greed; that we may seek earnestly to walk in the light as thou art in the light, in whom is no darkness at all; through Jesus Christ our Lord.

Frederick B. Macnutt

Section 9

THE ECONOMIC ORDER

A BETTER ORDER **704**

Behold, O Lord God, our strivings after a truer and more abiding order. Give us visions that bring back a lost glory to the earth, and dreams that foreshadow the better order which thou hast prepared for us. Scatter every excuse of frailty and unworthiness: consecrate us all with a heavenly mission: open to us a clearer prospect of our work. Give us strength according to our day gladly to welcome and gratefully to fulfil it; through Jesus Christ our Lord.

Bishop Westcott

REPENTANCE FOR SOCIAL DISORDER **705**

Almighty God, who hast entrusted this earth unto the children of men, and through thy Son Jesus Christ hast called us unto a heavenly citizenship: grant us, we humbly beseech thee, such shame and repentance for the disorder and injustice and cruelty which are among us, that, fleeing unto thee for pardon and for grace, we may henceforth set ourselves to establish that city which has justice for its foundation and love for its law, whereof thou art the architect and maker; through the same Lord Jesus Christ, thy Son, our saviour. *William Temple*

SOCIAL REFORMATION 706

Stir up, O Lord, the wills of thy people and kindle our understanding; that we may discern the way to a just and ordered society, where all may work and all may find a just reward, and thy people may serve thee and one another in peace and goodwill, in the spirit of thy Son, Jesus Christ our Lord. *Harold Anson*

SOCIAL JUSTICE 707

O God, the king of righteousness, lead us, we pray thee, in the ways of justice and of peace: inspire us to break down all tyranny and oppression, to gain for every man his due reward and from every man his due service; that each may live for all, and all may care for each, in the Name of Jesus Christ. *William Temple*

708

Almighty God, who hast created man in thine own image: grant us grace fearlessly to contend against evil, and to make no peace with oppression; and, that we may reverently use our freedom, help us to employ it in the maintenance of justice among men and nations, to the glory of thy holy Name; through Jesus Christ our Lord.
American Prayer Book

SOCIAL RIGHTEOUSNESS 709

Look, we beseech thee, O Lord our God, upon us thy people, and lead us in the way of righteousness and truth; that we may forsake those things that are contrary to thy will, and follow after all such things as be good and wholesome, to the glory of thy Name and the well-being of this realm; through Jesus Christ our Lord.
Frederick B. Macnutt

IN SOCIAL UNREST   710

O God, who art the Father of all, and who alone makest
men to be of one mind in an house: we beseech thee to
grant us, at this time of unrest and strife, a fuller sense of
our brotherhood in Christ; allay all anger and bitterness,
and help us to be true and just in our dealings one with
another; through the same Jesus Christ, thy Son, our Lord.
J. Armitage Robinson

                                                711

Guide us, O Christ, in all the perplexities of our social life;
uproot our enmities, and in thy good time bring us together
in love and unity; and make the kingdoms of this world thy
kingdom as thou willest; who with the Father and the
Holy Spirit art one God, world without end.
James Adderley

INDUSTRY AND COMMERCE   712

O God, who givest to every man his work and through his
labours dost accomplish thy purposes upon earth: grant thy
blessing, we beseech thee, to those who are engaged in the
industries and commerce of this land.   Inspire them with
the knowledge that in ministering to the needs of others
they are serving thee; defend them from injustice and
oppression, and give them the due reward of their labours;
that, seeking first thy kingdom and righteousness, all
things may be added unto them here and hereafter;
through Jesus Christ our Lord.   *Unknown*

EARNING AND SPENDING   713

O God, whose blessed Son, Jesus Christ, earned his bread
at Nazareth by the labours of his hands, and taught us that
our possessions are a trust from thee: help us to be faithful
stewards of what thou givest; that in earning we may be
just and honest, and in spending we may seek not our own,
but thy glory and the good of others; through the same our
Lord Jesus Christ.

UNSELFISHNESS   **714**

O strong Lord God, who wilt judge all mankind, grant to
the exalted humility, to the desolate thankfulness, to the
happy sympathy with sorrow; that so earthly eminence may
become a stepping-stone to heavenly heights, and loneliness may introduce to the full communion of saints, and
joy blossoming in time may bear eternal fruit. Be we high
or low, prosperous or depressed, wheresoever, whatsoever
we be, make us and ever more keep us well-pleasing in thy
sight; through Jesus Christ our Lord.   *Christina Rossetti*

EMPLOYERS AND EMPLOYED   **715**

O God, who art the Father of all mankind, we beseech thee
to give us a fuller realization of our brotherhood, man with
man, in thee; and raise up among us a deeper sense of truth
and equity in commercial dealings one with another. Give
grace, O Lord, to those who serve, that they may do their
work heartily as unto thee and not unto men; to masters,
that they may do what is just and equal as having themselves a master in heaven: and to all alike, that they may be
united in the common service of the Lord Christ, and
receive of thee the reward of their inheritance; through the
same Jesus Christ our Lord.   *From 'Sursum Corda'*

THE UNEMPLOYED   **716**

O God, thou Lord of the vineyard, who wouldest not that
any should stand idle in the market-place: hear our prayer
for all who are without employment or assurance of livelihood; and in the largeness of thy loving wisdom, declare
unto us thy counsels to help and heal all our distresses;
through Jesus Christ our Lord.   *E. Milner-White*

                                                         717

O Lord and heavenly Father, we commend to thy care and
protection the men and women of this land who are suffering distress and anxiety through lack of work. Strengthen
and support them, we beseech thee; and so prosper the
counsels of those who govern and direct our industries,

that thy people may be set free from want and fear to work in peace and security, for the relief of their necessities and the well-being of this realm; through Jesus Christ our Lord. *Industrial Christian Fellowship*

THE HOMELESS AND THE NEEDY **718**

O Lord, who rescuest the poor from need, and restorest the lonely to a home: look in mercy upon all who suffer the lack of livelihood and, like thee, O Son of Man, have not where to lay their head. And as thou hast assured those who do good to others that, inasmuch as they do it to thy brethren, they do it unto thee, let thy pity and compassion move us to house the homeless and to lighten the burdens of the needy and the distressed. Guide, we beseech thee, those who govern the nations, that thy people may be set free from want and fear, and that in thee all the families of the earth may be blessed; who livest and reignest in thy kingdom of righteousness and love, world without end.

Frederick B. Macnutt

THE NEEDY **719**

O God, the God of all righteousness, mercy, and love, give us all grace and strength to conceive and execute whatever may be for thine honour and the welfare of the needy; that we may become at last, through the merits and intercession of our common redeemer, a great and a happy because a wise and understanding people. *The Earl of Shaftesbury*

DAILY WORK **720**

Guide us, O Lord, amidst the trials and conflicts of our social life, and fill our centres of industry with thy presence; that daily work may become to us a high vocation, and that all may learn the dignity of labour and make it a freewill offering to thee; through Jesus Christ our Lord. *Anon.*

721

Almighty God, who by thy Son hast bidden us to ask of thee our daily bread: prosper the work of those who labour in the fields, and grant such favourable weather that we may gather in the fruits of the earth in their seasons; protect the sailors who carry food across the seas; and give us grace day by day to deny ourselves and to remember the needs of others.   *Unknown*

722

O God, who hast bound us together in this bundle of life, give us grace to understand how our lives depend upon the courage, the industry, the honesty, and the integrity of our fellow-men; that we may be mindful of their needs, grateful for their faithfulness, and faithful in our responsibilities to them; through Jesus Christ our Lord.
                Reinhold Niebuhr

723

O blessed saviour, who wast pleased thyself to be numbered among the craftsmen: we pray thee to guide and prosper all who labour with mind and hand, that their work may be done for thy honour and rewarded with thine approval; who livest and reignest with the Father and the Holy Spirit, one God, world without end.   *Unknown*

THE CITY   724

Grant us, O Lord, a vision of this city, fair as it might be in fulfilment of thy purpose: a city of justice, where none shall prey upon others; a city of plenty, where greed and poverty shall be done away; a city of brotherhood, where success is founded upon service, and honour is given to nobleness alone; a city of peace, where order shall not rest on force, but on love of all for each and of each for all. Hear thou, O Lord, our prayer and pledge of love and service; and hasten the day of the eternal city which cometh down from heaven to earth from thee; through Jesus Christ our Lord.   *After Walter Rausenbusch*

CHRISTIAN CITIZENSHIP   725

Eternal God, our heavenly Father, who hast given to us thy children an abiding citizenship in heaven, and in the days of our pilgrimage a citizenship also upon earth: give us thine aid, as we journey to that heavenly city, so faithfully to perform the duties which befall us on our way, that at the last we may be found worthy to enter into thy rest; through Jesus Christ our Lord. *Unknown*

726

O Lord, who hast taught us that our citizenship is in heaven: prosper, we pray thee, our efforts to fashion our citizenship here on earth after the pattern of the heavenly city, whose light is thy glory, and whose builder and maker thou art; through him whom thou hast sent to deliver us from all evil, in our cities and in our souls, Jesus Christ our Lord.

Section 10

THE FAMILY

FAMILY LIFE 727

Almighty God and heavenly Father, whose Son Jesus Christ was subject to Mary and Joseph at Nazareth, and shared there the life of an earthly home; send down thy blessing, we beseech thee, upon all Christian families. Grant unto parents the spirit of understanding and wisdom; give unto the children the spirit of obedience and true reverence; and so bind each to each with the bond of mutual love, that to all its members of whatsoever age, every Christian family may be an image of the Holy Family of Nazareth, and every Christian home a school of heavenly knowledge and of virtuous and upright living; through him who became a child, and learned obedience to thy will, that he might save us, even Jesus Christ thy Son our Lord, who now liveth and reigneth with thee, in the unity of the Holy Ghost, God world without end. *E. C. Ratcliff*

728

Almighty Father, from whom every family in heaven and on earth is named: we entreat thy mercy for the families of this and every land, for man and wife and child, and for all who have the care of children; that by thy hallowing our homes may be blessed and our children may grow up in the knowledge of thee and of thy Son, Jesus Christ our Lord.   *St. Paul's Cathedral*

A FAMILY IN TIME OF TRIAL   729

O eternal God, our most merciful Lord and gracious Father, thou art my guide, the light of mine eyes, the joy of my heart, the author of my hope, and the object of my love and worshippings; thou relievest all my needs, and determinest all my doubts, and art an eternal fountain of blessing, open and running over to all thirsty and weary souls that come and cry to thee for mercy and refreshment. Have mercy upon thy servant, and relieve my fears and sorrows, and the great necessities of my family; for thou alone, O Lord, canst do it.   *Jeremy Taylor*

A HOME   730

Merciful Saviour, who didst love Martha and Mary and Lazarus, blessing their home with thy sacred presence: bless, we beseech thee, this our home, that thy love may rest upon us and thy promised presence may be with us. May we all grow in grace and in the knowledge of thee, our Lord and saviour Jesus Christ.   Teach us to love one another as thou didst give us commandment; help us all to choose the better part that shall not be taken away from us. Hear us, O Jesu, who with the Father and the Holy Spirit livest and reignest, one God for evermore.

                                    Canadian Prayer Book

731

Almighty God, our heavenly Father, whose blessed Son did share at Nazareth the life of an earthly home: bless, we beseech thee, this our home, that thy promised presence may be with us, and that we may always live and work together in thy steadfast fear and love; through Jesus Christ our Lord.

732

O God, who art perfect love, grant that we who are born of thee, and eat of thy bread, may bear one another's burdens with sincere affection; that thy peace which passeth all understanding may keep our hearts and minds in Christ Jesus thy Son our Lord, who with thee and the Holy Ghost liveth and reigneth one God, world without end.

Edward Bouverie Pusey

733

Be present with us, O Lord, in our daily duties, and grant to those who dwell in this house the strength and protection of thy continual help; that thou mayest be known as the master of the family and the defender of this home; through Jesus Christ our Lord.

After Gelasian Sacramentary

734

Almighty God, in whose house are many mansions, we pray thee to surround our dwelling with the unseen wall of thy protection; that we may be devoted to thy service, and may serve one another in love; until we come at last to that home which thou hast prepared for them that love thee; through Jesus Christ our Lord.

HUSBAND AND WIFE   **735**

O heavenly Father, who hast taught us by thy Son that except we love one another we cannot fulfil thy law: grant that thy Holy Spirit may lead us thy servants in the way of love and peace unto our lives' end; that, obeying thy will and always being in safety under thy protection, we may be united at last in the life which has no ending; through Jesus Christ our Lord.

736

O God our Father, we thank thee for uniting our lives, and for giving us to each other in the fulfilment of love. Watch over us at all times; guide and protect us; and give

us faith and patience as we hold each other's hand in thine
every moment of every day and night, and draw strength
from thee and from each other; through Jesus Christ our
Lord.   *Frederick B. Macnutt*

WOMEN   737

O blessed Jesus, who by thy holy incarnation didst consecrate womanhood to thy glory: make us pure, we beseech
thee, by the vision of thy purity; make us lowly by the
example of thy lowliness; make us holy by thy indwelling
of thy Holy Spirit.   Strengthen us, we beseech thee, that
we may strengthen each other in courage and in faith; and
show us how to use all thy gifts in thy service; for thy
Name's sake.

                                                           738

O Lord, who wast born of a woman, and hast glorified
womanhood in the sight of all men: bless, we beseech thee,
the women of our nation upon whom are laid the burdens
of unwonted duties.   Strengthen them in hours of strain
and weakness; preserve in them the spirit of sympathy and
love; keep them steadfast in temptation; and grant them
the help of thy grace, that in all things they may be worthy
of their vocation; to the glory of thy Name, Jesus Christ
our Lord.   *Frederick B. Macnutt*

PARENTS AND CHILDREN   739

O God, our heavenly Father, who hast blessed us thy
servants with the gift of children (*or* a child): grant, we
beseech thee, that we may show our love and thankfulness
to thee in so ordering our home, that by the example of our
lives and teaching we may guide our children (*or* child) in
the way of righteousness, and at last become partakers with
them (*or* him, *or* her) of the life everlasting; through Jesus
Christ our Lord.   *South African Prayer Book*

CHILDREN   740

Almighty God and heavenly Father, we thank thee for the
children whom thou hast given to us; give us also grace to
train them in thy faith, fear, and love; that as they advance

in years they may grow in grace, and be found hereafter in the number of thine elect children; through Jesus Christ our Lord. *Bishop Cosin*

741

Lord Jesus, we beseech thee, by the innocence and obedience of thy holy childhood, and by thy reverence and love for little children, to guard the children of our land; preserve their innocence, strengthen them in their weakness, recover the wandering, and remove all that hinders them from being brought up in thy fear and love; who livest and reignest with the Father and the Holy Spirit, ever one God. *S. Gladstone*

742

O Lord Jesus Christ, who hast bidden us to suffer little children to come unto thee, and didst lay thine hands upon them and bless them: forgive our neglect of those who know thee not, and inspire thy Church with new zeal to guide them into the knowledge of thy love who hast redeemed them, that they may know thee as their friend and saviour, and serve thee unto their lives' end. *Anon.*

743

O ever-blessed Jesus, very God and very Man, who thyself wast a child, and didst submit thyself to the charge and care of earthly teachers: bless, we beseech thee, the children of this land who are taught in our schools. Grant that as they grow in years they may grow in knowledge of thyself; let them learn to love and serve thee truly, and daily order their lives according to thy will.

744

O God, our Father, we remember before thee all orphaned, homeless, and unwanted children, the children of loveless homes, and those who suffer from bodily defect and disease. Make our hearts burn within us for the children of our dark places, and teach us how to turn to good account the laws that protect them and the efforts of those who strive to succour them; through Jesus Christ our Lord. *Mothers' Union*

745

Almighty God, who in thy love didst give thy servant Nicholas a perpetual name for deeds of mercy both on land and sea: we pray thee that thy Church may never cease to work for the happiness of little children, and the poor, and those tossed by any tempests of doubt or grief; through Jesus Christ our Lord, to whom with thee and the Holy Spirit be thanks and praise from all the company of saints, now and evermore. *E. Milner-White*

A CHILD'S PRAYER **746**

O Lord Jesu Christ, who as a child didst learn and grow in wisdom: grant me so to learn thy holy word, that I may walk in thy ways and daily grow more like unto thee; who art my saviour and my Lord. *Irish Prayer Book*

RELATIVES AND FRIENDS **747**

Almighty God, we entrust all who are dear to us to thy never-failing care and love, for this life and the life to come; knowing that thou doest for them better things than we can desire or pray for; through Jesus Christ our Lord.
American Prayer Book

748

O almighty and eternal God, through whose providence men are bound together by ties of blood and holy affection: pour down upon our relations and friends the manifold gifts of thy grace; that, united in faith and love, we may labour together according to thy will for the establishment of thy kingdom; through Jesus Christ our Lord.
Bishop Westcott

FRIENDS **749**

O Lord, who hast graciously called us not servants but friends: increase in us daily that holy friendship, and bind us ever more closely to one another in our common love of thee; that we may do the thing which thou commandest, and receive at last what thou hast promised, in thy presence, which is fullness of joy and freedom, world without end.
Frederick B. Macnutt

750

Be pleased, O Lord, to remember my friends, all that have prayed for me, and all that have done me good. Do thou good to them, and return all their kindness double into their own bosom, rewarding them with blessings, sanctifying them with thy grace, and bringing them at last to thy glory. *After Jeremy Taylor*

IN ABSENCE FROM HOME **751**

O God, who hast bidden us to honour our parents, and by thy Son, our saviour, hast hallowed the life of home: bless, we beseech thee, with thy gracious protection all those who are bound to us by ties of kindred and affection, from whom we are now absent. Keep them in health and safety; help us to fulfil our duty to them; and knit us evermore closely together in thee; through Jesus Christ our Lord.

Unknown

752

Almighty God, our heavenly Father, whose blessed Son incarnate did share the life of an earthly home: into thy hands we commend our parents, our families, and our homes. Watch over them in hours of trial and danger; grant to them thy strength and protection in their going out and their coming in; and unite us all together in thy steadfast fear and love; through Jesus Christ our Lord.

Frederick B. Macnutt

THE ABSENT **753**

O God, who art everywhere present, look down with thy mercy upon those who are absent from among us. Give thy holy angels charge over them, and grant that they may be kept safe in body, soul, and spirit, and be presented faultless before the presence of thy glory with exceeding joy; through Jesus Christ our Lord. *Richard Meux Benson*

754

O God, who art present to thy faithful people in every place, mercifully hear our prayers for those we love who are now parted from us: watch over them, we beseech thee,

and protect them in anxiety, danger, and temptation; and
assure both them and us that thou art always near, and
that we are one in thee for ever; through Jesus Christ our
Lord.   *Unknown*

755

O God, the Father and defender of thy people, whom
neither space nor time can separate from such as continue
in thy keeping: be present, we beseech thee, with those
who are parted from us; prosper them and do them good;
guide and direct them in all their undertakings; let nothing
hurtful beset them and no evil befall them; and grant that,
upheld by thy right hand, they may arrive in safety at their
journey's end; through Jesus Christ our Lord.

FOR TRAVELLERS   **756**

O God, who didst call Abraham to leave his home, and
didst protect him in all his wanderings, grant to those who
now travel by land, sea, or air a prosperous journey, a quiet
time, and a safe arrival at their journey's end. Be to them
a shadow in the heat, a refuge in the tempest, a protection
in adversity, and grant that when life's pilgrimage is over
they may arrive at the heavenly country; through Jesus
Christ our Lord.   *Anon.*

TRAVELLERS BY SEA   **757**

O eternal Lord God, who alone spreadest out the heavens
and rulest the raging of the sea: be pleased to receive into
thy protection all those who go down to the sea in ships and
occupy their business in great waters. Make thou their
voyages safe to their persons and their goods; and be
thyself their way and light till journeyings shall end.

TRAVELLERS BY AIR   **758**

Eternal God, who dwellest afar in the heavens, yet abidest
in the hearts of the sons of men: we beseech thee for all
who journey in the air, that they may know thee near them,
to pilot and to protect; through Jesus Christ our Lord.

TRAVELLERS BY ROAD   759

Almighty God, giver of life and health, guide, we pray
thee, with thy wisdom all who are striving to save from
injury and death the travellers on our roads. Grant to
those who drive along the highways consideration for
others, and to those who walk on them or play beside them
thoughtful caution and care; that so without fear or disas-
ter we all may come safely to our journey's end, by thy
mercy who carest for us; through Jesus Christ our Lord.
                                        Bishop Douglas Crick

Section 11

YOUTH AND EDUCATION

TEACHERS   760

O Lord and master, who thyself didst come into the world
to bear witness to the truth, and didst say that the good and
faithful teacher should be greatly accounted of in thy
kingdom: send, we beseech thee, thy blessing upon those
who are engaged in the work of education. Give them
clearness of vision and freshness of thought, and enable
them so to train the hearts and minds of the children committed to them that they may fill their appointed places in
the work of this life, and be ready for the service of the life
to come.   *Arthur W. Robinson*

                                                     761

O Lord God Almighty, who through thy Son Jesus Christ
didst reveal thine exceeding love for children: graciously
look upon those to whom thou hast entrusted the work of
teaching. Let them all be taught of thee; and so fill them
with love to thee that through them thy love may be
implanted in the hearts of those who are committed to
their care. In weariness and disappointment let thy comfort refresh their souls; that so continuing in thy service
they may receive from thee at last their full reward.

TEACHERS AND CHILDREN   762

Almighty God, our heavenly Father, who hast committed
to thy holy Church the care and nurture of thy children:
enlighten with thy wisdom those who teach and those who
learn; that, rejoicing in the knowledge of thy truth, they
may worship thee and serve thee from generation to
generation; through Jesus Christ our Lord.

American Prayer Book

STUDENTS   763

O Lord Jesus Christ, who on the night of thy Passion didst
pray to thy Father that all they who believe on him through
thee might be perfected into one: we pray thee to pour thy
Spirit upon the students of all nations, that they may
consecrate themselves to thy service, even as thou for their
sakes didst consecrate thyself; and so, being joined together
by their common faith and obedience, they may come
more perfectly to love and understand one another, that
the world may know that thou hast been sent by the Father
to be the saviour and Lord of all men; who livest and
reignest, one God world without end.

Bishop Philip Loyd

SCHOOLS   764

O Lord Jesus Christ, child of Bethlehem, everlasting God,
bless, we beseech thee, the boys and girls of our schools;
and grant that they may be truthful, pure, obedient, and
ready to do their duty in that state of life to which it shall
please thee to call them. Give grace to those whom thou
dost set over them so to bring them up for thee, that
teachers and scholars may meet with joy in the day of thy
appearing; who livest and reignest with the Father, and the
Holy Spirit, world without end.

A SCHOOL OR COLLEGE   765

Vouchsafe, O Lord, to prosper with thy blessing the work
of this school (*or* college). Grant that all who serve thee
here, as teachers or learners, may set thy holy will ever
before them, and do that which is well-pleasing in thy

O

sight; that so both Church and Commonwealth may be bettered by their studies, and they themselves may finally attain to thy perfect service; through Jesus Christ our Lord. *Unknown*

766

O God, who through the love and labour of many hast built us here a goodly heritage, and crowned our school with honour and length of days: for these thy gifts and for thyself we thank thee; for past achievements and future hopes; beseeching thee that both we and all who follow after us may learn to live as in thy presence, and help thee to build up the city of God. *Bishop E. A. Burroughs*

A SCHOOL **767**

O dearest Saviour, thou Word and revelation of the Father; purge us by the power of thy love from pride and prejudice, from boasting over the past and ambition for the future; take our lives and our school into thine own hands, and so use us in prosperity, in poverty or through death that, so far as lies in us, thy kingdom may come and thy will be done in earth as it is in heaven. *William Temple*

768

Almighty God, in whom we live and move and have our being: make this school as a field which the Lord has blessed; that whatsoever things are true and pure, lovely and of good report, may here abound and flourish. Preserve in it an unblemished name, enlarge it to a wider usefulness, and exalt it in the love of all its members as an instrument of thy glory; through Jesus Christ our Lord.
King's School, Canterbury

OLD AND YOUNG **769**

O God, who dost turn the hearts of the fathers unto the children, and hast granted unto youth to see visions and to age to dream dreams: we beseech thee to draw together the old and the young, that in fellowship with thee they may understand and help one another, and in thy service find their perfect freedom; through Jesus Christ our Lord.
Unknown

YOUTH OF ALL NATIONS 770

O God our Father, we give thee hearty thanks for the inheritance which thou hast entrusted to us and the vocation wherewith thou hast called us; for those who have taught and helped us on our way, and for our vision of the years of hope and promise and the tasks that lie before us. Guide us, we pray thee, with thy continual help; that the truth of thy Gospel may enlighten our hearts, and thy law may be a lantern unto our feet. Preserve our integrity and guard us from evil; accept our lives as we dedicate them to thee this day; and unite the youth of all nations in the kingdom of Christ our redeemer, and in service of the cause of justice, freedom, and peace; through Jesus Christ our Lord. *Westminster Abbey*

FOUNDERS AND BENEFACTORS 771

O Lord, we glorify thee in these thy servants our founders and benefactors departed out of this present life; beseeching thee that, as they for their time bestowed charitably to our comfort the temporal things which thou didst give them, so we for our time may fruitfully use the same to the setting forth of thy holy word to thy laud and praise; and finally that both they and we may reign with thee in glory; through Jesus Christ our Lord. *Elizabethan*

COMMEMORATION 772

O Lord God, the Father of lights, the maker and builder of every house not made with hands: we give thee thanks for all members of this school who have served thee with fruitful labour for the increase of knowledge and wisdom, and for the nurture of faithful servants of thy Church and kingdom. As thou didst enable them to add their share to thy work, wrought out by many hands from age to age, so teach and strengthen us, we pray thee, to do thy will in the task which thou hast apportioned us in this our generation; and grant that with them we may enter into thy joy in the fulfilment of thine eternal counsel; through Jesus Christ our Lord. *Unknown*

CHURCHWORKERS AMONG THE YOUNG 773

O Lord Jesus Christ, who art the saviour and friend of age
and youth: look graciously, we beseech thee, upon those
who give themselves to serve and help the young, and bless
their works undertaken in thy Name. Enlighten those who
teach and those who learn; renew their strength that they
may not grow weary in their work; let their lamps burn
bright in the days of darkness, and their hearts be strong in
times of disappointment. And so inspire them with thy
Spirit that old and young may be builded together as living
stones into the temple of thy Church; who livest and
reignest with the Father and the Holy Spirit, ever one God,
world without end. *Unknown*

SUNDAY SCHOOL TEACHERS 774

O Lord Jesus Christ, who art the life and light of all thy
servants: we beseech thee to help and inspire those who
teach in our Sunday schools, and those also who prepare
them for their work. Pour out upon them the spirit of
unceasing prayer and faithful service; encourage them with
good success; strengthen their faith and purpose when
they are weary and disheartened; and fortify them with
thy assurance that they are fellow-workers together with
thee. *Anon.*

SCIENTIFIC STUDY AND RESEARCH 775

Almighty God, of whose only gift cometh insight and
understanding: guide and prosper, we beseech thee, those
who labour in societies and associations devoted to
scientific study and research, that through them knowledge
may be increased and flourish; and grant that in thy light
they may see light, who art the fountain of all wisdom;
through Jesus Christ our Lord. *Unknown*

776

O God, the giver of wisdom, who in the beginning madest
man to have dominion over the works of thy hands: grant
that with every increase of knowledge and of power we may
seek to render service to mankind, and thereby to set
forward thy eternal purpose; through Jesus Christ our
Lord. *J. Armitage Robinson*

Section 12

SIN AND SUFFERING

THE TEMPTED   777

O God, who art faithful, and sufferest us not to be tempted
above that we are able, but with the temptation also makest
a way of escape, that we may be able to bear it: we humbly
entreat thy Majesty that thou wouldest graciously
strengthen with thy heavenly aid thy servants who rely on
thy mercy; and keep them with thy continual protection,
that they may evermore wait on thee, and never by any
temptation be drawn away from thee; through Jesus Christ
our Lord.   *Edward Bouverie Pusey*

778

O God, who willest not the death of a sinner, we beseech
thee to aid and protect those who are exposed to grievous
temptations; and grant that in obeying thy commandments
they may be strengthened and supported by thy grace;
through Jesus Christ our Lord.
                    Adapted from Gregorian Sacramentary

SINNERS   779

Almighty God, who gavest thine only-begotten Son, Jesus
Christ, to die for the sins of the whole world: have mercy
upon all who are in temptation and upon all who through
weakness or wilfulness fall into sin; make known to them
thy gracious love, and so teach them the evil of hatred and
malice, of envy and contempt, of lust and greed, that turning to thee for help, they may be led into fellowship with
thee and obedience to thy will; through Jesus Christ our
Lord.   *William Temple*

780

Almighty God, we beseech thee to hear our prayers for
such as sin against thee or neglect to serve thee; that thou
wouldest vouchsafe to bestow upon them true repentance
and an earnest longing for thy service; through Jesus Christ
our Lord.   *Office of Sext*

781

O Lord Jesus Christ, we beseech thee by thy love for out-
cast sinners, and by thy pity for those who put thee to an
open shame: have mercy upon all who have been unfaithful
to thee and have sold themselves to sin, and recover them
from the shame into which they have fallen.   Hear us, O
Saviour, who with the Father and the Holy Spirit livest
and reignest, one God, for evermore.   *S. Gladstone*

782

O Lord, by thy divine presence raise my soul, grievously
paralysed by all kinds of sin and evil deeds, as of old thou
didst raise the sick of the palsy; that, being healed, I may
cry unto thee: O merciful Christ, glory be to thy power!
Eastern Orthodox

THE SUFFERING WORLD   783

O thou who art love, and seest all the suffering, injustice,
and misery which oppose thy sway: have compassion, we
beseech thee, upon the work of thine hands; look mercifully upon the wounded world and its inhabitants, laden
with errors, labours, and sorrows; fill our hearts with compassion for those who suffer; and bring near thy kingdom
of mercy and peace; for the sake of Jesus Christ our Lord.
After Eugène Bersier

SUFFERERS   784

Remember every Christian soul, afflicted and oppressed,
and struggling and needing thy mercy and succour; and
our brethren that are in captivity and in prisons and bonds
and bitter thraldoms: supplying return to the wanderers,
health to the sick, deliverance to the captives, and rest to
them that have fallen asleep aforetime.
Lancelot Andrewes

785

We thank thee, O Father, for all who hallow suffering; for
those who in their thought for others leave no room for pity
for themselves; for those whose faith brings light to the

dark places of life; and for those whose patience inspires others to hold on. And grant, O loving Father, to all who are bound in the mysterious fellowship of suffering the sense of comradeship with others and the knowledge of thy love, and give them thy peace which passes all understanding; through Jesus Christ our Lord.   *H. L. Johnston*

786

O God, remember in thy mercy the poor and needy, the widow and the fatherless, the stranger and the friendless, the sick and the dying. Relieve their needs, sanctify their sufferings, strengthen their weakness; and in due time bring them out of trouble into the blessed peace of thy children; through Jesus Christ our Lord.   *Mothers' Union*

787

Merciful Lord, who art the strength of sufferers, and the comfort of those who are heavy of heart: incline thine ear, we beseech thee, to the prayers of all who cry unto thee in their troubles; succour the distressed, uphold the fainting, relieve the suffering, console the sad; and make thy face to shine upon them, O Lord, thou lover of souls.
Frederick B. Macnutt

HEALTH OF BODY   **788**

O God the Father of lights, from whom cometh down every good and perfect gift: mercifully look upon our frailty and infirmity, and grant us such health of body as thou knowest to be needful for us; that both in our bodies and in our souls we may evermore serve thee with all our strength and might.   *Bishop Cosin*

THE SICK   **789**

O Almighty God, who art the giver of life and health and the aid of all who seek thy succour: mercifully grant that thy help and goodness may be showed upon the suffering and the sick, that being healed of their infirmities they may give thanks unto thee in thy holy Church; through Jesus Christ our Lord.

790

O Lord and heavenly Father, who dost relieve those who suffer both in soul and body: stretch forth thine hand, we beseech thee, to heal the sick and to ease their pain; that by thy mercy they may be restored to health of body and mind, and show forth their thankfulness in love to thee and service of their fellow-men; through Jesus Christ our Lord.

Frederick B. Macnutt

IN ILLNESS 791

O Lord and heavenly Father, in whom we live and move and have our being: grant to me thy servant grace to desire only thy most holy will; that whether living or dying I may be thine; for his sake who loved us and gave himself for us, Jesus Christ our Lord. *Canadian Prayer Book*

THE DYING 792

O most merciful Lord, who dost so love the souls which thou hast created that thou wouldest not the death of any sinner, but that all should be converted and live: we pray thee by thy dying agony on the cross to purify through thy precious blood all the sinners in this world (*or* this thy servant) who are now in their (*or* who is now in his) agony, and who must this day die, and be called to appear before their (*or* his) judge. *Edward Bouverie Pusey*

793

O Lord Jesus Christ, who in thy last agony didst commend thy Spirit into the hands of thy heavenly Father: have mercy upon all sick and dying persons, and grant that they omit nothing which is necessary to make their peace with thee before they die. Deliver them, O Lord, from the snares of fear and the bands of evil, and grant them an end in peace; who livest and reignest with the Father and the Holy Spirit, one God, for evermore. *Sarum*

THOSE IN TROUBLE **794**

Almighty, everlasting God, comfort of the sorrowful and strength of the weary: may the prayers of all that call upon thee in any trouble come into thy presence; that they may rejoice that in their necessity thy mercy hath been with them; through Jesus Christ our Lord.

Edward Bouverie Pusey

IN TIME OF TROUBLE **795**

O God, who hast warned us of the troubles that shall come upon the earth; grant that thy Church may not be moved by any distresses that beset us, but may walk in the light, and serve thee with unshaken faith, waiting for the final manifestation of thy Son, Jesus Christ our Lord; that so we may be found abiding in the kingdom which cannot be shaken; through his merits, who liveth and reigneth with thee and the Holy Ghost, one God, world without end.

Richard Meux Benson

THOSE IN TROUBLE **796**

We humbly beseech thee, of thy goodness, O Lord, to comfort and succour all them who in this transitory life are in trouble, sorrow, need, sickness, or any other adversity: help us to minister to them thy strength and consolation, and so endow us with the grace of sympathy and compassion that we may bring to them both help and healing; through Jesus Christ our Lord. *1549 Prayer Book*

DOUBTERS **797**

O Lord our God, who givest light to them that sit in darkness and in the shadow of death: lift up, we pray thee, the light of thy countenance upon those who wander doubtful and uncertain in the night of this world. Open their eyes to behold thy glory in the face of Jesus Christ; make known to them the way of truth and peace; and keep them steadfast in this faith, that they may daily increase in the knowledge of thee and of thy Son by the Holy Spirit; through the same Jesus Christ our Lord.

THE DESPONDENT   **798**

Comfort, we beseech thee, most gracious God, all who are cast down and faint of heart amidst the sorrows and difficulties of the world; and grant that, by the energy of thy Holy Spirit they may be enabled to go upon their way rejoicing and give thee continual thanks for thy sustaining providence; through Jesus Christ our Saviour.

Richard Meux Benson

THE BLIND   **799**

O God, who art the Father of lights, with whom is no darkness at all: we thank thee for the good gift of sight which thou hast bestowed upon us. Fill us, we pray thee, with thine own compassion for those who have it not; direct and prosper the efforts that are made for their welfare: reveal to them by thy Spirit the things which eye hath not seen, and comfort them with the hope of the light everlasting; to which, of thy great mercy, we beseech thee to bring us all; through Jesus Christ our Saviour.

Arthur W. Robinson

THE DEAF AND DUMB   **800**

O God, the Father of our Lord Jesus Christ, who went about doing good, and both opened the ears of the deaf and made the dumb to speak: teach thy people, after his example, to pity and succour thy deaf children who need their help. May thy Holy Spirit bless our efforts to carry to them the knowledge of thy saving grace, and may they so serve thee in the body of their humiliation, that hereafter they may wear the body of thy glory; through Jesus Christ our Lord.   *Bishop Mandell Creighton*

THE DEAF AND THE BLIND   **801**

Almighty Father, who in the afflictions of thy people art thyself afflicted, whose blessed Son, Jesus Christ, went about doing good, healing all manner of sickness, opening the eyes of the blind, and unstopping the ears of the deaf: look, we beseech thee, upon those to whom is denied the gift of hearing or of sight. Give them the inward vision of

the spirit, and amid the silence of their lives make music in
their souls. Speak as of old and let them hear the inward
voice of thy compassion; and may thy new *Ephphatha* give
them new joy and fellowship with thee and with us thy
servants who minister to them; for the sake of Jesus Christ
our Lord.

IN OLD AGE 802

O Lord Jesus Christ, who didst hearken unto the prayer of
thy two disciples and abide with them, when it was toward
evening and the day was far spent: abide, we pray thee,
with thine aged servants in the evening of life. Make
thyself known unto them, and whensoever they shall pass
through the valley of the shadow of death, be with them
unto the end. *Unknown*

803

O Lord God, who hast promised that they who wait upon
thee shall renew their strength, and that as their days so
shall their strength be: comfort thou me according unto
thy Word; cast me not away in the time of age, and forsake
me not when my strength faileth; make thy face to shine
upon thy servant, and at evening time it shall be light;
through Jesus Christ our Lord. *Frederick B. Macnutt*

ENDURANCE OF SUFFERING 804

O my dear Lord, though I am so very weak that I am not
fit to ask thee for suffering as a gift, and have not strength
to do so, at least I will beg of thee grace to meet suffering
well, when thou in thy love and wisdom dost bring it upon
me. Let me bear pain, reproach, disappointment, slander,
anxiety, suspense, as thou wouldest have me, O my Jesu,
and as thou by thy own suffering hast taught me, when it
comes. *Cardinal Newman*

SERVICE OF THE NEEDY 805

O Christ, who being rich, for our sakes wast made poor;
King of glory, who didst will to become the man of
sorrows: teach us to serve thee in the person of our needy

brethren, weak, suffering, and set at naught; in fear lest at the last day we be of those to whom thou shalt say, Depart from Me.   *Eugène Bersier*

THE BEARING OF BURDENS   806

Lord, teach me the art of patience whilst I am well, and give me the use of it when I am sick. In that day either lighten my burden or strengthen my back. Make me, who so often in my health have discovered my weakness presuming on my own strength, to be strong in my sickness when I solely rely on thy assistance.   *Thomas Fuller*

807

O God, who art love, grant to them that are born of thee, and eat of thy Bread, out of sincere love to bear one another's burdens; that thy peace, which passeth all understanding, may keep our hearts and minds in Christ Jesus, thy Son our Lord.   *Edward Bouverie Pusey*

THE MEDICAL PROFESSION   808

O Lord, the healer of all our diseases, who knowest how the sick have need of a physician; bless all whom thou hast called to be sharers in thine own work of healing with health alike of body and soul; that they may learn their art in dependence upon thee, and exercise it always under thy sanction and to thy glory; who livest and reignest with the Father and the Holy Ghost, one God, world without end.
From 'Sursum Corda'

809

Almighty God, who art the Father of truth and understanding: shed forth, we beseech thee, upon those who are engaged in medical and surgical research the light of thy heavenly guidance; grant unto them the spirit of patient discernment, that they may be skilled to discover the way of health and healing; and strengthen them with the assurance that they are fellow-workers together with thee; through Jesus Christ our Lord.   *Frederick B. Macnutt*

810

O Lord Jesus Christ, who hast said that, inasmuch as we do it unto one of the least of these thy brethren, we do it unto thee: look upon thy servants who are called to nurse the sick and suffering children. Give them patience and fortitude, wisdom and love, and the grace and guidance of thy Holy Spirit; that they may faithfully minister to those to whom thou shalt send them, and be found worthy at the last to receive thy eternal reward.

Section 13

THE DEPARTED

DEATH 811

O God, who hast appointed unto men once to die, but hast hidden from them the time of their death: help us so to live in this world that we may be ready to leave it; and that, being thine in death as in life, we may come to the rest that remaineth for thy people; through him who died and rose again for us, thy Son Jesus Christ our Lord.

William Bright

LIFE AND DEATH 812

Good Lord, give me the grace so to spend my life, that when the day of my death shall come, though I feel pain in my body, I may feel comfort in soul; and with faithful hope of thy mercy, in due love towards thee and charity towards the world, I may through thy grace part hence into thy glory. *Sir Thomas More*

AT THE APPROACH OF DEATH 813

O my most blessed and glorious creator, that hast fed me all my life long, and redeemed me from all evil: seeing it is thy merciful pleasure to take me out of this frail body, and to wipe away all tears from mine eyes, and all sorrows from my heart, I do with all humility and willingness consent and submit myself wholly unto thy sacred will. My most loving redeemer, into thy saving and everlasting arms I commend my spirit: I am ready, my dear Lord, and earnestly expect and long for thy good pleasure. Come quickly, and receive the soul of thy servant which trusteth in thee.

Henry Vaughan

THE LIVING AND THE DEPARTED   **814**

Thou which art Lord at once of the living and of the dead; whose are we whom the present world yet holdeth in the flesh; whose are they withal whom, unclothed of the body, the world to come hath even now received: give to the living mercy and grace, to the dead rest and light perpetual: give to the Church truth and peace, to us sinners penitence and pardon.   *Lancelot Andrewes*

815

O Lord, we praise thy holy Name for all thy servants departed from amongst us in thy faith and fear; and we humbly beseech thee so to bless us that remain on earth, that, being protected from all evil, ghostly and bodily, we may ever serve and please thee with quiet minds and thankful hearts, and together with those that are gone before may have our refreshment in paradise and our portion in the resurrection of the just.

Frederick Temple

THE DEPARTED   **816**

O Lord our God, from whom neither life nor death can separate those who trust in thy love, and whose love holds in its embrace thy children in this world and in the next: so unite us to thyself that in fellowship with thee we may be always united to our loved ones whether here or there; give us courage, constancy, and hope; through him who died and was buried and rose again for us, Jesus Christ our Lord.   *William Temple*

817

O eternal Lord God, who holdest all souls in life: we beseech thee to shed forth upon thy whole Church in paradise and on earth the bright beams of thy light and heavenly comfort; that we, following the good example of those who have loved and served thee here and are now at rest, may with them at length enter into the fullness of thine unending joy; through Jesus Christ our Lord.

Bishop John Wordsworth

818

Remember, O Lord, the souls of thy servants and of thy handmaids, who have gone before us with the sign of faith, and slumber and sleep in peace. We beseech thee, O Lord, graciously to grant to them and to all who rest in Christ a place of refreshment, light, and peace; through the same Christ our Lord.   *The Roman Canon*

819

Into thy hands, O God, we commend the souls of all our loved ones (especially . . .) as into the hands of a faithful creator and most loving saviour; beseeching thee to grant unto them pardon and peace and, of thine infinite goodness, wisdom and power, to work in them the good purpose of thy perfect will; through Jesus Christ our Lord.

R. W. D. Lee

820

We commend unto thy mercy, O Lord, all thy servants who are departed hence from us with the sign of faith, and now do rest in the sleep of peace: grant unto them, we beseech thee, thy mercy and everlasting peace; and that at the day of the general resurrection we and all they who are of the mystical body of thy Son, may altogether be set on his right hand, and hear that his most joyful voice, Come, ye blessed of my Father, inherit the kingdom prepared for you from the foundation of the world. Grant this, O Father, for Jesus Christ's sake, our only mediator and advocate.   *Non-Jurors' Prayer Book*

821

Almighty God, whose love is over all thy works in this and every world: into thy hands we commit the souls of those whom thou hast taken into the world of light, beseeching thee to grant unto them the unutterable joys of thine eternal kingdom, and unto all who mourn them grace to abide thy will in fortitude of spirit and in perfect faith.

Anon.

822

Remember, O Lord, thy servants and thy handmaidens who have departed hence in the Lord, especially . . . and all others to whom our remembrance is due. Give them eternal rest and peace in thy heavenly kingdom, and to us such a measure of communion with them, as thou knowest to be best for us. And bring us all to serve thee in thine eternal kingdom, when thou wilt, and as thou wilt, only without shame or sin; through Jesus Christ our Lord.

Edward Bouverie Pusey

823

O Saviour of the world, whose nature and property is always to have mercy and to forgive, whose will is to have pity on all men, and whose loving-kindness is like the great deep: stablish my . . . , who has passed from this world of affliction and the shadow of death, in the place where light shineth for ever.

Anon.

A CHILD DEPARTED　**824**

O merciful Father, whose face the angels of thy little ones do always behold in heaven: grant us steadfastly to believe that this thy child hath been taken into the safe keeping of thine eternal love; through Jesus Christ our Lord.

American Prayer Book

825

Blessed Lord, who knowest thy sheep and callest them into thy fold, where none can harm them: we give thee thanks that it hath pleased thee to give to this thy child with thy flock in paradise a place of refreshment and rest. Keep her (*or* him) in peace, good shepherd, in the joy of thy presence; and grant her (*or* him) at last a portion with thy saints in the fullness of life everlasting; where thou livest and reignest with the Father and the Holy Spirit, one God, now and for ever.

Frederick B. Macnutt

THE SAINTS IN LIGHT   826

O King eternal, immortal, invisible, who in the righteousness of thy saints hast given us an example of godly life, and
in their blessedness a sure pledge of the hope of our calling;
grant, we beseech thee, that being compassed about with so
great a cloud of witnesses, we may run with patience the
race that is set before us, and with them receive the crown
of glory that fadeth not away; through Jesus Christ our
Lord.

THE LIFE OF HEAVEN   827

Bring us, O Lord God, at our last awakening into the house
and gate of heaven, to enter into that gate and dwell in that
house, where there shall be no darkness nor dazzling, but
one equal light; no voice nor silence, but one equal music;
no fears nor hopes, but one equal possession; no ends nor
beginnings, but one equal eternity; in the habitation of thy
glory and dominion, world without end.

After John Donne

MOURNERS   828

O heavenly Father, whose blessed Son Jesus Christ did
weep at the grave of Lazarus: look, we beseech thee, with
compassion upon those who are now in sorrow and
affliction; comfort them, O Lord, with thy gracious
consolations; make them to know that all things work
together for good to them that love thee; and grant them
evermore sure trust and confidence in thy fatherly care;
through Jesus Christ our Lord.

Canadian Prayer Book

                                                  829

O merciful Lord God, who hast given us thy Son to be the
bright and morning star, and to give light to them that sit
in darkness and in the shadow of death: look, we pray thee,
upon all whose hearts thou hast troubled by the loss of
those whom they love; draw them beneath the shadow of
thy wings; enlighten their eyes that they may endure as

P

seeing the invisible; and cheer them with largeness of hope and confidence in thy eternal purpose; through Jesus Christ our Lord. *J. Armitage Robinson*

830

O Lord Jesus Christ, who didst have compassion upon the widow of Nain and say unto her, Weep not, and by thine Apostle hast bidden us not to be sorry as men without hope for them that sleep in thee: visit, we beseech thee, with thy compassion those who mourn the loss of their beloved, and when thou comest in thy kingdom, wipe away all tears from their eyes; who livest and reignest with the Father and the Holy Spirit, ever one God, world without end.

In use at Salisbury

NOTES

These Notes are to be read in conjunction with the Index of Principal Authors immediately following; and also with the attributions printed beneath the Prayers.

1 and 5. *The Breastplate (Lorica) of St. Patrick, c. 373–463.* Best known in the metrical English version by Cecil Frances Alexander, *The Lorica* is preserved 'in a vellum manuscript of the eleventh century in the Library of Trinity College, Dublin,' known as 'The Irish Liber Hymnorum,' containing 'Hymns and Prayers in Latin and Irish which were used in the worship of the early Celtic Church.'

2. *Meditations and Devotions*, Part III.

3. Adapted from *Acts of Devotion*, p. 39.

6. Leonine, adapted Cf. *The Priest to the Altar*, p. 305.

9. *The Primer*, 1559. See in *Private Prayers of the Reign of Queen Elizabeth* (Parker Society, 1851).

10. *The Primer*, 1557: in *Godly Prayers* (Parker Edition) p. 294.

12. Adapted. Cf. *A Book of Prayers for Students*, p. 28.

14. *Village, Town, and Country Sermons, III.* The Transfiguration, p. 212.

15. From *A Thanksgiving by those relieved by the Waters*, shortened.

18. Part of the Morning Prayer of Martin Luther, printed in three languages for the Amsterdam Assembly of the World Council of Churches.

20. For Remembrance Day, November, 1946.

21. *Imitation of Christ*, Book IV, Chap. v. Translation by Charles Bigg, p. 205.

22. See A. W. Robinson, *Prayers New and Old*, p. 87, adapted.

23. From *A Collection of Letters on the most important and interesting Subjects* (Letter XI), published by two of his friends, George Ward and Thomas Langcake, in 1760.

24. Derived from the Coptic Liturgy of St. Cyril.

25. *Ecclesiastical History of the English People*, Book V, Chap. xxiv. A new translation.

26. *A Collection of Forms of Prayer* (Bristol, 1745), p. 11.

27. A Prayer of King Henry VI. A translation by Dean Milner-White, in 'Collegium Regale Beatae Mariae De

Etona Die Natali Fundatoris Regis Henrici Sexti,'
which is usually attributed to M. R. James, late Provost
of Eton.

28. Quoted in *Horae Mysticae*, p. 132. Slightly varied.
29. Author unkown. Adapted from *The Kingdom, the Power,
and the Glory*, p. 75.
30. Adapted from the Roman Breviary.
31. *The Splendour of God*, p. 13.
32. After an introductory sentence, this prayer combines two
fragments of prayer widely attributed to St. Francis.
33. *Prayers and Meditations*, edited by H. E. Savage.
35. Derived from S. Baring-Gould (1834–1924): *Golden Gate*,
p. 225.
37. Suggested by and derived from the 'Preacher's Prayer'
of Fulgentius Ruspensis (468–533), which is quoted by
Bishop Lancelot Andrewes: *Preces Privatae*, Before
Preaching.
39. *Ancient Collects*, p. 233.
40. Slightly varied from the adaptation by Dean Milner-
White in *After the Third Collect* of a prayer from
Speculum Ecclesiae.
41. See W. A. Knight, *Prayers Ancient and Modern*, p. 58.
Slightly altered.
42. *A Form of Compline and Additional Prayers*, p. 23.
Adapted from St. Fulgentius, for use at Westcott
House, Cambridge, by Bishop Westcott.
43. A retranslation of a famous Latin prayer of Erasmus from
Precationes, 1535, prayers written for use at Dean
Colet's School (St. Paul's School). This prayer is
contained in successive English Primers; e.g. 1545,
1552, 1557, etc. ('A prayer at your Uprising').
44. *Ancient Collects*, p. 234.
45. *Prayers Ancient and Modern*, p. 223.
46. *A Poet's Prayers*, XLVI.
48. The Prayer Book of Aedeluald the Bishop, commonly
called *The Book of Cerne*, edited by Dom A. B.
Kuypers, Benedictine of Downside Abbey (Camb.,
1902). *The Book of Cerne* is a collection of 74 prayers
and hymns, etc., attributed by Dom Kuypers to Mercia
in the first half of the ninth century. The prayers were
for use in private devotion, and are 'specimens of the
devotional, as distinguished from the liturgical, prayers
current in England in VIIth and VIIIth centuries.'
49. From *The Book of English Collects*.
50. A translation of the Vesper Hymn of the Greek Evensong
known as 'The Thanksgiving of the Lighting of the
Lamps.' St. Basil the Great described it as 'of un-

known authorship.' In English it is best known in Keble's fine translation, 'Hail, gladsome light' (*A. & M.*, 24), which, after appearing in a magazine, was published in *Lyra Apostolica*, 1836. The *Yattendon Hymnal* includes another translation (cf. *E. H.*, 269), 'O gladsome light, O grace.' There is a prose version in Newman's translation of Andrewes' *Preces Privatae* in *Tracts for the Times*, No. 88. J. M. Neale's prose translation will be found in *The Living Liturgy*, by M. H. Shepherd. See also Brightman's translation and note in his edition of Andrewes. Longfellow also translated it in *The Golden Legend*.

51. Henry Martyn was the well-known Anglican missionary. The prayer will be found in Bishop Boyd Carpenter's *The Communion of Prayer*.

52. *Prayers and Meditations on the Life of Christ*, Treatise II, Part II, Chap. vi. Translation by W. Duthoit, p. 326. Shortened.

53. *Preces Privatae*. Translation by F. E. Brightman.

55. Quoted from *The Tent and the Altar*, 1847, by William Boyd Carpenter, Bishop of Ripon (1884–1912), in *The Communion of Prayer*, p. 69.

56. *The Daily Service for Schools*. Slightly altered.

57. *Works*, edited by J. A. Giles (1843), Vol. I, p. 242.

58. The Liturgy of St. James: from the *Parastasis* (Prayer of Standing before the Altar), slightly adapted.

59. *Preces Privatae*.

60. See *Prayers of the City of God*, p. 19.

61. Adapted from several Eastern Orthodox Troparia. See *A Manual of Eastern Orthodox Prayers*, pp. 46, 49, 50.

63. Prayers in use at Cuddesdon College, 1929, p. 94. Sometimes ascribed to William Bright.

64. Thomas Becon was chaplain to Archbishop Cranmer. From *The Flower of Godly Prayers*.

66. Adapted from Leonine Sacramentary.

67. Sarum Prime. Cf. 1928 Prayer Book, *An Order for Prime*; and *The Hours of Prayer* (Mowbrays).

68. The distinguished prison reformer.

70. *Christian Praiers* (Parker Society), p. 169.

71. *Preces Privatae*. A third Form of Evening Prayer.

72. Benedict Pictet (1655–1724) was a theologian and pastor of the Reformed Church of Geneva. From *Psalms and Prayers* for the World Conference on Faith and Order, Edinburgh, 1937.

74. *A Summarie of Devotions*, Monday.

77 and 84. *The Mount of Olives*, edited by Grosart (1871), Vol. III. Shortened.

78. From the dean's private notebook.
79. Adapted by Archbishop Laud from Gregorius Nazian-
    zenus, Orat. 8.
81. Sixteenth century. Cf. H. J. T. Bennetts, *Devotions to
    the Holy Spirit*.
82. From *A Pocket Manual of Prayers*, 1860.
83. The author was a Nonjuring bishop deprived of his see
    in 1691. From his *Manual of Prayers for Winchester
    Scholars*. Clearly a variation upon the *Gloria in
    Excelsis*. The opening, e.g., adopts the Greek Morning
    Prayer version.
85. *Sacra Privata*, Evening.
86. See *A Plain Man's Prayer Book*, p. 35.
87. *Common Prayers for Family Use*.
88. *Salisbury Book of Occasional Offices*. Slightly revised.
90. *Sacra Privata*, Noon, and Sunday.
91. Translated from the Latin version of *The Spiritual
    Exercises*, 'Contemplation for obtaining Love.' See
    edition by W. H. Longridge (Mowbrays), p. 155,
    where there is a briefer translation from the Spanish.
    The Latin version is given in *St. Ignatius*, by Chris-
    topher Hollis (Sheed & Ward, 1931).
92. *A Call to Prayer* for the Life and Liberty Movement.
93. The author (died 1370) was a Carthusian prior at Stras-
    bourg. From *Vita Christi*.
94. From *Sursum Corda*: Thanksgiving, Friday, p. 194.
96. The Primer, 1553.
97. *Meditations on the Life and Passion of our Lord Jesus
    Christ*. (Trans. Cruikshank.)
98. *The Daily Service for Schools* (L.C.C. Edition), p. 71.
99. *Private Devotions*.
100. From his *Spiritual Exercises*.
101. *Precationes*. Abridged from the first paragraph of a long
     prayer, 'ad Filium.' Cf. *Imitation of Christ*, Book IV,
     Chap. lvi. 'I am the Way, the Truth, and the Life.
     Without the Way there is no going; without the Truth
     there is no knowing; without the Life there is no
     living. I am the Way which thou must follow; the
     Truth which thou must believe; the Life which thou
     must hope for.'
102. *Repton School Sermons*, p. 83.
103. *Devotions for Ordinary Days*, VI.
104. *Holy Living*, Prayers for Several Occasions, Chap. iv.
105. *Prayers*, p. 30. The Address, 'Lord,' is added.
106. Extracted from a prayer which occurs in *The Spirit of
     Prayer*. Cf. *Prayers for the City of God* (G. C. Binyon),
     p. 16.

108. Suggested by Gelasian III, 84, *Ad Matutinas*. Muratori, Col. 774.
109. Adapted by A. W. Robinson: *Prayers New and Old*, p. 81.
110. *Common Prayers*, p. 25.
111. *Prayers Ancient and Modern*, p. 206.
112. *Christian Prayers*, 1566.
113. Form of Service for the National Day of Prayer, March 26, 1941.
114. From the Gallican Liturgy of Alcuin of York (735–804): Migne, *Liber Sacramentorum*, Vol. I, Col. 450, 10.
115. See *Sursum Corda*, p. 201.
116. See Bishop Walsham How, *Daily Family Prayers*, p. 24.
117. The Liturgy of St. Chrysostom. From the Thanksgiving.
118. St. Ignatius of Loyola: or, perhaps more accurately, after St. Ignatius
120. *Preces Privatae*. (Trans. Brightman.)
122. From *The Mount of Olives*, 'A Prayer for the Evening,' p. 37.
123. From *Homily on St. Matthew xvi.* 24.
124. See *Private Prayers of the Reign of Queen Elizabeth*, 1564. (Parker Society.)
125. *Private Prayers*, 1836.
126. Adapted from Gregorian Sacramentary.
127. *Common Prayers*.
129. *Fellowship with God*, p. 243.
130. *Preces Privatae*, trans. Newman: *Tracts for the Times*, Order of Evening Prayer, p. 15.
131. *Common Prayers*, etc.
132. This translation of Alcuin's prayer is by Miss Helen Waddell, who in a private letter describes it as 'one of the great unknown prayers contained in a letter from Alcuin to Arno of Salzburg.'
133. *Gebete*: translated from the German for *Psalms and Prayers* of the World Conference of Faith and Order, Edinburgh, 1937.
134. Quoted in the 'Memoir of B. K. Cunningham,' the much-loved Principal of Westcott House, Cambridge, by John Moorman. Very slightly adapted.
135. Weimarischer Gesangbuch, 1873.
136. Source untraced, but ascribed to Thomas à Kempis in *Prayers Used at Cuddesdon College* (1929).
137. *Daily Office*. Sunday, Ninth Hour.
138. Liturgy of the Lutheran Swedish Church. Translated from a French version contained in *Venite Adoremus*.
140. Gelasian: *Oratio ad Matutinas;* III, 84. Muratori, Col. 743.

141. *Creation and Redemption.*
143. *Preces Privatae*, Morning Prayers. (Trans. Brightman.)
144. St. Nerses, Patriarch of the Armenians. Shortened.
146. *Out of the Deep*, 'Prayers and Confessions,' VII, 179. Other, adapted, versions of this prayer are in general circulation.
147. Ephraem of Edessa (*c.* 308–373), a famous 'Desert Father.' Another version will be found in Bishop Boyd Carpenter's *The Communion of Prayer.*
148. The source of this noble prayer which is in wide circulation cannot be traced.
149. Dwight L. Moody, the American evangelist. Quoted by Bishop Boyd Carpenter in *The Communion of Prayer.*
150. *Preces Privatae:* Praise, Blessing, Thanksgiving. (Trans. Brightman.)
151. *Daily Office*, Thursday.
152. *Patres Ecclesiae Anglicanae*, edited by J. A. Giles.
154. *Prayers Public and Private:* from Some Greek Devotions, abbreviated.
155. See *Sursum Corda*, p. 201.
156. This prayer is sometimes attributed to the Gelasian Sacramentary; while it originated there it has been much changed and adapted.
158. *Liturgie*, 1874, from the Order of Service for Sunday Evening.
159. Adapted from Mozarabic Rite.
160. *A Poet's Prayers.*
162. Derived from Thanksgivings in the *Order of the Opening Service* at the Bournemouth Church Congress, 1935.
164. *Private Devotions*, Vol. II, p. 166.
166. Malcolm Spencer, Congregationalist minister, for many years associated with the Student Christian Movement.
168. The Collect from the Lutheran Liturgy.
169. The Primer, 1545. From *The Third Hour.*
170. *Meditations and Devotions*, XXIII.
172. *A Summarie of Devotions*, 1705, p. 19.
174. *Sacra Privata*, Tuesday.
175. *The Non-Jurors' Prayer Book* (1718–19), *Fragmenta Liturgica*, V, 41.
176. Works, Vol. II. Prayers for the Evening.
178. *Preces Privatae*, Daily Prayers. Taken from *The Book of Common Order* (Knox's Liturgy, 1564).
179. *Prayers for the Home*, p. 61.
180. Taken from *The New Christian Year* of Charles Williams.
181. *Religio Medici*, Part II, Section xv. See *Golden Treasury* Edition.

182. *A Collection of Offices or Forms of Prayer in Cases Ordinary and Extraordinary*. Morning Prayer.

183. Based on a Gelasian collect for Pentecost: Muratori, I, 601.

184. The author was martyred in 1555. Quoted in *Westminster Prayers*.

185. *Preces Privatae:* Comprecation, A Prayer for Grace.

186. *Daily Office*, etc.

187. The Liturgy of St. James. At the beginning, 'Standing before the Altar.'

188. *The Flower of Godly Prayers* (Parker Society).

189. An anonymous translation of a Priest's Prayer of the Thirteenth Century. Sometimes ascribed to St. Francis of Assisi.

190. *Out of the Deep*, Prayers and Confessions, VII, 178.

191. Liturgy of St. Chrysostom. Post-Communion.

192. *Meditations*, IV. (Trans. C. C. J. Webb.)

193. *A Call to Prayer* for the Life and Liberty Movement.

195. Adapted from R. A. Reeves, Bishop of Johannesburg, in *A Quiet Room*.

197. After Walter Hilton, *The Scale of Perfection*. Cf. *A Pilgrim's Book of Prayers*, by Gilbert Shaw, Note, p. 154.

198. *Proslogion*, Chap. xxvi. (Trans. C. C. J. Webb).

199. Form for the Day of Remembrance, 1946.

200. Adapted from Mozarabic Use. Cf. R. M. Benson, *Manual*, p. 168.

202. Cf. Lancelot Andrewes, *Preces Privatae*.

203. Thomas Dekker: 'After St. Augustine.'

204. *Salisbury Book of Occasional Offices*, p. 73.

205. *Daily Offices*, etc. From 'Prayers added since the restoring of this book to me, which was taken from me in a search by Mr. Prynne, 1643, and with much difficulty restored unto me, Nov. 6, 1644.'

206. *Daily Office*, etc.

207. The authorship of this very widely used prayer is still uncertain. With variations of wording it is contained in P.B. 1928 (at the end of *Occasional Prayers*), the Scottish P.B. (in Compline), and the American P.B. (in Family Prayer). Printed with Tudor spelling ('troubelous,' 'buisy,' 'lodgeing,' etc.), it has been described as 'sixteenth century' and 'Elizabethan.' Some have erroneously attributed it to Bishop Lancelot Andrewes or Bishop Phillips Brooks, and others—with more probability—to Cardinal Newman. See a letter in *The Times*, April 13, 1935, by the late Dr. Vernon F. Storr, Canon of Westminster. In Newman's

Sermon, 'Wisdom and Innocence,' number XX in *Sermons bearing on Subjects of the Day* (2nd edit., 1844, p. 347), the following passage occurs without any suggestion of quotation: 'Let us beg of Him (our divine Lord) to stand by us in trouble, and guide us on our dangerous way. May He, as of old, choose "the foolish things of the world to confound the things which are mighty!" May he support us all the day long, till the shades lengthen, and the evening comes, and the busy world is hushed, and the fever of life is over, and our work done! Then in his mercy may he give us a safe lodging, and holy rest, and peace at the last!' This may seem decisive; but the fact of Tudor spelling in some current versions is not explained; and, after all, Newman may have been quoting.

208. *The English School Service Book*, p. 76.
209. *A Manual of Eastern Orthodox Prayers*, Part III, Kontakion, p. 23.
210. See *Venite Adoremus* (World's Student Christian Federation Prayer Book), Vol. I, p. 30. 'This prayer is an abridged text taken from the Order of Service prepared by Eugène Bersier,' and is incorporated in *Liturgie à l'usage des Eglises Réformées*.' For the French text with a different English translation ese *Venite Adoremus*, as above.
211. Derived from Gelasian III, 84, *Ad Matutinas*. Muratori, Col. 744.
212. From *Suspiria Animae*.
216. Liturgy of St. Chrysostom: The Prayer before the Gospel.
217. After Leonine Sacramentary.
218. *Sacra Privata*.
220. From *A Collection of Offices*.
221. Adapted from *Westminister Prayers*, 51.
222. From *An Horology* from Lancelot Andrewes (John Keble): *Sursum Corda*, p. 239.
223. An Ancient Homily by an unknown author sometimes described as 'The Second Epistle of St. Clement to the Corinthians.'
224. *Meditations and Devotions*, VII (2).
225. See Gasquet, *The Rule of St. Benedict*.
226. *A Collection of Offices*.
227. From *Repton School Sermons*.
228. *A Manual of Eastern Orthodox Prayers*, Part I.
229. The best of the varying translations
230. *Proslogion*, Chap. xviii. (Trans C. C. J. Webb.)
231. Adapted. Cf. *Westminster Prayers*, 49.
233. *Common Prayers for Family Use*.

234. 'A free translation of a prayer of Fr. Condren of the French Oratory' (Dean Milner-White, in *Liturgy and Worship*, p. 755).

235. See *Oremus*, Prayer Book of the Cambridge Delhi Brotherhood.

237. Derived from Gelasian III, 84. *Ad Matutinas:* Muratori, Col. 744.

238. *A Cambridge Bede Book*, LXIII.

239. From *Suspiria Animae*.

240. Dean Milner-White writes: 'This comes from the Founders' Day Prayers of Eton College and King's College, Cambridge. It dates from Queen Elizabeth's reign.'

242. Derived from a Collect in Bishop Walter Frere's *Collects, Epistles, and Gospels for the Lesser Feasts* (St. Jerome).

243. *The Church Looks Forward*, p. 92.

244. Ancient Scottish Collects in *The Iona Books* (1595).

246. *Daily Service*.

247. Adapted from Bright's *Ancient Collects*, p. 235.

248. *A Collection of Offices, etc.:* Morning Prayer for a Family.

250. *A Manual of Eastern Orthodox Prayers*, Part II, Evening Prayers.

251. The author was well known as Vicar of St. Martin-in-the-Fields, and later Dean of Canterbury.

252. Quoted in *A Prymer of the Holy Eucharist*.

253. Adapted from Eastern Orthodox.

254. Sermon 53, *De Diversis*.

255. From *Basic Convictions*.

256. The Primer, 1557, from 'The Suffrages' at the end of the Litany.

257. Derived by Dean Milner-White from a passage in the writings of John Donne. See *Daily Prayer*, p. 117.

258. American P.B. Ending shortened.

259. *Prayers and Meditations on the Life of Christ*. First chapter. (Trans. Duthoit.)

260. *English Prayers*. 'Prayers on the Passion,' p. 28.

261. The Primer, 1559.

262. See *The Communion of Prayer* by Bishop Boyd Carpenter.

264. *The Flower of Godly Prayers*, p. 68. Elizabethan 'Prayers,' etc.

265. *Daily Office*, etc. Sunday, Ninth Hour.

266. The Primer, 1558.

267. See *A Book of Prayers for Students*.

268. *A Diary of Private Prayer*, p. 115.

269. *Common Prayers for Family Use*, p. 34.

270. *Christian Praiers and Holy Meditations* (1566).

271. *Family Prayers.*
272. Shortened.
275. *Meditations and Devotions*, Part III.
276. *Common Prayers for Family Use.* Saturday.
278. *Prayers*, 'Act of Self-dedication.' From a manuscript prayer, shortened.
279. *The Church in Germany in Prayer*, p. 47. Slightly varied.
280. Adapted from *Salisbury Book of Occasional Offices.*
282. The Geneva Bible of 1560; Edition of 1578.
284 and 287. The Primer, 1559. See in *Private Prayers of the Reign of Queen Elizabeth* (Parker Society, 1851).
285. Used daily in the bishop's private chapels.
286. American P.B.: Prayers and Thanksgivings, For Christian Science.
288. From *Prayers of the World-Wide Church.* Based on the three opening suffrages of the *Litany for Missions*, in *Prime and Hours* and *The Priest's Book of Private Devotion.*
289. *A Collection of Private Devotions for the Hours of Prayer.*
290. From *The Daily Service for Schools* (L.C.C. Edition).
291. Adapted as a thanksgiving from the Oblation in the Liturgy of St. Mark.
292. *Prayers for the City of God*, p. 83.
293. W. Gray Elmslie (1848–89), Professor and Minister of the Presbyterian Church.
294. *Family Prayers for a Week*, p. 43. Slightly altered.
295. *Prayers*, printed privately. Translated and adapted from the Leonine Sacramentary.
296. *The Great Exemplar*, Part III, Section xv, Discourse xix.
298. Cf. another version in *Uncommon Prayers*, collected by Cecil Hunt (1898).
299. *A Cambridge Bede Book*, LXVI.
300. Sarum from Gregorian, 135. See First P.B. Edward VI, Advent III.
301. *A Book of Christian Prayers collected out of the Ancient Writers* (1578).
302. From a long prayer of Invocation: *Works*, Vol. III.
303. The opening of *An Evening Prayer.*
305. *Prayers Public and Private*, p. 39. Forms for Schol. Cancell. Lincoln.
306. From *The Treasury of Devotion*, p. 31.
307. *Sacra Privata.*
308. *Meditations and Devotions*, III (1).
309. Author unknown. *Prayers in use at Uppingham School.*
310. *A Cambridge Bede Book*, XXX.

311. This prayer is generally attributed to Francois de la
     Mothe Fénélon (1651–1715), Archbishop of Cambrai.
312. Derived from *The Book of Deer*. See Scottish P.B., 1929.
314. P.B. Collect for Epiphany I. Adapted by Archbishop
     Laud. *Daily Office.*
316. Supplement to *Sacra Privata.*
318. Canadian P.B., Forms of Prayer to be used in Families:
     Evening.
319. *A Manual of Eastern Orthodox Prayers*, Part V, p. 54.
320. From *A Devotion of the Eucharist.*
321. A much longer prayer, shortened. For a fuller version
     see *A Prymer of the Holy Eucharist*, pp. 65–6.
322. *Preces Privatae.* A Second Form of Morning Prayer.
     (Trans. Brightman.)
323. *Devotions*, The Office for Every Day.
324. *Prayers Public and Private*, pp. 107–8.
325. Adapted by the Rev. G. C. Binyon from a passage in
     the writings of Bishop F. Westcott. Cf. *Prayers for the
     City of God*, p. 11.
326. Official Form of the Day of Thanksgiving for Victory, 1945.
327. John Hunter, Minister of Trinity Church, Glasgow:
     Devotional Services for Public Worship (1901).
328. Mrs. Reinhold Niebuhr, *Radical Religion*, 1938. See
     Venite Adoremus II, p. 111.
329. From *Psalms and Prayers* for the World Conference on
     Faith and Order, Edinburgh, 1937. Professor Clavier
     of Strasbourg writes to me: 'This remarkable prayer is
     the famous "Confession des Peches" which is still
     used in most parishes of the Reformed Church of
     France.' It is ascribed to Calvin or his assistant,
     Theodore of Beza.
330. Liturgy of Geneva, *Confession*, by John Calvin (1509–
     1564). Part only of the appointed 'Confession.'
331. Adapted from *Venite*, A Book of Worship for Schools,
     Acts of Penitence, III.
332 and 333. Derived from various Biblical and liturgical
     sources.
335. Adapted from a translation of 'The Penitential Prayer of
     St. Ephraem the Syrian' (died 378) contained in *A
     Manual of Eastern Orthodox Prayers*, p. 38. Cf. Helen
     Waddell, *The Desert Fathers*, p. 302, for a much longer
     Confession.
336. *Prayers*, 'A Penitential Prayer,' p. 68. Shortened from a
     manuscript prayer.
337. A section of the prayer, 'To be offered each day before
     an image of Christ,' which appears in the Primers with
     the title, 'A Fruitful prayer to be said at all Times.'

338. Undated. *Prayers and Meditations*, ed. Savage, p. 130.
     Dr. Johnson's Prayers, ed. Trueblood, p. 37.
339. *Sacra Privata*.
340. *Prayers and Meditations*, ed. Savage, p. 119. *Dr. Johnson's Prayers*, ed. Trueblood, p. 36.
341. Derived from an ancient form of Absolution.
342. From Lydney's *Praiers*, a section of Henry Bull's *Christian Praiers and Holy Meditations*, 1568.
343. *Preces Privatae*. Translated by Cardinal Newman for *Tracts for the Times*, No. 88. Slightly altered.
344. Adapted by Archbishop Laud from the P.B. Litany. *Daily Office*, etc.
345. *Sacra Privata*.
347. Adapted from a prayer in a pamphlet issued by the Archbishops' Advisory Committee, *A Way of Renewal* (1932), p. 17.
348. *Confessions*, Book I, Chap. vi. (Trans. C. Bigg.)
349. Adapted from Gothic: *Sanctorum Decus*. Cf. *Sursum Corda*, p. 119.
350. Sarum for Trinity XXV (i.e. XXVII post-Pent.) and P.B., 1549, from Gregorian II, 176.
351. Sarum for Advent I, from Gregorian, 133. The Sarum Collects for Advent I, II, and IV, and the Sunday next before Advent. All began with the word 'Excita,' 'which had been used in the Gelasian Advent collects in connection both with man's heart and God's power' (Bright, *Ancient Collects*, p. 220). Of these four collects there only remain two in the Anglican Prayer Book, Advent IV and Trinity XXV, the Sunday next before Advent. For the Latin original, etc., of these collects see Brightman, *The English Rite*, Vol. I, p. 200, etc., or Procter and Frere, *A New History of the Book of Common Prayer*.
352. Sarum for Advent IV from Gelasian II, 80. This and the Collect for Trinity XXV (next before Advent) are the only 'Excita' collects which remain in the Anglican Prayer Book. This and Trinity XXV have been in-included to accompany the others which were appointed in the old English Service Books.
353. The first part of this prayer, from Gelasian II, 81, introduced the Collect which was replaced in 1549 by the present Collect for Advent II.
354. Gelasian II, and Bright, *Ancient Collects*, p. 16.
355. *The Non-Jurors' Prayer Book*, 1734.
356. *A New Prayer Book* (1924). Collect for Advent IV.
357. For the phrase 'thine eternal pact and promise' see Archbishop Matthew Parker's prayer for Psalm cxxxii.

358. From an unpublished prayer.

359. Derived from Mozarabic Use. Cf. Alcuin Club *Prayer Book Revision Pamphlets*, No. 3, *A Century of Collects*.

361. See *The Book of English Collects*, by Jonh W. Suter, p. 448 and note, 'From the Altus of St. Columba,' and the Scottish P.B., Post-Communions: Collects, 3.

362. Adapted from three of the great Sarum Advent Antiphons sung before *Magnificat* on the last days of Advent. (Bright, *Ancient Collects*.)

363. Derived from *A Priest's Book of Private Devotion*, p. 363.

364. The opening was suggested by Gelasian (Bright, *Ancient Collects*); and the phrase 'no more need of light from lamp or sun' is taken from Mgr. R. Knox's translation of Revelation xxii. 5.

365. Gregorian, 135. Cf. Collect Advent III before 1662.

366. *A New Prayer Book*, p. 37. 'The First Coming.'

367. Adapted from Leonine through Roman, Ordo Missae 222, At the Benediction of the Oblations; and Sarum Christmas II.

368. From Leonine: Scottish P.B., Christmas II.

369. Written for the Service at the Crib in York Minster.

370. *Daily Prayer*, p. 23.

371. Sarum from Gelasian II, 84. (In Vig. Nat. Dom. ad Nonam.)

373. *A New Prayer Book* (1923), Part I: Collect for Christmas.

374. *Prayers* (1899). From a manuscript prayer.

375. Adapted from *The Kingdom, The Power, and The Glory*. Prayers and Biddings, p. 73.

376. Adapted from the Collect for New Year's Day appointed in the 1928 Prayer Book, and the longer versions in the Scottish, Irish, and Canadian Prayer Books.

377. *Prayers and Thanksgivings*, Collect for New Year's Day.

378. Derived from the opening of a long Mozarabic prayer for the New Year. See Bright, *Ancient Collects*, p. 164.

379. W. E. Orchard, former Minister of King's Weigh House Church, London: *Divine Service*, Proper Collects of the Season, New Year's Day, p. 143. Slightly adapted.

380. *Collects etc. for Various Occasions*, August 7th.

381. Based on Gelasian. Cf. Bright, *Ancient Collects*, p. 27.

382. See *The Treasury of Devotion*, p. 161.

383. Charles Henry Brent, late Bishop of Western New York: from *With God in Prayer*. Bishop Brent was one of the early pioneers of the Oecumenical Movement.

384. From the Service of the Hallowing of the Bells, Clock, and Chimes of Leicester Cathedral 1937.

385. 'From the prayer with which Calvin concludes his exposition of Habakkuk.' See Sir George Adam

Smith, *The Book of the Twelve Prophets*, Vol. II, p. 159.

386. This is a revision of the 1549 Prayer Book collect of the Epiphany, written for the Prayer Book of the Church in Persia by request.

387. Scottish P.B., Post-Communions, Epiphany and seven days after.

388. Cf. Bright, *Ancient Collects*, p. 29.

389. Suggested by several Epiphany collects in Bright, *Ancient Collects*, pp. 28–30.

390. After Mozarabic. Cf. Bright, *Ancient Collects*, p. 87.

391–4. After Gelasian. Cf. Bright, *Ancient Collects*.

396. From an unpublished manuscript.

397. From a longer prayer written for the Guild of Health. See *Prayers of Health and Healing*, p. 11.

399. Adapted from a Roman collect in the Palm Sunday Office of the Blessing of Palms.

400. Adapted from a Sarum Collect. Cf. E. A. L. Clarke, *A People's Missal*.

401. From the Office for the Royal Maundy in Westminster Abbey. Wording slightly revised.

402. Cf. the many editions of the 'Hours.' See *The Priest's Book of Private Devotion*, p. 61.

403. Peter Abelard (1079–1142). This is a prose version of Abelard's *Solus ad Victimam procedis, Domine* (*In Parasceve Domini: III. Nocturno: Good Friday, the third Nocturn*), one of the collection of 93 hymns which form part of the Breviary of the Paraclete, composed for the use of the Sisterhood at the request of Heloise, after she had become Abbess of the Paraclete. For the original Latin lyric and a charming verse translation see Helen Waddell, *Mediaeval Latin Lyrics*, pp. 166–7, 336–7.

404. From *The Treasury of Devotion*.

405. From a long prayer: *Coram Imagine Christi Crucifixi*, Tom. I, p. 101. *Christian Prayers*, 1578.

406. Adapted from Gallican Use. Cf. *Freedom, Love, and Truth* (W. R. Inge), p. 337.

407. The last passage in a Good Friday sermon quoted in his *Life*, Vol. I, p. 250.

409. *The Worthy Communicant*, Chap. v, Section vii.

410. Cf. *Wells Office Book*, p. 113.

412. P.B., 1928.

413. *A Harvest of Myrrh and Spices*, XLIX. Adapted from Draper's translation.

414. *Prayers*, I. (Trans. C. C. J. Webb.) Shortened.

415. *The Church in Germany in Prayer*, p. 51. The opening

sentence is slightly varied from the original translation, and 'ones' is added after 'faithful.' In *Venite Adoremus* this prayer is ascribed to Löhe (1808–72).

416. After 1 St. Peter i. 3, 4, 8. Cf. Dean Milner-White, *After the Third Collect.*

417. Hebrews xiii. 20–21, in prayer form. See *Daily Prayer*, p. 36.

418. P.B., 1549, from Gregorian; P.B., 1928, as 'An additional Collect on Easter Day and seven days after'; and the American P.B.

419. Frequently used by Archbishop William Temple (and his Father, Archbishop Frederick Temple) in his private chapel and otherwise on great festivals. The author is unknown.

422. *A New Prayer Book*, 1923, p. 75. Derived from Gelasian in the first half, and from Colossians iii. 1 in the second.

423. Adapted from Old Gallican. Cf. Bright, *Ancient Collects*, p. 57.

424. Adapted from Mozarabic. Cf. Bright, *Ancient Collects*, p. 58.

425. *Prayers*, p. 16. W.P. 279.

426. Quoted in *Horae Mysticae*, p. 148.

428. Including phrases from the Resurrection narratives of St. Luke and St. John, and from the Epistles of St. Paul and St. Peter.

429. Adapted from Scudamore, *Manual of Daily and Occasional Prayers* (1874).

431. Collect for Ascension Eve (*Alternative Form of the Order for the Administration of the Holy Communion*, 1938).

432. Post-Communion for *Ascension Day and until the Vigil of Whitsunday inclusive.*

433. Derived from *A New Prayer Book*, 1923: Sunday after Ascension.

434. Adapted from (*a*) Phrases in the *Salisbury Book of Occasional Offices*, p. 12; (*b*) The A.V. of Ephesians i. 10, 22–3.

435. *A Cambridge Bede Book*, XLIV.

436. See *Preces Veterum*, CXXX; and Bright, *Ancient Collects*, p. 79. Sometimes erroneously ascribed to Phillips Brooks, Bishop of Massachusetts, who may have quoted a translation.

437. Cf. *The Priest to the Altar*, p. 98. Slightly varied.

440. Derived from (*a*) the Proper Preface for Ascension Day, 1662; (*b*) Colossians iii. 1; (*c*) St. John xiv. 3.

Q

441. Antiphon for Ascension Day. This is the Evening Anthem for Ascension Day in Magdalen College Chapel, Oxford.

442. Tom. I, p. 120. 'A Prayer to Christ ascending and reigning in glory.' Slightly shortened.

443. Scottish P.B., Post-Communions, Whitsunday.

444. *Prayers of the Spirit*, p. 24.

445. Gelasian: Muratori I, 602. Cf. Bright, *Ancient Collects*, p. 63.

446. Derived from Gelasian. Cf. Bright, *Ancient Collects*, p. 62.

447. See A. W. Robinson, *Prayers New and Old*, p. 54.

448. Scottish P.B., Post-Communions, Trinity Sunday.

449. For The Transfiguration, August 6th.

450. The Transfiguration. The Scottish P.B. Collect.

451. American P.B. (by William R. Huntingdon, 1892).

452. Based on the American P.B. (1918).

453. Adapted from Troparion and Kontakion for the Festival of The Transfiguration (August 6th) of the Eastern Orthodox Church.

454. *The English Liturgy*. Edited. by Dr. Percy Dearmer, assisted by Bishop Frere and Bishop S. M. Taylor.

455. In section *Saint's Days in the Kalendar not otherwise provided for*. 'Thy saints' is substituted for 'thy servant, Saint N.'

456. South African P.B. Appendix, and cf. P.B., 1928: *Collects, Epistles, and Gospels for the lesser Feasts and Fasts*, 'Of any Saint.'

457. Adapted from the Preface appointed in P.B., 1928, 'Upon All Saints' Day, and the Feasts of Apostles, Evangelists, etc.' Suggested by a similar use of this Preface by the Archbishop of Canterbury at the closing service of the Lambeth Conference, 1948, held in St. Paul's Cathedral.

458. *Ancient Collects*, p. 236, slightly altered as suggested by Dean Milner-White, *Occasional Prayers*, 1928, *Reconsidered*.

459. Adapted. Bright, *Ancient Collects*, p. 69.

460. Derived from Gregorian. The original Latin will be found in *A Century of Collects* (57), p. 25.

461. Collects, Epistles, and Gospels for the lesser Feasts and Fasts; November 8.

462. Written in 1926 for the Dedication of Westcott House Chapel, Cambridge.

463. Written for the annual commemoration in Canterbury Cathedral of St. Thomas à Becket, murdered on December 29, 1170.

464. Cf. *Prayers in Use at Uppingham School*. Slightly altered.

465. Contained in *A Suggested Prayer Book* (known in Church Assembly as 'The Green Book').

467. Canadian P.B. (1918): 'On Rogation Days and at other times.'

468. *Salisbury Book of Occasional Offices*, p. 164.

470. *Works*, Vol. II (Lib. of Anglo-Cath. Theol.).

472. *Prayers Public and Private*, p. 70.

473. Scottish P.B., At the Thanksgiving for Harvest.

474. Adapted from a Collect of Harvest Thanksgiving in the American P.B. dating back to 1792, when there was appointed 'a Day of Thanksgiving to Almighty God, for the Fruits of the Earth, and all other blessings of his merciful Providence.'

475. Authorized by Convocation for use at Harvest Festivals, 1862.

476. Convocation, 1862.

477. Adapted from the prayer after the Tract of the 8th Prophecy (Isaiah iv) in the Roman Office for Holy Saturday.

478. Convocation, 1862. In general use.

479. The Primer, 1557. Parker Edition, p. 45, at the end of 'Grace' before and after meals. Cf. Primer of Henry VIII, 1545, etc.

480. Included in the Office for the Feast of Corpus Christi prepared by Aquinas at the command of Pope Urban IV. Opera (edit. Parma, 1864), Vol. XV, *Opuscula*, p. 253.

481. *The Priest to the Altar*, P. G. Medd (1898), p. 149.

482. Prayer used in the Sacristy before Celebrations of Holy Communion at Canterbury Cathedral, adapted by Canon A. J. Mason (died 1928). See Bright, *Ancient Collects*, p. 137.

483. Cf. Percy Dearmer, *The Sanctuary*, p. 97.

484. *Ancient Collects*, p. 16.

485. Adapted from the prayer of the Roman Benediction of the water and the sine at the Oblations. Cf. P.B., 1928, Christmas II, for another version.

486. *Salisbury Book of Occasional Offices*, p. 16. In the first line 'we' is substituted for 'they,' and 'in this place' is omitted.

487. Adapted from *A New Prayer Book*, Pentecost XXI.

488. Adapted from *A New Prayer Book*, Easter III.

489. Liturgy of St. James: The Priest's confession before reception. For the original see Brightman, *Liturgies Eastern and Western*, pp. 63–4.

490. Adapted from the translation of 'A Prayer of St. Chrysostom' contained in *The Orthodox Liturgy, according to the Use of the Church of Russia* (S.P.C.K., 1939).

491. Adapted from the conclusion of a translation of a prayer of St. Basil the Great, Bishop of Caesarea (330–79).

492. *The Great Exemplar*, Part III, Section xv, Discourse xix.

493. *The Daily Office* (1705); Sunday. In the Holy Sacrament.

494. *The Mount of Olives*, pp. 69–70. Shortened, but not adapted.

495. Scottish P.B. See J. W. Suter, *The Book of English Collects*, 162 and note.

496. See *A Simple Form of Compline*, B. K. Cunningham, p. 37.

498. Adapted from an Ante-Communion prayer in the *Wells Service Book*, p. 122.

499. *Liturgy of St. Chrysostom:* The Communion, For the original see Brightman, *Liturgies Eastern and Western* p. 394.

500. *Imitation of Christ*, Book III, Chap. i. Shortened. (Trans. Charles Bigg.)

501. From *Precationes*.

502. *A Collection of Offices:* An Office for the Holy Communion, Post Communion, Eucharistical Prayers I.

503. *The Mount of Olives* (1871), p. 70.

504. *Maxims of Piety and Morality*, p. 45.

505. *Village Sermons*, XVI, The Crucifixion, p. 126. Shortened.

506. This prayer to be said *At the Sanctus* is taken from *The Lay Folks Mass Book* (*c.* 1175). edited by T. F. Simmons, Canon of York (Early English Text Books, 1879).

507. Cf. Dearmer, *The Sanctuary*, p. 99.

508. Cf. Dearmer, *The Sanctuary*, p. 108.

509. *Piae Preces*, Oratorio post Communionem; Parma Edition, Vol. XXIV, p. 245. This is the best of many translations, and with slight variations it will be found in *The Cuddesdon Office Book* (1940), p. 166.

510. *The Worthy Communicant*, Chap. vii, Section ii, After the Communion.

511. The Prayer of Dismissal. The early part is said by the Deacon, and the latter part by the Priest 'as he goes from the Altar to the Sacristy.' See Brightman, *Liturgies Eastern and Western*, pp. 67–8. This translation is the result of comparing the Greek original with several translations current in modern English collections.

512. Adapted from Leonine. Cf. Bright, *Ancient Collects*, p. 151.

513. *Manual of Prayers* for Winchester scholars.
514. *The Daily Office*, etc. Edition 1705. Sunday: Immediately after receiving both Kinds, p. 102.
515. Gelasian: Muratori I, 364. Cf. H. J. T. Bennetts, *Devotions to the Holy Spirit*, p. 28.
516. Scottish P.B.: Collects for Various Occasions, At a Thanksgiving for the Institution of Holy Baptism. Derived from a Roman Prayer.
517. P.B. 1928: Collects, Epistles, and Gospels of the Lesser Feasts and Fasts.
518. *Manual*, p. 53. Slightly adapted.
520. *Prayers of Health and Healing*, for the Guild of Health, p. 70.
521. American P.B. Collect for St. Luke's Day.
522. After the Trisagion in the Liturgy of St. Mark. Cf. another version in *Prayers for Healing*, p. 17.
523. From *A Prayer Book Revised*, with the addition of the words 'and the use of thy provided means.'
524. This morning prayer dated 'May 21, 1890, Cuddesdon,' and found after the Archbishop's death among his private papers, was written on the eve of his Ordination as Deacon.
525. Adapted from a prayer in use in theological colleges, e.g. *Wells Office Book*, p. 28.
526. *Priest's Prayer Book*, p. 22. 'From among us' is substituted for 'in it.'
527. *Cuddesdon College Office Book*, Terce, p. 25.
528. *Daily Office*, etc. (1705).
529. Derived from the Ordinal and included, e.g., in a Service sometimes in use in St. Paul's Cathedral. Cf. *The Priest to the Altar*, p. 241.
531. *A Call to Prayer*, Life and Liberty (1917).
532. *Preces Privatae:* Morning Prayer, second form, Intercession.
533. Included in a leaflet *Prayers*, issued for use in Peterborough diocese by Bishop F. T. Woods in 1921.
534. Gelasian: Muratori I, 560. Cf. Duchesne, *Christian Worship*, p. 109.
535. Liturgy of St. Chrysostom. For the original see Brightman, *Liturgies Eastern and Western*, p. 397; and for another translation, see, e.g., Neale and Littledale, *Translations of the Primitive Liturgies*, p. 124.
536. Cf. Bright, *Ancient Collects*, p. 103.
537. From the Prayer for the Church in the Liturgy of the Swedish Lutheran Church (*Lutherische Hochmesse*).
538. *The Golden Grove.* Litanies for all Things and Persons IV, Vol. VII, p. 637.

539. *Holy Living:* Prayers for Several Occasions, Section 7.

540. From *Ecclesia*, in *A Summarie of Devotions*. Lib. Ang. Cath. Theol., Laud's Works. Vol. III, p. 68.

541. See *Prayers New and Old*, A. W. Robinson, p. 48.

542. The first of a sequence of three prayers in *A Litany of Fellowships*, Life and liberty (1918).

544. The first Post-Reformation form of Accession Service was issued in 1576. See *Liturgical Services of the Reign of Queen Elizabeth*, Parker Society, pp. 548 f. This was altered and added to in subsequent reigns. 'At the Accession of George I the Prayer for Unity was added.' (Procter and Frere, *A New History of the Book of Common Prayer*, p. 645, Note 5.)

545. The Liturgy of St. Mark: The Prayer of the Kiss of Peace. For the original see Brightman, *Liturgies Eastern and Western*, p. 123. Adapted.

547. *Gebete*. Translated from the German for *Psalms and Prayers* of the World Conference on Faith and Order, Edinburgh, 1937.

548. Dean Milner-White reprints this prayer with two others in his article 'Modern Prayers and their Writers,' in *Liturgy and Worship*, pp. 749 f., with the words: 'In 1845 ... Keble, Pusey, and Marriott circulated some short prayers for use at the traditional Hours. Which of these was the actual author we do not know.'

549. *A Call to Prayer*, Life and Liberty Movement, 1918.

550. After *The Splendour of God*, p. 12.

552. Adapted from Mozarabic Use. Cf. Bright, *Ancient Collects*, p. 76

554. For Diocese of Gibraltar. See Gibraltar Diocesan Journal, 1938.

555. Cf. R. M. Benson, *Manual*, p. 143.

556. *Prayers and Intercessions for the Lambeth Conference*, 1930, arranged by Bishop F. T. Woods.

557. After P.B., 1662: *The Form of Ordaining or Consecrating of an Archbishop*. As adapted for use at the Enthronement of an Archbishop in Canterbury Cathedral. 'Who is now' is omitted before 'enthroned.'

558. P.B., 1662. *The Form of Ordaining or Consecrating of an Archbishop or Bishop:* The Collect.

559. See Archbishop E. W. Benson, *Prayers Public and Private*, p. 45.

560. A widely-used version of the previous prayer.

561. Prayer from the Enthronement Service of Dr. J. W. C. Wand as Bishop of London in St. Paul's Cathedral, October 9, 1945.

562. *Daily Office* (1705), p. 208.

563. Canadian P.B., 36. *The Form of Institution and Induction.*
565. Adapted from a Latin Prayer composed by Canon A. J. Mason (died 1928), regularly in use by the Chapter of Canterbury Cathedral.
567. Written by the late Ven. A E. Daldy, Archdeacon of Winchester, for the division of the Diocese of Winchester, 1927.
568. For the Diocese of Leicester.
570. S. African P.B.: *For Several Occasions,* 8. Ember Days, Collect 3. (Alternative Form of H.C.)
571. In R. M. Benson's *Intercessions Manual,* p. 41.
572. *Oremus,* Prayer Book of the Delhi Christian Brotherhood, p. 63.
573. *Hours of Prayer for Daily Use throughout the Year,* 1856.
574. Contained in his private note-book with the title 'For the Clergy of St. Margaret's' (Westminster).
575. *Manual,* p. 236.
576. *A Book of Parish Intercessions,* p. 28.
578. *Prayers, Public and Private,* p. 36.
579. *Salisbury Book of Occasional Offices,* p. 175.
580. *Manual of Intercessory Prayer,* p. 40. For a revised version see Dean Milner-White, *The Occasional Prayers in the 1928 Book Reconsidered,* p. 14.
581. *Intercessory Manual.*
583. The Prayer for the Order of Deaconesses approved by the Council for the Order, and authorized for use in the Diocese of Canterbury.
584. From the *Form and Manner of Making of Deaconesses,* adopted by the Upper House of the Convocation of Canterbury and York.
585. For the work of Church Extension in the Diocese of Leicester.
586. Written in the first instance in 1939, in connection with the building of Guildford Cathedral.
587. Adapted by H. P. Liddon.
588. *Manual:* For the Church at Large, 10, p. 34.
589. *Manual,* p. 129.
590. Adapted from a prayer in the *Salisbury Book of Occasional Offices,* p. 107.
591. Used in Salisbury Cathedral at Choral Festivals and Organ Recitals.
595. A vestry prayer at The Temple, London.
596. This is the complete version of this prayer. See *Sursum Corda,* p. 108, which is erroneously attributed to R. M. Benson.
597. Cf. another version in *A Book of Prayers for Schools,* p. 154.

598. Derived from several Salisbury prayers.

600. *Hours of Prayer for Daily Use through the Year*, Sext (1856).

601. A prayer widely used in the bishop's dioceses and elswhere.

602. *Ancient Collects*, p. 237.

603. Adapted from *A New Prayer Book*, 1923, commonly known as 'The Grey Book': Collect for Pentecost XXI.

604. From a Southwark Diocesan Form for the *Licensing of a Lay Woman Worker*.

605. Cf. *Sursum Corda*, p. 85.

608. *Salisbury Book of Occasional Offices*, p. 196. Slightly altered.

609. Scottish P.B. Thanksgiving for Harvest, 2.

610. *The Hours of Prayer* (Sarum Breviary), p. 395, edition 1928. Collect for the Feast of Christ the King.

611. The original version of this prayer.

612. Official Form for the National Day of Prayer, 1940.

613. *Sacra Privata*. Extracted from some longer prayers.

614. Derived from passages in the Epistle to the Ephesians and from phrases in a missionary prayer once widely in use.

615. Irish P.B.: *Prayers and Thanksgiving*, Mission Districts of the Home Church.

616. *A New Prayer Book*, Collect of Epiphany V.

617. Widely circulated at the time of the 'Way of Renewal,' and also in more recent years, in slightly varying versions: author unknown.

618. Adapted from Gelasian: Whitsunday. Cf. *The Priest to the Altar*, p. 102.

619. *Intercessory Manual*, p. 47.

622. Eugène Bersier was one of the chief leaders of the French Reformed Church for half a century. He was pastor in Paris, 1855–c. 1895, and was celebrated as a preacher. One of his best-known works is his *Liturgie à l'usage des Eglises Réformées*, published 1874. This prayer occurs (p. 47, Edit. 1876) in the *Ordre à suivre pour le service ordinaire du Dimanche Matin*.

623. This and many other Missionary Prayers are contained in *Prayers of the World-wide Church* (S.P.G., 1947).

624. In wide circulation. Author unknown.

625. *A Poet's Prayers*, LVI.

626. Bishop Cotton of Calcutta, 1856. Canon J. R. Peacey writes in the *Guardian* of July 11, 1947, stating that this prayer originally contained the phrase 'all the people of this land,' and not 'all the peoples of the world,' and that, as thus written by Bishop Cotton,

it 'is used in almost all the Churches in India after the Collect for the day by the authority of the Bishops.' See P.B., 1928, *Occasional Prayers*, 9, for the version in general use elsewhere, as in the text.

628. Divine Service, Missionary Litany, p. 81 (1919).

629. *A Naval Prayer Book*, by D. J. N. Wanstall, p. 45. Slightly altered.

630. Adapted from a Collect in the Roman Good Friday Office of the Mass of the Pre-Sanctified.

631. From *A Suggested Prayer Book* by the Church Union in view of the proposed Revision which led to the issue of P.B., 1928. The Collect for the Missionary Work of the Church.

633. From *A New Prayer Book*, Pentecost.

634. Derived from a missionary prayer: author unknown.

635. From *Sursum Corda*. Slightly altered.

636. *Manual of Offices* of St. Augustine's College, Canterbury, p. 47.

637. Bishop Bardsley was at one time Hon. Secretary of the Church Missionary Society, and Secretary of the Missionary Council of the Church Assembly.

638. Cf. *Wells Office Book*, p. 143.

639. Cf. *Prayers in Use at Uppingham School*, p. 45 (1929). Slightly altered.

640. Derived from a prayer of the Church Missionary Society, which is included in *Morning Prayers and Readings for School and Family*, compiled by Mrs. Guy Rogers.

641. Authorized by Convocation for use at Harvest Festivals, 1862.

643. *The Kingdom, the Power, and the Glory:* Prayers and Biddings, 36b, p. 76.

644. This prayer was written on a loose leaf in the dean's notebook with the bidding, 'Let us lift up our hearts unto the one God and Father of all, that grace may be given unto us to preach unto the heathen the unsearchable riches of Christ, and to set forward the salvation of all men.'

646. *Salisbury Book of Occasional Offices*, p. 195.

647. *Sacra Privata*.

648. Adapted from a prayer, S.P.G. Cf. *Prayers of the Worldwide Church*, p. 14.

649. Scottish P.B.: *Prayers and Thanksgiving*, 15. Cf. 19 and P.B., 1928. *Occasional Prayers*, 9.

650. Adapted from the Collect for June 5th (St. Boniface) in *Collects, Epistles, and Gospels for the Lesser Feasts according to the Calendar set out in 1928.* Arranged by Bishop Frere.

651. The Collect of the Communion of the *Order of Service for the Coronation*, 1937. Adapted.

652. From *A Chaplet of Prayers for the Coronation*, 1937. Adapted.

653. From the *Order of Service for the Coronation*, 1937.

654. From *A Chaplet of Prayers for the Coronation*, 1937. Adapted.

655. P.B. Collect of the Accession Service, brought up to date (1952).

656. Adapted from a prayer in wide use at youth services.

657. From the *Form of Service for the National Day of Prayer*, August 4, 1918. Widely in use 1918–38. Adapted.

658. A prayer of the Oxford Mission to Calcutta.

661. From *Acts of Devotion*. Adapted.

662. The prayer appears in a Peterborough Diocesan Leaflet of Prayers issued by the bishop in 1919.

663. An adaptation of two prayers: (*a*) one from Westminster Abbey Intercession Paper, November, 1938; and (*b*) a prayer in use in Leicester Cathedral before 1938.

664. *Acts of Devotion*, p. 49; widely used with variations of wording.

665. From *A Chaplet of Prayers for the Coronation*, 1937.

666. The original version of this prayer by Archbishop Laud will be found in his *The Daily Office of a Christian*, 1705. The version in the text was suggested by Dean Milner-White in *The Occasional Prayers of the 1928 Book Reconsidered*.

667. Source unknown.

668. Author unknown. Traced only as far back as 1928, when the revision of the Prayer was before Parliament.

669. From 'Prayers for the Parliament,' used daily before the meetings of the House of Lords and the House of Commons. The prayer is said to have been used in the Commons from 1660 onwards.

670. Adapted from a prayer by Hugh Johnston. See *When Two or Three*.

671. Adapted from the *Form of National Thanksgiving for Peace*, November, 1918.

673. A Prayer of the Most Noble Order of the Garter (1348).

675. American P.B.: Prayer for Independence Day, July 4th.

676. *Prayers and Thanksgivings*, For Social Justice.

677. Derived from the Five Peace Points of Pope Pius XII, and the Four Freedoms affirmed by President Roosevelt in his Message to Congress on January 6, 1941 as re-stated by him and Mr. Winston Churchill in the Atlantic Charter of August 12, 1941.

678. Official Form of Prayer, October 1, 1939.
679. Adapted by Dean Milner-White from words used by Dr. Cyril Garbett, the late Archbishop of York. Included in the official *Form of Service for the Day of Remembrance*, 1946.
680. *After the Third Collect*.
681. See *Prayers* (privately printed), the official Forms of Service for use in the War of 1914–18, and *A War Primer*, 77.
682. Official Form of Prayer, May 26, 1940.
683. Written for the official *Form of Prayer and Dedication for Use on May 9th 1937*, the Sunday before the Coronation of their Majesties King George VI and Queen Elizabeth.
684. Slightly adapted: used in Westminster Abbey at a Memorial Service on November 25, 1947.
685. See Alcuin Club Prayer Book Revision Pamphlet, No. III, *A Century of Collects*.
687. *Prayers for Occasional Use*, issued by the Archbishops of Canterbury and York after the World War, 1939–45. Author unknown.
688. The collect recommended by the Archbishops of Canterbury and York 'for use in connection with the San Francisco Conference and on other occasions as a summary of the prayers which Christian people will offer both in public services and in their private devotions.'
689. Of several current versions, this seems the best. See E. Milner-White and G. W. Briggs, *Daily Prayer*, p. 166.
690. Suggested by Chapter vii of the Archbishop of York's Visitation Charge, 1947, *Watchman, what of the Night?* and the Report of the Archbishops' Commission, *The Church and the Atom*, 1948.
691. From *Family Prayers*. Included in *Daily Prayer*, E. Milner-White and G. W. Briggs, p. 97.
693. Adapted from a prayer in use after the First World War.
694. Written for private use during the Second World War.
695. *Acts of Devotion*, p. 109. Widely used after the War of 1914–18.
696. From *Daily Service for Schools* (L.C.C. Edition), edited G. W. Briggs.
697. Derived from a prayer once widely in use.
699. A revision of a collect in *A New Prayer Book*, 1923: Part. I.
700. A slight variation of a prayer by the late Canon Percy Dearmer, which G. C. Binyon remembers as appearing

in *The Commonwealth*. See *Prayers of the City of God*, p. 146.

701. From the *Form and Order of a Service in Westminster Abbey* attended by the Lord Chancellor, Judges, and Members of the Legal Profession, October 13, 1947.

702. From the dean's notebook.

704. Adapted by G. C. Binyon in *Prayers of the City of God* from a passage in the writings of Bishop Westcott. Widely used as a prayer in the Life and Liberty Movement.

705. The exact occasion of this prayer has not been traced.

706. From an unpublished prayer.

707. *A Call to Prayer* for the Life and Liberty Movement, 1918.

708. *Prayers and Thanksgivings*, for Social Justice.

710. Dated August 19, 1911. Taken from his private notebook.

711. Canon James Adderley, one of the pioneers of the Christian Social Union (founded 1889), with Bishop Westcott, Bishop Gore, Canon Scott Holland, and others, and Editor of *Goodwill*, 1894–1910.

712. A revised version of a current prayer.

713. Adapted from *A New Prayer Book* (1923), Pentecost XIV.

714. *A Poet's Prayers*, VII.

715. Phrases from this prayer have passed into several others now in wide use.

716. *After the Third Collect*. Slightly altered.

718. In the opening, the phrase 'rescuest the poor,' etc., is from Monsignor R. A. Knox's translation, *The Book of Psalms* (Vulgate), 105, 41, and 'restorest the lonely', etc., is from W. O. E. Oesterley's *The Psalms*, Vol. II, p. 321. (Psalm lxviii. 6).

719. Anthony Ashley Cooper, 7th Earl of Shaftesbury (1801–1885). The prayer is dated 1841, when he was working on behalf of factory workers in their struggle for just legislation.

721. Adapted from a wartime prayer, 1914–18.

722. Reinhold Niebuhr: Professor of Christian Ethics, Union Theological Seminary, New York, and author of *The Nature and Destiny of Man*, etc. *Venite Adoremus*, II, p. 45.

723. *The Sanctuary*, p. 208, one of 'Six Collects, from a Prayer Book Revised, 1913.' Authorship not stated. A longer version appears in *Sursum Corda*, and yet another in *Acts of Devotion*, p. 25.

724. Several versions of this prayer are current. This is adapted by permission from a long prayer by the late

Professor Walter Rauchsenbusch, Rochester, New York contained in *Prayers of the Social Awakening*, 'For our City' (S.C.M.), pp. 125–7.

725. *Daily Prayer*, p. 65.

726. A revised version of a prayer issued for use on Industrial Sunday.

727. Written by Professor E. C. Ratcliff at the suggestion of Dr. J. W. C. Wand, Bishop of London. See London Diocesan Leaflet for December, 1948.

728. This prayer was composed for and used at the Service held in St. Paul's Cathedral on the occasion of the Silver Wedding of their Majesties the King and Queen on April 26, 1948.

729. *The Doctrine and Practice of Repentance:* Chap. vi, Prayer 1.

730. *Forms of Prayer to be used in Families:* Morning. Canadian P.B. Derived from a prayer in Bishop Walsham How's *Family Prayers*.

731. Adapted. The first sentence is derived (like the beginning of 'The prayer for the Home' in the Baptismal Office in P.B., 1928) from a prayer in Bishop Walsham How's *Family Prayers*.

732. *Prayers for Common Use*, p. 225.

733. *Ancient Collects*, p. 103.

734. Adapted from a *Salisbury Benediction of a Rectory*, p. 149.

735. Derived from (*a*) S. African P.B., Solemnization of Matrimony (Alternative Order); (*b*) *A New Prayer Book*, 1921, as revised in (*c*) the Alcuin Club's *Survey of the Proposals for the Alternative P.B.*, Part II, p. 58 (1924); and (*d*) P.B., 1928, Solemnization of Matrimony, 'The Communion, The Collect.'

737. Prayer in use at the Greyladies College, Blackheath.

739. South African P.B.: The Churching of Woman (Alternative Order). Adapted.

740. *Private Devotions*, Vol. II.

741. See *Sursum Corda*, p. 62. Slightly adapted.

743. *Salisbury Book of Occasional Office*, p. 144. Slightly altered.

744. From *The Mothers' Union Book of Offices and Prayers*, p. 11.

745. *A Cambridge Bede Book*, p. 1. St. Nicholas.

746. *Prayers and Thanksgivings*. Slightly altered.

747. *Family Prayer*, For those we love.

748. A Prayer from a MS. lent by the Rev. Arthur Westcott.

749. The clause is based upon St. John xv. 15, and the second half has in it echoes from the Collect for Easter IV.

750. Adapted. Source unknown.
751. *A Naval Prayer Book*, D. J. N. Wanstall, p. 38.
753. *A Manual of Intercession*, No. 76.
754. Cf. A. W. Robinson, *Prayers New and Old*, p. 140.
755. Suggested by Gelasian III, xxiii. Cf. Bright, *Ancient Collects*, p. 107.
756. From 'The Priest's Prayer Book.'
757. A version of P.B., 1928, *Occasional Prayers*, 22; suggested by Dean Milner-White. Substituting for the standing conclusion a sentence from Jeremy Taylor's *Devotions for Several Occasions*.
758. Adapted from a prayer by Canon G. W. Briggs in *The Daily Service for Schools* (L.C.C. Edition).
759. Douglas Crick, Bishop of Chester since 1939. Written for use in the Diocese of Chester during Road Safety Week, 1949.
760. *Prayers New and Old*, p. 37.
761. Adapted from *Salisbury Book of Occasional Offices*, p. 144.
762. American P.B., and P.B., 1928. 'All the Days of their Life' is substituted, as in P.B., 1928 (*Occasional Prayers*, 17), for 'from generation to generation.'
763. *A Book of Prayers for Students*, p. 159. Approved by the Archbishops of Canterbury and Armagh for use on behalf of Students and of the Student Christian Movement.
764. *Priest's Book of Private Devotion* (Edition 1870).
765. In circulation with variations.
766. See *A Book of Prayer for Schools*, p. 373.
767. *Repton School Sermons*, p. 312.
768. From a Book of Prayers in use at the King's School, Canterbury, compiled by the Headmaster, Dr. F. J. Shirley. Author uncertain—attributed to Thomas Field, D.D., sometime King's Scholar and later Headmaster.
770. Adapted from a prayer in the Order of Service used in Westminster Abbey at the Empire Service of Youth on May 19, 1937, a week after the Coronation of their Majesties King George VI and Queen Elizabeth.
771. From Elizabethan *Form of Commemoration for use in the Colleges of Cambridge University*, 1570.
772. In use at Eton, King's College, Cambridge, and other foundations. See *Daily Prayer*, edited by E. Milner-White and G. W. Briggs, p. 71.
774. See also P.B., 1928: *Occasional Prayers*, 17.
775. This prayer was included in the Order of Service for an Association of those engaged in Scientific Study and Research; its origin cannot be traced.

776. Dated August 13, 1919, 'For James Watt Celebration,' in his private notebook. A prayer directly and profoundly relevant to this 'atomic age.'

777. *Prayers*, p. 49.

779. An unpublished prayer found among the archbishop's papers after his death, and lent by Mrs. Temple.

781. Intercessions on behalf of Social Purity. Slightly altered.

782. Adapted from Eastern Orthodox Kontakion for 'The Sunday of the Paralytic.' See *A Manual of Eastern Orthodox Prayers*, p. 43.

783. Several translations of this prayer are in circulation, e.g. *Freedom, Love, and Truth*, edited by W. R. Inge, p. 203, and *Westminster Prayers*, etc.

784. *Preces Privatae: Daily Prayers*, Wednesday, Intercession. (Trans. Brightman.)

785. *Prayers of Health and Healing*, p. 34.

786. *Mothers' Union Book of Offices and Prayers*, p. 13.

788. *Prayers for the four Ember Weeks*.

789. Adapted from a prayer circulated by the Alcuin Club in *A Survey of the Proposals for the Alternative Prayer Book* (1924), Part II, which states that their prayer 'is an adaptation from the Latin Collect, *Omnipotens sempiterne deus salus eterna credentium*.'

790. Suggested by Gelasian: cf. *Prayers for Healing*, p. 32.

791. *The Visitation of the Sick: A Prayer for submission to the Will of God. Changed from the third person to the first.

792. *Prayers*, p. 40. From a notice to *The Companions of the love of Jesus*.

793. Adapted from Sarum; None.

794. *Prayers*, p. 49. From an unpublished manual.

795. From a prayer leaflet of the Society of St. John the Evangelist, Cowley. Slightly altered.

796. Prayer Book of 1549, etc., with an addition to the intercession in the prayer *For the whole state of Christ's Church* in the Office of the Holy Communion.

797. Derived from the South African P.B. Slightly shortened and adapted.

798. S.S.J.E., *Manual*, p. 110.

799. *Prayers New and Old*, p. 139.

800. This is a prayer of the Central Advisory Council for the Spiritual Care of the Deaf and Dumb, included in the Council's leaflet of prayers for use on Ephphatha Sunday, Trinity XII.

801. Derived from a prayer in the Ephphatha leaflet of the Central Council as above.

802. See *A Plain Man's Prayer Book*, p. 37.

804. *Meditations and Devotions*, V (2).

805. *Liturgie*, 1874, p. 49, from the Order of Service for Sunday Morning. Cf. Edinburgh, 1937, *Psalms and Prayers*, pp. 14 and 31.

806. *Good Thoughts in Bad Times*, Personal Meditations, II, edited by E. R. Waller, p. 6.

807. *Prayers*, p. 46. 'From an unpublished Manual.' This prayer and Thomas Fuller's, which precedes it in the text, recalls the moving prayer by the Very Rev. C. Tugman, Dean of Bloemfontein, quoted by H.M. King George VI in his speech at Pretoria on March 30, 1947. 'Nothing', said the King, 'has moved me more than to hear as I did in church a few Sundays ago (at Bloemfontein Cathedral) a South African congregation offer up a prayer which stirred me so deeply that I have kept a copy of it.' The prayer was as follows: 'O Lord, our heavenly Father, Almighty and everlasting God, look down with compassion, we beseech Thee, upon our brethren in Britain, and lighten the burden of these rigorous days: a burden of cold, a burden of shortages, a burden of industrial difficulty and international uncertainty, and a burden of disappointment and of hope deferred. And grant to us who have lived so gently throughout all these years that we may have true sympathy with them in their struggle and follow the example of their courage.'

808. Intercession, Saturday; p. 140.

810. Adapted from a prayer in a nineteenth-century Manual for Nurses.

811. *Private Prayers for a Week*, p. 12. Slightly adapted.

812. *English Prayers*, etc. Prayers on the Passion, p. 27.

813. *The Mount of Olives* (1871), pp. 127–8. A Prayer in the Hour of Death. Shortened, but not adapted.

814. *Preces Privatae*, Intercession. Trans. Brightman, p. 273.

815. This prayer, 'a commendation of absent and departed friends, was composed by himself, and it is a characteristic expression of his strong love of home' (*Life*, Vol. I, p. 570).

816. This prayer was written for Mrs. Temple at the time of her mother's death.

817. *Salisbury Book of Occasional Offices*, XIX, p. 121, Commemoration of the Faithful Departed. Included with slight alteration in P.B., 1928; *Occasional Prayers*, 32.

818. For the original Latin see Procter and Frere, *A New History of the Book of Common Prayer*, p. 443.

820. *The Non-Jurors' Prayer-Book* (1718–19). Fragmenta Liturgica, V, 41.

821. From the Form of Service used at Westminster Abbey on July 10, 1947, at the Unveiling and Dedication of the Battle of Britain Chapel.

822. Prayers gathered from the *Writings of Edward Bouverie Pusey*, by E.H. and F.H. This prayer has the note, 'Used by the Rev. John Keble.'

824. The Burial of a Child.

825. In Memoriam of Margaret, March 5, 1939.

826. *Acts of Devotion*, p. 35.

827. Derived from a sermon by John Donne. For this arrangement of the extract as a prayer, see Milner-White and Briggs, *Daily Prayer*, p. 118.

828. 'At the Burial of the Dead', Additional Prayers, 2. 'The same' is omitted in the conclusion. See also the Scottish P.B.: A prayer for those in sorrow, where 'his friend' follows 'Lazarus.'

829. *Prayers*, printed privately.

830. Cf. *Salisbury Book of Occasional Offices:* The Form of Consecration of a Churchyard, p. 34. Slightly altered.

ACKNOWLEDGEMENTS

ON behalf of my husband I desire to acknowledge with gratitude permission by the following authors, owners of copyright, and publishers to include prayers in this volume. In many cases my husband had already received 'permission.' Care has been taken to verify doubtful cases. If I have overlooked any copyrights I hope such mistakes will be pardoned as unintentional:

His Grace the Archbishop of York, the Bishop of Chester, Bishop P. H. Loyd, the Dean of St. Paul's, the Dean of York, Dr. J. W. Suter (late Dean of Washington), Canon Harold Anson, Canon G. W. Briggs, Canon Peter Green, and Professor E. C. Ratcliff.

Mrs. Temple and Messrs. Macmillan for prayers by Archbishop William Temple: also Student Christian Movement for prayers by Archbishop William Temple from *Palm Sunday to Easter*.

Colonel F. C. Temple for prayers by Archbishop Frederick Temple.

Mrs. Theodore Woods for prayers by Bishop Woods.

Deaconess Bardsley for prayers by the late Bishop of Leicester.

The Rev. G. C. Binyon and Messrs. Longman for prayers from *Prayers for the City of God*.

The Principal for prayers from *Prayers in Use at Cuddesdon College*.

Lady Sykes and Messrs. Rivington for prayers from Canon Percy Dearmer's *The Sanctuary* and other sources.

Student Christian Movement for prayer by A. Clutton Brock in *Prayers of Health and Healing*.

The Superior of the Community of the Resurrection for prayers by Bishop W. H. Frere.

The Rev. R. A. S. Martineau and Messrs. Mowbray for prayers from *The Church in Germany in Prayer*.

Messrs. J. W. Dent for prayers by Professor W. A. Knight from *Prayers Ancient and Modern*.

The Dean of Westminster for prayer by Archbishop Lang.

Messrs. Longmans, Green for prayers from *A Cambridge Bede Book* by Dean Milner-White, and prayers from *The Treasury of Devotion*.

The Principal of Westcott House for prayer by Professor Alexander Nairne.

The Rev. D. J. N. Wanstall and Messrs. Mowbray for prayers from *A Naval Prayer Book*.

Mrs. J. Armitage Robinson for prayers, privately printed, by Dean Armitage Robinson.

S.P.G. for prayers from *Prayers of the World-Wide Church*.

The Bishop of Salisbury for prayers from *The Salisbury Book of Occasional Prayers*.

Mrs. A. W. Robinson and the Student Christian Movement for prayers from Canon Arthur Robinson's *Prayers New and Old*.

The Rev. A. Westcott and Messrs. Macmillan for prayers from Bishop B. F. Westcott's *Common Prayers for Family Use*.

The Principal of Wells Theological College for prayers from *Wells Office Book*.

The Dean of Windsor for a prayer of the Most Noble Order of the Garter.

Professor J. Baillie and the Oxford University Press for prayer from *A Diary of Private Prayer*.

Oxford University Press for prayers from *A New Prayer Book*, 1923; *The Kingdom, The Power, and The Glory*; and *The Daily Service*.

Messrs. Methuen for extracts from Professor Charles Bigg's translation of *St. Augustine's Confessions* and *The Imitation of Christ*; also for translations by Dr. F. E. Brightman from his edition of the *Preces Privatae* of Bishop Lancelot Andrewes.

Student Christian Movement for prayer by Dr. Malcolm Spencer.

The Society of St. John the Evangelist, Cowley, and Messrs. Longmans, Green for prayers from Father R. M. Benson's *Manual of Intercessory Prayer*.

Deaconess Lister for prayer in use at the Grey Ladies' College, Blackheath.

The Dean of St. Paul's for prayers in use in St. Paul's Cathedral.

The Dean of Westminster for prayers used in Westminster Abbey.

Father Bloomfield for prayer in use by the Oxford Mission of Calcutta.

The Publication Committee of the Episcopal Church of Scotland and the Cambridge University Press for prayers from the Scottish Prayer Book.

The Association for Promoting Christian Knowledge, Dublin, for prayers from the Irish Book of Common Prayer.

The General Synod of the Church of England in Canada for prayers from the Canadian Prayer Book.

The Authorities of the Church of the Province of South Africa for prayers from *The Calendar and Occasional Offices*, and from the *Alternative Holy Communion* of the Province of South Africa.

Messrs. Mowbray for prayers from *After the Third Collect, The Priest's Book of Private Devotion, Sursum Corda,* and *The Sarum Breviary.*

The Rev. Dr. F. J. J. Shirley for prayers from *A Canterbury Prayer Book* in use at King's School, Canterbury.

The Bishop of Lichfield for prayers from *The Splendour of God.*

The Headmaster of Uppingham for prayers from *Prayers in use at Uppingham School.*

Miss Helen Waddell for her translation of a prayer by Alcuin.

The Dean of Liverpool and S.P.C.K. for prayers from *Acts of Devotion.*

The Provost of Southwark for prayer from a *Southwark Diocesan Form for the Licensing of a Lay Woman Worker.*

The Cambridge Brotherhood, Delhi, and S.P.C.K. for prayer from *Oremus.*

The text of the Book of Common Prayer is Crown copyright and extracts from it are reproduced by permission.

Also extracts from the Prayer Book as Proposed in 1928 have been reprinted in this publication by permission of the holders of the copyright.

E. M. M.

INDEX OF PRINCIPAL AUTHORS

As a rule the dates following appointments (such as Bishop or Dean) are of the period during which the appointment was held.

SUBJECT INDEX